MOTHER TERESA

MOTHER TERESA

SAINT OF THE PERIPHERIES

INES ANGELI MURZAKU

Paulist Press
New York / Mahwah, NJ

Cover image courtesy Fr. Lush Gjergji, personal archive
Cover design by Joe Gallagher
Book design by Lynn Else

Library of Congress Cataloging-in-Publication Data
Names: Murzaku, Ines Angeli, author.
Title: Mother Teresa : saint of the peripheries / Ines Angeli Murzaku.
Description: Mahwah, NJ : Paulist Press, 2021. | Summary: "A biography of Mother Teresa that pays close attention to how her childhood in Albania affected her spiritual and pastoral development"— Provided by publisher.
Identifiers: LCCN 2020006875 (print) | LCCN 2020006876 (ebook) | ISBN 9780809153770 (paperback) | ISBN 9781587687501 (ebook)
Subjects: LCSH: Teresa, Mother, Saint, 1910-1997—Childhood and youth. | Missionaries of Charity—Biography.
Classification: LCC BX4700.T397 M87 2021 (print) | LCC BX4700.T397 (ebook) | DDC 271/.97 [B]—dc23
LC record available at https://lccn.loc.gov/2020006875
LC ebook record available at https://lccn.loc.gov/2020006876

ISBN 978-0-8091-5377-0 (paperback)
ISBN 978-1-58768-750-1 (e-book)

Published by Paulist Press
997 Macarthur Boulevard
Mahwah, New Jersey 07430
www.paulistpress.com

Printed and bound in the
United States of America

CONTENTS

ACKNOWLEDGMENTS

This book has been in the works since St. Mother Teresa's canonization on September 4, 2016. Working closely with a gifted scholar and inspiring colleague, Dr. Christopher Bellitto, on a splendid CNN special on Mother Teresa, made me think seriously about a book project on Mother. The book has involved much digging, discerning, journeying with Mother to the places she traversed in her life, and meeting with Mother's family members, people who knew Mother personally and intimately, or people who knew her close and extended family. This journey of discovery provoked more thoughts and new ideas about the book. All these venues of research and findings converged into one avenue: a new discovery and interpretation of Mother's roots, which stretched through continents, peoples, and cultures, connecting and dialoguing with all parties while applying Pope Francis's theology of the peripheries—I found Mother to be the incarnation of this theology. Mother never forgot her home in the Balkans and her people. She was rooted in her people and in that peripheral land. However, she was able to take a little bit of the soil from her native Albanian land and plant seeds elsewhere. One who knows Albania and Albanians can detect that influence. As the plant that retains the soil from the homeland to protect the roots, Mother persevered and cherished her Albanian roots, her people, and the wisdom she learned in the Balkan laboratory, which made her Mother Teresa of Kolkata, Mother of the Poor par excellence, and a canonized saint in the Catholic Church.

What a journey of discovery and reflection these three years have been for me! I did not write in solitude, but instead was in company and accompanied—in the company of Mother and accompanied by many people from around the globe who knew her. Her road to sainthood is inspiring for anyone who is searching for meaning and sainthood in little ways, or searching for the sacred and holy in the ordinary, in the simple things of everyday life. Mother's journey was tough; she did not settle for less but went for the best of love, service, and dedication. She thirsted and satiated that intense thirst with a similar tough love: her multiplicity of loves for the poorest of the poor, her sisters, her brothers, her family members was intense. Mother loved until it hurt, and in her life, she satiated all these loves by mirroring the prototype—Jesus.

I have shared her astute theology and her thought with my students and valued colleagues at Seton Hall University, and through scholarly presentations in several professional conferences in the United States and worldwide, with scholars around the world. I have been impressed with the reception Mother's theology has received among my professional academic peers. Besides my Seton Hall family, my family have read the drafts of my work and discussed them intensively around the dinner table. Mother makes a great deal of sense to my teenage sons—she is indeed a commonsense woman.

The list of those whom I want to thank is long, but I will be succinct and try to fit them all: my editor Dr. Christopher Bellitto, who read carefully the manuscript, making valued suggestions in every chapter; Dr. Maura Grace Harrington Logue, who skillfully edited the manuscript, making important suggestions; Fr. Lush Gjergji from Kosovo, for sharing his scholarly work and memories and special friendship with Mother; Fr. Brian Kolodiejchuk, MC, for his splendid scholarship and fundamental work on Mother and for opening many avenues to see and understand her; colleagues from Albania, Kosovo, and North Macedonia who gave me important leads to follow so I could experience Mother and Mother's early life among Albanians, whom she called her people; and Mother's close and extended family: especially her niece, the only remaining family member from the Bojaxhiu family living in Palermo, Italy—Ms. Agi Bojaxhiu was so kind to meet not only with me but share a meal with my Seton Hall students who were taking the Italy in the Footsteps of the Saints study abroad course with me; Prof. Inis Kraja from the University of Tirana, and Ms. Alma Bejtullahu, who was kind enough to share with me the memories of her mother, Vilma Antoni Bejtullahu, a cousin of Mother Teresa.

I thank my colleagues at Seton Hall University: Drs. Mary Balkun, Ki Joo Choi, Nancy Enright, Anthony Haynor, Christopher Kaiser, Peter Shoemaker, Dianne Traflet, Dermot Quinn, Allan Wright; Frs. Douglas Milewski, Joseph Laracy, and Gerald Buonopane; Msgrs. Robert Coleman, Richard Liddy, John Radano, and Anthony Ziccardi; Jean McArthur, Brenda Knight, and Sheila Riley. Ms. Gloria Aroneo, MBA, from Catholic Studies is more than a colleague to me. Gloria has made my journey with Mother a special one. Gloria and I not only work together, we share a common passion for everything that has to do with Catholic studies. This also goes for my colleague from Catholic Studies Ms. Danute Nourse. I am incredibly fortunate to share my passion and my life with these people at work. I have written quite a bit in the Catholic media on Mother—*Catholic World Report, The Catholic Thing, National Catholic Register, Crux, Salt and Light Media*, and other outlets, and I am grateful for all the feedback and questions raised by the readers and followers.

I also thank the Seton Hall students I have been privileged to teach, especially Catholic studies majors who were in the senior seminar while I was writing this book, who have been an incredible resource for testing arguments from the perspective of millennials and Generation Z. This incited me to dive even deeper and dwell more profoundly on Mother's thought. A 2018 Fulbright Specialist Grant at the Università Roma Tre (University of Roma Tre) in Italy gave me the opportunity to spend some incredibly rich time in the Eternal City and explore the archives, but also see her order— the Missionaries of Charity—in action serving the multitudes of poor, immigrants, and destitute in the streets and piazzas of the city. A 2019 Humboldt Research Summer Grant at the University of Münster (Ecumenical Institute, School of Roman Catholic Theology) provided some incredible resources and allowed discussions on Mother's theology to take center stage in many new and renewed scholarly friendships.

My husband, Dr. Alexander Murzaku, has been my lifelong friend and fan. His insights are brilliant even in theology, which is not his field of scholarly expertise. My sons, John and Matthew Murzaku, are the greatest asset I have at home. Over the three years I have been researching and writing the book, they have discussed Mother passionately, and they continue to tease and appease me by reminding me of Mother's teachings and sayings that go their way. My daughter, Era Caterina Murzaku, MD, and her husband, Mark Bauernfeind, MD, are the two grand joys of my life who know as much about Mother Teresa as everybody else in the family. My parents, Prof. Kristaq Angjeli and Mirela Angjeli, have also been of great help and support over the years. The research of my father-in-law, Prof. Thoma Murzaku, has been instrumental in helping me construct Mother's Balkan history; my mother-in-law, Vetima Murzaku, MD, has also been instrumental in her own way, sharing her experience of reading historical research that is beyond her field. This book on Mother is as much theirs as it is mine.

Special thanks go to the tireless editorial, production, and marketing teams at Paulist Press, who work hard to make sure the book is ready for dissemination to the public. Sister M. Victorija, a Missionary of Charity in Plainfield, New Jersey, is owed my special gratitude for granting permission to use Mother's direct sayings in this book. I will always cherish what Sister Victorija wrote to me in granting the copyright: "Dr. Murzaku has our permission to use Mother's words for her book. May it increase the love of Jesus for those who read it"—beautifully said, Sister Victorija. I can only add, may it increase the love for Mother, too, so that more people follow in her footsteps and become extraordinary-ordinary saints.

Acknowledgments

With every chapter I wrote and finished, I had the feeling that what I wrote and researched was not enough. Actually, I wanted to finish with a "to be continued" note. Probably this book is a to-be-continued project focusing on one of the most remarkable women of the twentieth century.

Sparta, New Jersey
November 13, 2019, Memorial of
St. Frances Xavier Cabrini, MSC

PROLOGUE

THE THEOLOGY OF PERIPHERY

Can anything good come from Nazareth?

John 1:46

POPE FRANCIS AND ST. MOTHER TERESA: THEIR THEOLOGY OF PERIPHERY

"Go out, head for the peripheries"—the leitmotif of Pope Francis's pontificate. Since the very start of his papacy in March 2013, Francis moved the Church from safe security to risk taking, from inward looking to outward looking, from the center to society's edges. There is, in fact, much convergence between St. Mother Teresa and Pope Francis regarding the periphery. Rather than a purely geopolitical or geo-economic construction, for Pope Francis and Mother Teresa the periphery refers to a multiplicity of peripheries: geographical, existential, mystical, moral, intellectual, religious, and extending in all of these cases to include the female periphery.[1] While recognizing that peripheries have a variety of meanings and connotations, this study will explore periphery and center in concert, as one cannot be concerned with the peripheries and justify neglect of the center. Mother Teresa certainly did not. As this book will explain, her mission was to bring the periphery to the center and vice versa. So, the center and periphery will be explored not in opposition but in partnership.

1

Close parallels can be drawn between Pope Francis's and Mother Teresa's theology of periphery. Both Francis and Teresa centered in the periphery and both served the Church from and in geographic peripheries—Argentina and India, respectively. However, there is a "peripheral distinction" between the two: Mother Teresa's geography of serving the Church went from the Balkan periphery—Skopje—to the Indian periphery. On the other hand, Francis moved from the Argentinian periphery to Rome—the center. Nevertheless, both Mother Teresa and Pope Francis equally brought the periphery to the center of the world's attention. They complemented each other.

Mother Teresa and Pope Francis met very quickly in person. During his apostolic journey to Tirana (Albania) on September 21, 2014, in the country where Mother Teresa came from, Francis told journalists that he had seen her briefly, twenty years before, in 1994, at the Synod of Bishops in Rome when he was the archbishop of Buenos Aires. As Fr. Lombardi, the then-Vatican spokesman explained, Bergoglio sat close to Mother Teresa, who was behind him, and often heard her intervene with great energy, without being intimidated by that vast assembly of bishops. From that moment, he developed great esteem for her as a strong woman who could give courageous testimony. Bergoglio admired her strength, her decisive interventions, and her humility not to impress the bishops' assembly but to bring the pressing problems of the Church of the peripheries to the Bishops' Synod's attention. She said what she intended to say—no big words, no beating around the bush. "I would have been afraid if she had been my superior, because she was very demanding," the pope added jokingly.[2]

Bergoglio might have been intimidated by the tough, tiny, and straightforward woman coming from the peripheries and making a case for the newfound periphery of India in the Bishops' Synod without blinking an eye, but the two are closely aligned in the way they centered their apostolates and worldviews in peripheries. He would have never fathomed that he, the pope of the peripheries, would canonize the mother of the peripheries after twenty-two years, on September 4, 2016.

Like Francis, Mother Teresa comes from the geographical and existential periphery. She was born and raised in Skopje, in today's Republic of North Macedonia.[3] Mother Teresa grew up in a multiethnic, multireligious society where the Catholic community was a minority. Like Francis, Mother Teresa knew firsthand the existential peripheries of poverty, misery, war, displacement, and ethnic cleansing. It was the "periphery of periphery" in the Balkans that taught and prepared Mother Teresa for her mission in India. It is that story of Mother Teresa that we will pursue in detail in this book, but first we must put her theology of the periphery into the context of Church history.

THE CHURCH'S THEOLOGY OF PERIPHERY

The concept of the periphery is not unknown in Catholicism. The popes of the Second Vatican Council dealt with the theology of and the evangelization of the peripheries. On January 25, 1959, from the Benedictine Abbey of St. Paul outside the Walls, Pope John XXIII, announcing his intention to convene an ecumenical council, spoke specifically of the poor and those living in the periphery surrounding Rome. He noted the internal Italian immigration, misery, and abandonment as well as the rapid urban transformation that was happening in Rome: "a cluster of houses, houses, homes, families, coming here [Rome] from all parts of Italy, from the surrounding islands, from all over the world. A real human beehive from which an uninterrupted buzz of confused voices, in search of chords."[4] He was concerned about the peripheries and all those living in and around Rome's fringes. Pope Paul VI, a champion of the Church's mission to promote social justice, never lost sight of the periphery and the plight of the people living in the margins nationally and internationally. His 1967 encyclical *Populorum Progressio* made an enduring contribution to the Church's understanding of development and progress. His visits to Uganda, the Philippines, Iran, Colombia, Australia, and India (where he met with Mother Teresa) took him to the peripheries, as well. Pope John Paul II inaugurated his pontificate by inviting people to not be afraid and to "open wide the doors for Christ."[5] This was the voice of a peripheral, non-Italian pontiff, coming from the Communist Eastern-bloc Poland, who was identifying and giving voice to all those who were suffering persecution. The pontificate of Benedict XVI pointed to a new periphery—specifically, to the intellectual periphery. Ratzinger started a fresh dialogue with the secular culture, focusing on the truth about humanity and the reasonableness of faith in God, emphasizing that the Catholic tradition "from the outset, rejected the so-called 'fideism,' which is the desire to believe against reason."[6]

However, Catholicism's concern with the periphery and the peripherals runs deep. Who set the model of the peripheral prototype that the Church has been following? Who identified with society's margins and the multitudes since the beginnings of Christianity?

GEOGRAPHICAL PERIPHERY

Human and social sciences, including history, sociology, and urbanism, might have their own definition and understanding of periphery, but to understand the multilayered theological meaning of periphery as acted and enacted by Mother Teresa and Pope Francis, the gospel is of paramount importance.

The periphery is the place and time where two of the most profound Christian mysteries, incarnation and Trinity, are made manifest. It was in the periphery of Galilee that Jesus began his mission and preaching, and it was Galilee that served as a training ground for him and his disciples to announce the kingdom of God. Jesus was the periphery's gift to the world. Moreover, the mystery of the resurrection happened in the periphery. The story of salvation is also periphery bound—no one is excluded from the redemptive power of the Lord. The same can be said for the story of God's compassionate love for the lowly. God chose to live among the marginalized in the periphery in order to start a new chapter in the history of humankind.

Jesus was not born in the center—Jerusalem. Instead, he was born in Bethlehem, around five miles from Nazareth and 120 miles away from Jerusalem. The angel Gabriel was sent from God to a town of Galilee called Nazareth (Luke 1:26); that was when Jesus's conception took place.

"Can anything good come from Nazareth?" (John 1:46) asked an inhabitant of a nearby village scornfully. The question seems to indicate some bad reputation of the people living in the periphery—Nazareth. So, Jesus-God indeed was conceived, born, and lived in a lowly place or a nonplace, a place that could not be good or bring anything good. However, peripheral Nazareth-Bethlehem became the focal point and origin of the incarnation and the Trinity, the nonplace, nondescript dot on the map, a periphery expected to produce no good. Nazareth was the site of a discreet and industrious mundaneness, which failed to understand and appreciate the unique identity of its special family. The Nazarenes were peasants who worked their own land, tenant farmers or craftspeople who served the inhabitants' needs.[7] Clusters of mostly poor houses within three to four miles from the regional city of Sepphoris in Jerusalem's periphery became the scene of revolutionary teaching and a revolutionary preacher; of encounters that witnessed to extraordinary events; of miracles that were kept secret by silence and discretion in order not to create false political, social, and religious expectations. Jesus was not afraid to cross borders and make his movement known. In fact, it was his courage in crossing borders that brought him to the cross.

But there is more to the geographical periphery: there is a periphery inside the periphery—Bethlehem and Nazareth were part of the province of Galilee, a traditional agrarian area[8] where numerous sites of biblical importance are located: "It happened in those days that Jesus came from Nazareth of Galilee and was baptized in the Jordan by John" (Mark 1:9); "on the third day there was a wedding in Cana in Galilee, and the mother of Jesus was there" (John 2:1). Moreover, Galilee was at the crossroads of diverse cultures, peoples, and languages. Jews, Phoenicians, Syrians, Greeks, Arabs, and other people—a mixture of races and cultures that Isaiah aptly calls "Galilee of the Nations" (Isa 8:23). Jews from Galilee were known to have a particular accent and probably lacked the religious purity and the cultural sophistication of the center—Jerusalem.[9] The synagogue in first-century Galilee was the local village assembly place, and its functions included local self-government and community celebrations and cohesion.[10] Moreover, Galilean Jews were looked down upon by the Jews of Jerusalem and Judea—especially by the Pharisees and the priests who saw themselves as the heirs of cultural and religious purity.[11] Galilee was for them synonymous with lowliness. They believed that neither good nor prophet nor prophecy nor a Messiah could come from Galilee. That is why the chief priests and Pharisees asked Nicodemus, "You are not from Galilee also, are you? Look and see that no prophet arises from Galilee" (John 7:52).

The trajectory Jesus traced during his early life was from periphery to periphery: he was born in the geographical and existential periphery in Bethlehem and raised in Galilee, returning there upon the arrest of John the Baptist after spending time in the desert, to preach and serve the people of the periphery. It was in the periphery of Galilee that Jesus began his public ministry and preaching, fulfilling the prophecy of Isaiah and enlightening the "people who sit in darkness" and those "dwelling in a land overshadowed by death" (Matt 4:16). So, it was in the periphery that God via Jesus embarked on the proclamation of the new world order. This was where he chose his first disciples: "As he was walking by the Sea of Galilee, he saw two brothers, Simon who is called Peter, and his brother Andrew, casting a net into the sea; they were fishermen. He said to them, 'Come after me, and I will make you fishers of men'" (Matt 4:18–20).

Jesus's Galilean ministry was the stage for his public preaching and proclamation of the gospel. He went about all Galilee, teaching in the synagogues, preaching the gospel of the kingdom among people, curing every disease and illness, and casting out devils from the multitudes who lived on society's margins (Matt 4:23). Thus, the place of Jesus's messianic message, the place where Jesus became a prophet, was centered in the periphery—Galilee—and from the Sea of Galilee, he sent out his disciples, who, as was their master, were from the periphery, to preach and teach after first commissioning, teaching, and training them on the peripheral ground (Matt 6). Galilee is thus the place where Christ established his messianic credentials, built the base of the messianic community, and began to experience his messianic sufferings for the world.[12] Galilee prepared him for his mission in the center-Jerusalem, bringing the problems of the peripherals to the center, and enabling him to argue with the center-Jerusalem, presenting a radical message for the arrival of the Messiah—the kingdom of heaven is at hand.

But as the Scriptures inform us, the evangelizing mission of Jesus was not going to end in the center of Jerusalem. There is yet another turn in the periphery for another ressourcement or aggiornamento and reenergizing of the followers. He asked the disciples to follow him into the periphery, saying, "But after I have been raised up, I shall go before you to Galilee" (Mark 14:28). This is what Jesus said after the Last Supper, preparing his disciples for the glorious mystery of the resurrection and providing a prototype to follow after the resurrection. Jesus chose the periphery even for the postresurrection establishment of discipleship—Galilee. He has been raised from the dead, and in Galilee the disciples will see him again (Mark 28:7). He left behind an empty tomb and the shroud, symbols of corruption, weakness, and imperfection, to be united eternally with God. After Jesus's crucifixion the disciples were scattered; they were overwhelmed with disillusionment by Jesus's arrest and crucifixion. They did not understand what Jesus was saying. They were probably embarrassed, and they missed his message: "But they did not understand the saying, and they were afraid to question him" (Mark 9:32).

Resurrection in Galilee brought hope and reestablished discipleship—the disciples had forgotten his teachings and his promise, and, in a way, had abandoned him. Jesus's was a full peripheral circle: Galilee was where he was born, grew up, started the mission, and started discipleship, and where he returned to redeem and restore, including the faith of his disciples in him and his message. So, the Galilean periphery is the locus of the postresurrection recovery and restoration. The proclamation of the gospel's good news started and spread from the geographical periphery, and Jesus the Galilean—the peripheral—set the model and the path to follow that is, in essence, a full-circle periphery: one that starts to return and returns to start in the periphery. Consequently, the periphery becomes a multilayered center.

EXISTENTIAL PERIPHERY

The most profound encounters of Jesus narrated in the Scriptures are his meetings with the marginalized men, women, and children of his time. Jesus did not have access to the traditional channels to God via the temple and the Torah, as did other Jews of his time. Instead, he came from Galilee, from the periphery, and also identified himself with the periphery, the rural, and the lowly.[13] The Galilean periphery was not only the geographical or ethnic marginal from Jerusalem but was also the economic periphery inhabited by the multitudes and those who were abandoned by the central government but not by God. Thus, the Galilean periphery was not only referred to as the events' setting, but as the best locus for people to recuperate a profound meaning of their existence and put on a new identity. Jesus was situated in the periphery as one of the peripherals, a man who identified with the poor and the powerless—and the message he was proclaiming was targeting the marginalized. This was due to the fact that they reflect the greatest evidence of the effect of sin and evil on human life, but also because of the biblical conviction that they are socially and historically closer to understanding the mystery of God's grace and the wonder of God's revelation.[14] The periphery of the multitudes was the favorite place for God to show his mercy for those who fear him and show the might of his arm and disperse the arrogant of mind and heart: the place where the lowly are lifted, the hungry are filled with good things, and the rich chased away empty-handed (Luke 1:50–53).

The poor Galilean periphery was also the preferred place for Jesus's miracles. Water into wine, in the Galilean village of Cana. Jesus and his mother, Mary, and his disciples were invited to the festivities, and witnessed the miracle and his power. This was the first sign of what was to come, and this first miracle happened in the periphery. The first miraculous catch of fish happened on the shore of the Sea of Galilee; the first calming of the storm; the first miraculous healing; feeding the crowd of five thousand people who were tired and hungry; and walking on water. The message is clear: the periphery is capable of miracles; actually, it is the preferred place for God, and God has never abandoned the abandoned and the forgotten. In a way, the periphery marked Jesus for life and forever. He strongly identifies with the least brothers, with the people who have suffered, who are hungry and thirsty, or with people who have suffered at the hands of persecutors because of their preaching to all the nations—with those who have supported the message of Jesus.

Jesus was one of them; he identified with the persecuted, as he said, "Amen, I say to you, whatever you did for one of these least brothers of mine, you did for me" (Matt 25:40). In Acts, Jesus again identified with the persecuted: "Saul, Saul, why are you persecuting me?" (9:4). This was the voice of Christ in his human nature, and who appeared visibly and in person, making a case for the persecuted as he was seen by the apostle. The emphasis on "me" is that identity mark Jesus was continuing to model. "I am Jesus whom you are persecuting" (Acts 26:15). So, the persecuted was none other than

Jesus. In the Gospel of Matthew, the Son of Man, as Jesus called himself, identified with the homeless, who had no fixed place to stay and no roof over their heads, saying, "Foxes have dens and birds of the sky have nests, but the Son of Man has nowhere to rest his head" (8:20). Foxes are safe because they make their "homes" down in the earth; birds can also be safe in their nests high up in trees; but the Son of Man could find neither safety nor security. He had no home he could call his own, no fixed dwelling where he could lay his head on a pillow and go to sleep at night. He lived his life out in the open, sometimes alone and sometimes sleeping rough at night. So, the homeless was none other than Jesus. In the picture of the last judgment described in the Gospel of Matthew (25:31–46), Jesus identifies with six kinds of peripherals: the hungry, the thirsty, the foreigner, the sick, the naked, and prisoners. Jesus identified himself with all categories of peripherals with the social and human reality of his time. These people are the very face of Jesus. In and through the lowly, Jesus continues his agony and suffering.

So, if one wants to find Jesus, he is to be found among the peripheries and the peripherals. This identification with the suffering periphery becomes Christianity's identifying mark. This essence of the christological message of the New Testament starts from the margins, working its way up to gain credibility and acceptance among the multitudes. The community of the marginals living in the society's periphery, who were without a shepherd, became a community of hope and witness to the power of God' message. So, the Galilean periphery was the geography of the birth of the first community that brought about the birth of Christianity. This explains why Christianity has always preserved the inherent connection with the periphery and the peripherals. God entered history from the margins, bringing salvation to and from the marginals.[15] Only after being tested among the marginals was the salvific message destined to spread and conquer the center. Peter and Paul preached and were martyred in the center—Rome. Two men from the periphery were brave enough to bring the periphery to the center, the salvific message tested in the Galilean periphery to the center of the empire and the entire world.

CENTER-PERIPHERY: STRAIN AND SYMPHONY

Christianity and the Christian Church came about from movements, disciples, and a community built in the periphery—but it was not a proletarian movement as Rodney Stark put it in his classic *The Rise of Christianity*, although it came from the frontiers of the Roman Empire.[16] Jesus was a revolutionary, controversial leader, who promised to bring division and disruption, to disrupt peace rather than to establish it (Luke 12:51; Matt 10:34). Religious movements and groups, sects, and philosophies of varying sizes and intensities abounded in antiquity, and Jesus most likely interacted with a number of these. Most of them flourished for a time and were not popular with the masses but had a strong influence in society. However, these religious movements died out, while the peripheral Christianity not only survived but expanded and thrived.

Why was Christianity so successful? How did a tiny, obscure religious movement coming from the frontiers of the Roman Empire become the dominant faith of the center? There is a plethora of reasons for Christianity's success. One important one is the accessibility of its message, which went a long way, from the people to elite politicians and to the emperor himself. Constantine's choice of Christianity as the new religion for the empire was motivated by the desire to form an alliance with the strongest God of all.[17] A deal was made with the center, the state, and a balance was achieved: Rome became Christian. Once Christianity was adopted, the center-periphery balance (despite tensions) was achieved. As a result, Christianity developed a strong institutional structure—one that would strengthen and make it outlast the empire itself. Rome as the See of Peter was established as the head of the world in pastoral honor, and whatever

Rome did not besiege with arms it held by religion. As St. Prosper of Aquitaine (370–465), known as the best disciple of Augustine, put it, *Sedes Roma Petri, quae pastoralis honoris facta caput mundo, quidquid non possidet armis religione tenet* (Rome, the See of Peter, which has been made head of the pastoral office on earth, holds in religion what it does not hold by arms.)[18] Rome was the Church of the Apostles, "of the first pastor of the Church, that is, of the most blessed Peter, chief of the Apostles, who...founded the Church of Christ at Rome," as Venerable Bede wrote in the *Ecclesiastical History of England*.[19]

By then, the Christian Church had developed into an ordered institution with an apostolic structure and a hierarchical center, which coincided with the center of the empire—Rome—whose ministry was to oversee the unity of the local churches in one catholic and apostolic Church. But the Church had also its geographical periphery, where people of different languages, cultures, races, liturgical traditions, and classes lived and followed the Church's tradition with fidelity and local creativity.

Yves Congar, OP, used the word *periphery* in an ecclesiological context in his important book *True and False Reform in the Church*. He argued that authentic reform in and of the Church comes about most effectively when the "center" is attentive to ecclesial life on the "periphery," and that this mutual responsiveness is achieved most effectively through councils.[20] Congar's center-periphery model of balance and synchronization is not outdated. Ideas and movements that emerge in response to regional or local opportunities need both the freedom to develop and the encouragement of authorities at the center. As was the case with the first Christian community founded by Jesus, and more generally with Christianity, the periphery is vibrant; it is impregnated with new ideas and new reforms; it is the little flock (Luke 12:32) that was capable of being the salt of the earth and the light of the world (Matt 5:13–14). Religious orders— the medieval Franciscans and Dominicans in addition to the modern Missionaries of Charity founded by Mother Teresa—all came from below; they were not created from above: the center, or Rome. These initiatives coming from the Church of the periphery followed the Galilean prototype. Even the reform within the reform of the religious orders in the fifteenth century came from below. For reform or renewal to become truly ecclesial, it must come from below, but according to Congar it must be accepted by Church authorities and "synchronized" or harmonized with what the Church is doing. This is how it eventually becomes integrated into ecclesial structures.[21]

Grassroots movements need structure. For example, initially the Italo-Greek monasticism of southern Italy was not structured. With the arrival of the Normans in the beginning of the eleventh century, this form of itinerant monasticism, made up of hermits, began to change. The Latin Normans favored a stable and well-regulated form of coenobitic monasticism, which in turn would boost the local economy, which was based almost exclusively on agriculture and animal husbandry, but would also provide a change for the Italo-Greek monasticism to survive.[22] Structure and uniformity replaced the fluidity and the multiplicity of monastic experiences. The stress on the structured, communal lifestyle was followed by an organized system of liturgical *typika*, which governed all aspects of monastic life.[23] With all these limitations and changing in nature, the Italo-Greek monasticism—due to centralized structure coming from Rome—survived.

Moreover, center and periphery need each other; they cannot do without each other. Initially, when the harmony with the center is missing, the innovations from the periphery might be a cause for suspicion.[24] The center, for Congar, was Rome and the periphery was the local churches. New movements and novelty come especially from the periphery of the Church, or its body, rather than its head or the center.[25] Freshness comes from people and ecclesial communities that live on the margins. For Congar it was a special calling of the center to assure unity and continuity, or progress within continuity, of the Church's tradition and bring these new ecclesial movements into the structural framework of the Church.[26]

The center's concern is that they develop in harmony and build on the structure, fitting in the overall plan of the center. Without the harmony with the center, the movements have no future to serve the Church. Reforms that come uniquely from the center without the acceptance and participation of the periphery are not effective either. So, the harmony between the two—center and periphery—is a must for the movement to mature. It is the institutional structure that protects the inspiration coming from the periphery, and all are part of the Mystical Body of Christ that is the Church. Thus, the center-periphery relation is a mutual relationship that matures in and within the Church, the Mystical Body of Christ, and approved by the center (hierarchy) and in the Church it finds its universality of expression. This is how the institution protects inspiration, how law protects life, in the Body of Christ that is the Church.[27]

This is the theology of the multiplicity of peripheries and how these peripheries are brought to the center's attention, are harmonized, and became part of the Mystical Body of Christ. The study will explore the trajectory as walked by Mother Teresa from periphery to periphery, and how she in an extraordinary way managed to incorporate the inspiration and rigor of her religious order into the Church with the center's assistance and support, and how center-periphery tensions and concessions brought about a new religious order incarnated in the Missionaries of Charity of Mother Teresa. Mother Teresa respected, obeyed, and patiently waited for the center's deliberations. Hers was a positive theology of peripheries, bringing them to the center but without dismantling the center or diluting the periphery. She did not treat the center with suspicion or seek pastoral autonomy, division, or separation from the Church. Her order, coming from the peripheries, respected the center-periphery balance without searching to delegitimize the Church's hierarchy and structure. She had a strong Roman-centered sentiment that she cherished throughout her life, but she never forgot where she came from or where she ministered.

PART I

PERSONAL PERIPHERIES

And what should I do in Illyria?

William Shakespeare, *Twelfth Night*, act 1, scene 2

CHAPTER 1

GONXHE BOJAXHIU

A CHILD OF THE PERIPHERY

FORMATIVE YEARS IN THE PERIPHERY

> Viola: What country, friends, is this?
> Captain: This is Illyria, lady.
> Viola: And what should I do in Illyria?

This is how William Shakespeare, in his comedy *Twelfth Night*, introduces the main character, who has survived a shipwreck and learned from the captain that they were on the coast of Illyria. Viola seems highly perplexed: Where was she? What could she do there? Shakespeare thought of it as an unfamiliar, remote, exotic, and peripheral land, which made it the perfect setting for intrigue, romance, and lost and found loves. Illyria offered much more to the Shakespearean characters than they would have ever imagined: lost and found family members, fresh and stolen loves, intrigue, dukes and countesses, changed identities and genders, and much more. Illyria was the ideal setting for this exciting Shakespearean play because it was an area that Western Europeans knew only as a place of mystery. "The Illyrians barely make footnotes" in history, whether ancient or modern. Illyria was a world closed to outsiders, and Illyrians were dismissed as barbarian savages.[1] But in fact, Mother Teresa's home country of Albania is part of Illyria. In her case, the footnote made it to the text, the margin made it to the center, and the periphery gave birth to one of the most remarkable women—one of the saints the moderns and millennials celebrate most. Mother brought the center's attention to the periphery and the periphery to the center in her life's trajectory from periphery to periphery—the Balkans to India.

Mother Teresa and the Missionaries of Charity, the order she founded and headed until her death in 1997, are known worldwide. However, not very well known are her formative years in the Balkans, which in itself is a combination of many peripheries, including geographical, geopolitical, imperial, ethnic, religious, and existential peripheries. Mother Teresa took great pride in her Albanian family roots in the Balkans: "By blood, I am Albanian," she told the media when she was awarded the Nobel Peace Prize in 1979.[2] Family, friends, and neighbors coming from the Balkan periphery meant everything to her, and they formed the future Mother Teresa. This corner of the world, as unknown to many Westerners as Illyria was to Shakespeare, was the cradle of a future world-renowned and beloved saint; it indeed was the laboratory of mercy in action Mother experienced firsthand. During her entire religious life, Mother Teresa modeled the values and the virtues she learned and experienced in the Balkan periphery to her religious order, following the traditions she knew best: those experienced in her family in Skopje, the current capital of the Republic of North Macedonia. The happy and tight-knit family of Gonxhe Bojaxhiu[3] (the future Mother Teresa) included her parents, Dranafile and Nikollë Bojaxhiu, her older brother, Lazër, and sister, Age, and left indelible marks on the character of the future saint of mercy canonized by Pope Francis during the Jubilee Year of Mercy on September 4, 2016.

WHO WAS MOTHER TERESA BEFORE BECOMING MOTHER TERESA?

What is the trajectory of Mother Teresa to sainthood? Periphery to periphery: from the Balkan periphery to South Asian periphery; from Skopje to Kolkata, where she established her lifelong mission of mercy. The future saint easily understood the peripheries because she herself was peripheral. She was born there and became acquainted with the reality and life-experiences of people in the periphery in her native Skopje.

Little is known about Mother Teresa's early life in Skopje, in the Ottoman Balkans. Kathryn Spink, her biographer, wrote, "Asked about her family background, Mother Teresa's reply was characteristic: 'It was a happy family. I had one brother and one sister, but I do not like to talk about it. It is not important now.'"[4] In the past, scholars of Mother Teresa have asked this question: Why was Mother not particularly keen to talk about her family or her early life? Indeed, she kept everything related to family and Albanian Skopje strictly private. Neither was she interested in her own biography, as David Porter states in the preface of his book: "Mother Teresa's interest in her own biography is minimal."[5] Mother Teresa's general practice was not to speak of her loved ones back home, not to talk of self. There are many reasons why Mother Teresa preserved her memories of her early life in Skopje unblemished, untouched, and almost "sacred" from the media and biographers' requests. The Balkan geopolitics and intricate history when she was growing up were more complicated than the average educated Westerner would have been interested to hear about, and certainly beyond what the average educated Westerner would have been prepared to grasp. The wounds of wars, ethnic cleansing, and unresolved boundaries between nations and ethnicities that made up Yugoslavia were not healed.

In fact, all these divisions were dormant and ready to explode at the opportune moment, as, in fact, happened in the early 1990s—a series of conflicts and political upheavals that caused the breakup and dismantling of Yugoslavia. But there were more historical, existential, and political reasons for Mother's silence about her early life in Skopje: since 1934, her mother, Drana, and her sister, Age, had been living and eventually died in Tirana, Albania's capital, enduring the most rigid and severe communist dictatorships, religious persecutions, and human rights violations of any in the Soviet-bloc countries. Mother Teresa was seriously worried about Drana's and Age's well-being, their safety, and their lives—she was concerned that she would put them in harm's way if she were public about her family relations in Albania when she was one of the most celebrated Catholic figures in the world. Enver Hoxha, the dictator who ruled Albania for almost fifty years, created the first atheist state on the planet.[6] Their lives under the dictatorship were a real "Calvary, but faith in Jesus was the light which illuminated and consoled all their existence."[7] From an Albanian family perspective, Mother must have deeply suffered that she was not able to visit her mother for forty-six years, as she wrote when she learned that her mother had passed: "Months before she died, she kept calling, and longing to see me, her youngest child. Albania being what it is, no Indian is allowed to go. I could go so near, and yet not to her."[8]

On a psychological level, looking at her remarkable and redeeming service to the poorest of the poor and especially her joy in serving, Mother Teresa had made peace with her past. Gonxhe was loved, cared for, and supported by her mother, her immediate and extended family, friends, relatives, and neighbors. Agi Bojaxhiu, Mother Teresa's niece, agrees that Mother Teresa spoke very rarely about her childhood and her early years in Skopje with the media. However, Agi admits that her father, when they themselves were alone and in private, spoke constantly about the past and the family's time growing up in Skopje: "They remembered the games they have played together, family vacations by the sea, Gonxhe's love of music."[9]

Neither self-focus nor narcissism were Mother Teresa's character traits. She was not preoccupied with maintaining social dominance over people, an inflated self-view, or focus on herself. However, humility does not mean holding a low opinion of self. The opposite of humility is pride. Humble people tend to practice self-forgetfulness, as they think of themselves less and of others more. Mother practiced what psychologists call strengths of transcendence, as her focuses were the poor and her religious community, never diminishing others.[10] This is exactly the reason why Mother was ready to shift attention elsewhere in conversation and interviews: to her poor on the margins and peripheries, and definitely to the all-powerful God, which represented a far bigger reality related to her lifelong vocation of serving the poorest of the poor. On the other hand, Mother Teresa was not made for public speaking: "I was not made for encounters and conferences. I and public speaking do not get along," as she used to joke.[11]

Moreover, Mother was humble and focused on others instead of herself, following in the footsteps of Mary—the Virgin of Charity, who had completely emptied herself of any residue of self-centeredness or egocentrism, offering herself as the handmaid of the Lord. Mary was neither full of herself nor self-protective. She completely surrendered herself to love and humility. Mother Teresa, imitating Mary who treasured everything in her heart, confided the workings of her soul to only a few. Even those close to her had no idea what had transpired in her soul because she kept it so hidden. Humbly keeping all attention off herself, she pointed only to Jesus, seeing and finding God in all things and loving her vocation. That is one of the reasons why Mother refused to talk about her past. She had given to God her all, her *totum*, to use the words of a woman saint she emulated and was named after, St. Thérèse of Lisieux (the Little Flower): "My Vocation is Love."[12]

Mother Teresa's lack of desire and her reluctance to speak about her past, her childhood in Skopje, or her family can be understood only within this theological, religious, historical, and existential framework. Although she was unwilling to speak about her past, her life in her native Skopje, she brought and "planted" her past, her Balkan periphery, in all 139 countries her order of women and men are serving either actively or contemplatively. As an unrooted rosebud (*gonxhe*) brings its original roots and its original soil when planted in a new flower bed, so did Mother Teresa—she never forgot her family, her country, and her people in everything she touched. The periphery that prepared her for the world's mission remained sacredly in her although she was neither keen nor ready to talk about her past.

IMPERIAL, GEOPOLITICAL, RELIGIOUS, ETHNIC, AND LINGUISTIC PERIPHERY

Before Gonxhe Bojaxhiu's birth in 1910, Macedonia shifted from being a central Ottoman province to the margins, so Mother indeed was born in the imperial periphery. This shift happened especially after the developments related to what is known as the Great Eastern Crisis of 1875–81.[13] At the time of her birth, Skopje was part of the Ottoman Empire. When Gonxhe was born, the geopolitical situation of the Albanian population in the Ottoman Empire, including Albanians of Skopje, was different from that of their neighbors. After the decay of the Ottoman Empire, most ethnic groups in the region were quick to gain territorial independence and draw borders that coincided, for the most part, with the corresponding regions they were inhabiting. One would think that the same would apply to the Albanian ethnic populations, which were awakening after five hundred years under Ottoman dominance of the Balkans. This was not the case.

In comparison to the other nationalisms in the region, Albanian nationalism developed relatively late, and national revival emerged only after 1878,[14] but what made Albania's fight for statehood different and in a sense peripheral to other new and emerging Balkan nationalisms was the fact that Albanians were not united, and the elites, who for the most part belonged to the landowning class of Islamic beys, played their role in causing disunity.[15] Why were Albanians who had lived under the Ottoman Empire not united? Religious, social, and linguistic factors were at play. By estimates, more than 65 percent of the Albanian population living under the Ottomans had converted to Islam. Conversions to Islam were happening up until the fall of the Ottoman Empire. Ten percent of the Albanians were Roman Catholic and were living primarily in northern Albania, in and around the historic Scutari, Montenegro, Kosovo, Skopje, and other major cities of the empire who made Albania's territories prey to their nationalist appetites. Gonxhe Bojaxhiu's family belonged to this minority. The Greek Orthodox Albanians, who were approximately 20 percent of the population, were living in southern Albania. Conversion to Islam, because of either conviction or convenience, paid back: Muslim Albanians enjoyed far more benefits, government jobs, and government protections compared to Christians (Roman Catholic and Orthodox Albanians). For the Ottomans, religion equaled ethnicity, so Albanians who belonged to different religions were different ethnicities that could not be united as were other ethnicities in the region within the progressively decaying empire. So, Albanian Christians (and particularly Catholics, as were Mother Teresa's family) were a minority within a minority, a periphery within a periphery, the last to enjoy benefits from the Ottoman establishment. The Ottoman Empire had traditionally tried to preserve and reward adherence to Islam by pursuing a divide and rule policy, openly encouraging divisions between Albanian Muslims, Catholics, and Orthodox Christians.[16]

Albanians under the Ottoman Empire were not allowed to learn their own language. Turkish, Arabic, Greek, Italian, or German were the teaching languages in Muslim, Greek, and Italian schools, corresponding to the religious affiliations of the Albanian students. Common language and common schools did not unite and consolidate the sense of the nation—*Albaniandom*—although Albanian language and the culture were religiously preserved at home, as was the case with Mother Teresa and her family. From 1902, the Turkish orders made punishable not only the possession of Albanian books but even the use of the Albanian language.[17] In fact, in 1910, the year Gonxhe was born, the battle of the alphabets to be used by the Albanian populations was underway. Even from a linguistic point of view, Albanian language, Gonxhe's mother tongue, was an endangered and marginalized language, so from a young age, Gonxhe must have experienced marginalization and exclusion in expressing her national identity and her native language.

The decline of the Ottoman Empire and the vacuum of power it created—especially in the peripheries—caused the Balkans to be called the "powder keg" of Europe, where the European superpowers Austro-Hungary, France, Italy, England, and Russia clashed with the rising nations and nationalities and their desire for self-governance. The drawing of the new national borders brought out the worst among the neighbors, who, until this point, had been co-sufferers under the Ottomans. Macedonia and Albania became apples of discord among the pretentious neighbors who had cast a covetous eye on their territories and were fighting among themselves to see who would get the biggest piece of the pie. Triple pressure was building from within the new and emerging Balkan nations and from the European superpowers who wanted to safeguard their areas of influence and power on one side, and an Ottoman Empire on the verge of death who once in a while woke up and was ready to attack the new emerging nationals and indirectly the supporting European superpowers. The territorial problem in the Balkans was a crucial problem because none of the Balkan nations was able to include within its borders all the members of an ethnicity. Thus, the principle "a state for a nation" become extraordinarily hard, if not impossible, to apply. Additionally, the developments in the Balkans were such that no solution would ever be satisfactory to all stakeholders.[18] Consequently, entire ethnicities were either left out or scattered and divided within the new borders of the new Balkan nations; the Albanian population, especially Muslims and Catholics, suffered unspeakable acts of genocide and ethnic cleansing. This was the case of Albanians in Skopje, including Gonxhe's immediate and more distant family, who were living in Prizren and other cities of the Ottoman Balkans.

When the Ottoman Empire had finally disintegrated, dividing the territorial spoils of the empire became the new apple of discord among the Balkan contenders. After the Serbian victory in the Battle of Kumanovo (a city in Macedonia) on October 23–24, 1912, which ended the First Balkan War, with little effort the Serbian army occupied the city of Skopje, the city of Gonxhe's birth, on October 26, 1912. The Serbian victory of Kumanovo created hope for the liberation of the Serbo-Croatian ethnicity living in the Ottoman Empire. The application of "a state for a nation" principle by the winners resulted in ethnic cleansing and assimilation of the non-Serbs and consequently non-Eastern Orthodox (Serbs were Eastern Orthodox), that is, the Roman Catholics and Muslims of Skopje. Consequently, thousands of ethnic Albanians were killed, women raped, others tortured, and entire Albanian villages burned to the ground. Leon Trotsky, the war correspondent of the Russian newspaper *Kievskaja Misl*, visited Skopje a few days after the Serbian victory at Kumanovo and reported the atrocities happening in Gonxhe's Skopje: "Entire Albanian villages had been turned into pillars of fire—far and near, right up to the railway line. This is the first real, authentic instance I had seen in the theatre of war, of ruthless mutual extermination between men. Dwellings, possessions accumulated by fathers, grandfathers, and great-grandfathers, were going up in flames. In all its fiery monotony this picture was repeated the whole way to Skoplje [*sic*]."[19]

Under the bridge near Gonxhe's house were "heaps of Albanian corpses with severed heads."[20] Gonxhe was just a young child, but Drana and Nikollë Bojaxhiu had witnessed these atrocities committed against ethnic Albanian Catholics and Muslims. As if this was not enough, Skopje became a theater of fresh conflict waged between the

European powers on one side and Bulgaria and Serbia on the other side. After Belgrade fell in 1915 and the Austro-Hungarian and Bulgarian alliance was victorious, Skopje and many other Albanian regions including Kosovo were placed under Bulgarian rule, and the Bulgarians did not treat Albanians much differently than did the Serbs before them, in terms of ethnic cleansing and assimilation.

After the end of World War I in 1918, Serbia, as a member of the Triple Entente, was able to be at the center of the emerging southern Slav state—the Kingdom of the Serbs, Croats, and Slovenes—and was able to enlarge Serbian territory, occupying the northeast territories inhabited by Albanians, which included Skopje, the city where the Bojaxhius lived. No resolution was provided for Macedonia, and the Macedonian question continued to be the apple of discord, dividing the Balkan states and peoples throughout the interwar period—and even down to current times.[21] During January–February 1919, according to statistics published in Italy, 6,040 people were killed and 3,873 homes were destroyed by the Serb troops in Kosovo.[22] In Skopje, the Albanian resistance led to the creation of the Islamic Association for the Defense of Justice to represent the rights of the Albanian Muslims of Kosovo and Macedonia. The Albanian population, who were a majority, was reduced to a minority, and in the case of Catholics they had become even more peripheral within a periphery, given the Albanian Muslims of Skopje outnumbered Catholics. The new state ruled by the Serbian elites did not recognize Albanian nationals living in Macedonia, and although agreements were signed to recognize minority rights,[23] Albanians became strangers in their own lands. Albanian-language schools, books, and newspapers were prohibited. This situation caused many families to emigrate to Turkey, Albania, and elsewhere in the Balkans, as was the case with Drana and Age Bojaxhiu, Gonxhe's mother and sister, who moved to Albania—first to Scutari in North Albania, and later to the Albanian capital, Tirana.

Why was this highly intricate Balkan history important in forging the future Mother Teresa?

On the Macedonian periphery of the Ottoman Empire, Gonxhe Bojaxhiu witnessed firsthand the Ottoman model, with diverse ethnic and religious groups living together: east and west, Rome and Byzantium, Slavic and Muslim worlds met and coexisted. She was exposed to "Macedonian fruit salad."[24] Growing up in the Balkan periphery, Gonxhe witnessed wars, famine, ethnic cleansing, religious persecution, and immense human suffering. This early exposure benefited the future Mother Teresa and her mission to the Indian periphery—her remarkable trajectory from periphery to periphery. The Balkan-Skopje periphery prepared Gonxhe Bojaxhiu for her future mission; in fact, her religious vocation started in and through her family in the Balkan periphery. By living through the Balkan and imperial intricacies, Mother Teresa might be one of the women religious who has been most exposed to and "trained" in mercy and actively living the gospel. Her message was credible because she was peripherally credible—her family lived the gospel while living through the political and economic upheavals and instability of "the Sick Man of Europe," the Ottoman Empire, as well as the struggle for power between the European superpowers and the lesser powers. Land partitions, wars, new borders drawn, families separated, ethnic cleansing, assimilation, rising nationalisms and new nations, national revivals, religious strife, human suffering—Gonxhe's life is a synthesis of human history and human suffering in the Balkan periphery. For this, Gonxhe's life was ordinary in an extraordinary way.

VALUES OF THE PERIPHERY

Where was Mother Teresa born? There is much confusion about her birthplace. The historically and geopolitically accurate answer is the city of Skopje named Üsküp by the Ottoman Turks, province of Kosovo in the Ottoman Empire, of Albanian parents—so, of an

Albanian ethnicity and language that after the division of the Ottoman Empire among the Balkan contenders were marginalized.

Here is what we know about Mother's early life spent in her
"beloved land" in Skopje, as she calls it when saying her farewell:

> I am leaving my dear house,
> And my beloved land.[25]

Gonxhe Bojaxhiu was born in Skopje, on August 26, 1910.[26]
Gonxhe was born to Albanian parents Dranafile (short name Drana,
Albanian for rose) and Nikollë (short Kolë) Bojaxhiu. Drana and
Gonxhe, rose and rosebud, mother and daughter, proved to be
more organically connected than even their names would suggest.
In Christian tradition, the rose has always represented martyrdom
and purity and has more recently become a privileged symbol for
Virgin Mary. "Why are you so enamored of my face that you do
not turn your gaze to the beautiful garden which blossoms under
the radiance of Christ? Here is the Rose, in which the Word Divine
became incarnate; here the Lilies are, whose scent led men to take the
righteous path,"[27] wrote Dante in his description of heaven. Indeed,
much is said in the names Drana and Gonxhe and their symbolism
in the Christian tradition, but their names also hint at their inherent
connection to each other. Gonxhe followed persistently in Drana's
footsteps; Gonxhe lived in her as a rosebud to later bloom into a
rose. Mother Teresa would say later when asked about her nuclear
family that "I was very close to my mother" and described Drana as
a "very holy"[28] woman, a closeness not unusual for the youngest in
the family—especially for Gonxhe, who had lost her father. Gonxhe
was Drana's favorite child, petted and loved by her siblings, similar
to St. Thérèse of Lisieux, whose name Mother Teresa would take
when she would become a religious sister.[29] Gonxhe was loved, cared
for, and supported by her mother, her immediate and extended
family, and friends. The mother-daughter bond was important in
overcoming the years of forced separation as explained later in this

book. Mother Teresa later would write, Drana "died with Gonxhe's name in her mouth."[30]

Fr. Jozef (Zef) Ramaj, a close friend of the Bojaxhiu family, baptized Gonxhe in the Sacred Heart Cathedral in Skopje, one day after her birth, on August 27, 1910,[31] according to her baptismal certificate preserved in the Albanian Institute of St. Gallen in Switzerland.[32] Agnes was her baptismal name—a tradition common among Catholics and other Christians is to assign a saint's name at baptism. St. Agnes of Rome (291–304), a virgin and martyr during the time of Diocletian and patron saint of chastity and virginity, is also connected to her first name Gonxhe, a symbol of martyrdom and purity. Names are significant and in the case of what became of Gonxhe-Agnes-Mother Teresa's journey to her canonization, her names are highly indicative: "What's in a name? that which we call a rose / By any other name would smell as sweet," said Juliet to Romeo when she suggests that he deny his Montague name.[33] In the case of Mother Teresa (rosebud-Gonxhe), in fact, "the sweet smell" was also in the name: Gonxhe—martyrdom and purity, followed by Agnes—chastity and virginity. The periphery assigned a mission to Gonxhe that would "bloom" into a religious vocation and a religious order that would respond to Christ's call to chastity and obedience as a way to become more Christlike, "molded into His image until He is formed in us," as the *Constitutions of the Missionaries of Charity* indicates.[34] Christ and imitating Christ, becoming Christlike, was the core of the life and mission of Mother Teresa. If Christ—the center—is removed, then there is no mission. If one tries to understand Mother Teresa without the center—Christ—one misses the theology of Mother Teresa. In fact, one misses Mother Teresa and what she stood for as she said to a group of reporters: "If you remove Jesus from my life, my life is reduced to a mere nothing."[35]

Besides the birth and baptismal dates and the rite in which she was baptized (the Latin rite), the certificate indicates the names of her parents, Kolë Lazër Bojaxhiu and Dran(j)a *e* (of) Lavrencit (Lorencit). Gonxhe's godmother was Tada *e* Pjetrit. Interestingly, at the bottom, the certificate indicates her confirmation, which Gonxhe received in the same church in Skopje on November 26, 1916. Traditionally, the sacrament of confirmation in the Catholic Church was conferred by the bishop, and in her case by the Catholic bishop of Skopje, Msgr. Lazër Mjedja. Agnes's confirmation sponsor was Simon Shiroka according to the certificate. Judging from the dates the certificate was released (August 11, 1928) and Gonxhe's religious calling and preparation to leave her native Skopje for Ireland, these documents were probably made in preparation for her departure. One month later (on September 12, 1928) she wrote in her native Albanian to her aunt Lis, announcing her upcoming departure from Skopje on September 26, 1928.[36]

What is in the name Bojaxhiu? The family's last name was popular in Prizren, Albania, and in Skopje, where Mother Teresa's family settled. The origin of the surname Bojaxhiu in Albanian refers to either a painter (*bojaxhiu*) or a merchant/trader of paints (*boja* translates to "paint").[37] The second meaning is probably the case with Mother Teresa's family's last name. Why did the Bojaxhiu family leave Prizren and disperse in various areas, including Scutari, in what became Albania?[38] The possible reasons are many. Business reasons might be the most probable, given the family had been merchants for several generations, looking for new and expanding markets and commerce opportunities, and cities offered more business prospects to merchants. The second is be the cholera pandemic (1846–60), which reached the Balkans from Europe and decimated the population of Prizren, forcing many families to take their belongings and move to safer areas. The third reason is to escape from persecution and conversion to Islam.[39] All reasons apply to the case of Mother Teresa's family moving to Skopje, although the second and third reasons have more historical grounding.[40] Part of Gonxhe's family was settled in the *vilayet* of Scutari, which held a prime location in commerce, given it had seven *sanjaks* (subunits of a vilayet governed by a *sanjakbey* or *sanjak*-chieftain) within the Ottoman Empire. Additionally, Scutari was known for its international trade with Austria, Turkey, Italy, Malta, Tunisia, France, Southern Dalmatia, and Montenegro.[41] Gonxhe's cousin from her father's side of the family confirms that the main reasons the Bojaxhius had left Prizren were commerce and trade.[42]

Mother Teresa's ancestors from her father's side of the family were originally from the city of Prizren in Kosovo. Nikollë Bojaxhiu was born in 1878 in Prizren to an Albanian merchant, a member of an important and prosperous Catholic family, with several relatives who were Catholic clergy. Msgr. Nikollë Mini, parish priest of Prizren, was a relative of Mother Teresa on her father's side of the family.[43] Gonxhe's paternal grandmother, Cecilia (Çilja in Albanian), was an extraordinarily strong woman who partnered in commerce with her husband. As Agi Bojaxhiu, Mother Teresa's niece, recalls, she was a woman "with a strong and decisive character, who directed everything and everyone,"[44] while Nikollë's father was a "lovely man."[45] Mother Teresa's father, Nikollë, spent his early youth in Prizren, where the entrepreneurial Albanian Catholic community engaged in many religious-recreational activities centered around the church and the bishopric of Prizren. Nikollë was well-educated and a creative entrepreneur and merchant, always in search of new markets and business opportunities. The Bojaxhius had moved to Skopje probably sometime before 1903, given the family was present and settled in Skopje, when the Sacred Heart Cathedral of Skopje was consecrated in 1903.[46] The Bojaxhius owned more than one property in Skopje, but their main residence, the house where Gonxhe grew up, was located a few meters away from the old cathedral, in the Catholic quarter in the city's center, and near the old railway station of Skopje. As elsewhere in the Balkans, the urban structure of the Ottoman cities was organized in quarters: at the city's heart stood the mosque surrounded by the shopping district. The city was divided into distinct Muslim, Christian, Jewish, and Roma quarters. Gonxhe would write in her memoirs that all her family grew up in the church's courtyard although their house had a large yard. In the yard there were two shops and an inn. One shop was for the sale of construction tools, and the other was a dyer's specialized shop,[47] thus the name *bojaxhiu* (painter). In a picture in the *Music Band Zani I Maleve* (the voice of the mountains), Nikollë poses in the center, where, according to tradition, the most important people stand.[48]

According to most recent archival findings, Mother Teresa's mother, Drana, was a native of Skopje of Albanian ethnicity.[49] Other scholars maintain that Drana Bernaj's family came from the village of Gramacel, in the parish of Novosella, in the Gjakova region, Kosovo, where the majority of the population is Catholic. In Gonxhe's baptismal and confirmation certificate Drana is referred to as Dran(j)a *e* (of) Lavrencit, meaning that her maternal father was in all probability called Lorenc, a popular Albanian-Catholic name. Both families were Catholic and highly involved in the Catholic life of the parish and the nation. Drana and Nikollë's marriage was an arranged marriage, the tradition among Albanians at the time: "a girl does not become a bride without a matchmaker."[50] This custom was codified in the *Kanuni i Lekë Dukagjinit* (the Code of Lekë Dukagjini), which was applied from the fifteenth through twentieth centuries in Albania and Kosovo, and especially in the village of Gramacel, where Drana came from. Usually senior members of the families who knew each other acted as intermediaries. Intrafaith marriages were the rule.

The couple eventually married in Skopje,[51] where they started a family. Their five children, Age (1906), Lazër (1908), and Gonxhe (1910)—and two girls who died in infancy[52]—were born there. The family went beyond the patriarchal structures of the traditional Albanian family, including values, roles within the family, and expected social roles and mores. For example, there was not an absolute subordination of Bojaxhiu women to men in the family. Nikollë Bojaxhiu did not dominate Drana and his three children as in traditional Albanian families. Instead, the Bojaxhiu children willingly showed love and respect for their father. Nikollë and Drana's marital relationship was respectful and gentle. Women in the Bojaxhiu household were not treated as second-class citizens as women were generally treated. Nikollë, from what is written about him and the interviews his son, Lazër, gave, never treated Drana as a child bearer or child rearer. Theirs was a respectful partnership and complementarity in raising a healthy and faithful family within a patriarchal societal structure.

Besides his involvement in trade, Nikollë Bojaxhiu was an ingenious entrepreneur who with ease practiced other skills including architecture, carpentry, and construction, while contributing to the church and the political developments in his country. The family was well-to-do, and owned property in Skopje and elsewhere. Navin Chawla in his study on Mother Teresa indicates that Nikollë Bojaxhiu was also a city council member who was fluent in a number of foreign languages, including Serbo-Croatian, Turkish, Italian, and French, in addition to his native Albanian.[53] Eventually, Nikollë's involvement in Balkan politics and his patriotism for the Albanian cause would cost him his life. In sum, Mother Teresa's family belonged to the merchant class, which was well-to-do, well-traveled, educated, and among Skopje's elites.

VIRTUES OF THE PERIPHERY

The household in which Gonxhe grew up was one with a strong sense of values and strict commitment to them, writes Eileen Egan—who knew Mother Teresa for thirty years and traveled extensively with her—in her in-depth account of Mother Teresa's life.[54] God, family, honor, and hospitality were values and the order of priorities ingrained in the Albanian lifestyle that Mother Teresa learned at an early age. She matured, holding fast to these values all her life. Love of God obviously came first: "Love the LORD, your God, with your whole heart, and with your whole being, and with your whole strength" (Deut 6:5). "The calling to what have I done for Christ was an early calling" for Gonxhe that took root when she was young. Early in her life, following the example of her parents, she realized why people should give all first to God, and then to the neighbor as she later would reflect: "If God who owes nothing to us is ready to impart to us no less than Himself, shall we answer with just a fraction of ourselves?"[55] Moreover, Gonxhe believed in faith as a special "gift from God"[56] infused into the souls of the faithful, being these Catholic or from other religions, because the "righteous by faith will live" (Rom 1:17). The God-given faith ran naturally in the members of the Bojaxhiu family, and in the case of Mother Teresa and her road to sainthood, the natural faith in the periphery rose up from her heart and in a way caused the supernatural faith to happen naturally. She knew how to find focus in Jesus. Lazër, Mother Teresa's elder brother, recalls her mother's strong faith, which she imparted to her three children naturally.[57]

"Every evening we said our prayers together,"[58] following what Jesus said, "For where two or three are gathered together in my name, there am I in the midst of them" (Matt 18:20). "There am I…" in the family, Jesus actually comes to you, into your midst. He is there. And if Jesus is with you, one becomes mighty—indestructible. Mother Teresa would enshrine this family tradition, her theology of prayer, in her order: "Every Missionary of Charity will pray with absolute trust in God's loving care for us. Our prayer will be the prayer of little children, one of tender devotion, deep reverence, humility, serenity and simplicity."[59]

During her early years in Skopje, Gonxhe was an active participant in the Albanian language school and other cultural activities organized by the church. Lazër remembers that Gonxhe was a good student, an exceptionally good example to everybody. She was outgoing, and people were attracted spontaneously to her.[60] From early on she developed an interest in poetry and later writing poetry, like the "Farewell" poem she wrote when she left her native land, her family, and home on board of the ship for Ireland. Church was home, and home was the domestic church for the Bojaxhius. Her relative remembers how Gonxhe stood out from other students in intelligence and organizational abilities, but above all she was kindhearted.[61] Gonxhe had a beautiful voice, and she sang as a soloist in church. She also sang with her sister Age.[62] The concerts and other artistic performances were organized and held in the cathedral of Skopje.[63]

Family, the fundamental building block of Albanian society, is the most important treasure to keep, safeguard, and cultivate; families provide a foundation from which a healthy society grows. First think of your family then the others—Agi Bojaxhiu Guttadauro, Mother Teresa's niece who lives in Palermo, Italy (Lazër Bojaxhiu's daughter) remembers her famous aunt's advice.[64] Mother Teresa's theology of the family was learned from and practiced in her Albanian family in Skopje. Family is at the core of Catholic teaching as explained by Pope John Paul II, a pontiff with whom Mother Teresa had a very special bond, in his apostolic exhortation *Familiaris Consortio*—the family is the first and vital cell of society.[65] Mother Teresa, who was usually hesitant to talk about her nuclear family and her early childhood in Skopje, would say with her usual joy and simplicity: "Mine was a happy family"[66] full of love and happy children.[67] The Bojaxhius were a happy, joyful, and tight-knit family who knew how to support and sustain each other for better or for worse. Gonxhe was surrounded by much affection from her family members. Mrs. Vilma Antoni Bejtullahu, Gonxhe's relative, had the following family story to share from Mother Teresa's early life in Skopje:

> When the grown-ups were preparing to celebrate the feast of St. Catherine[68] Gonxhe Bojaxhiu and her sister Age, Vitore (Vilma's mother) and (Vilma's) Aunt Katarina, together with Cana and Lajde Gashi, who were close friends of the Bojaxhiu family, all young girls went to skate on River Vardar, which at the time [in winter] was frozen. After skating, they were tired and freezing, they returned home for the celebration and ran to the room with the stove where the fire was burning. Somewhat carelessly, the girls dislocated the chimney pipe, and the room was filled

with smoke. The girls were mortified that their parents would reprimand them and with their small and freezing hands managed to adjust the dislocated chimney pipe and escaped giggling that their parents did not scold them.[69]

In fact, they never even noticed anything. Probably they were too busy feasting.

Living faith "work[s] through love" (Gal 5:6), and this was the case with the Bojaxhius home, which was open to the poor and destitute of Skopje. Mother Teresa remembered her father saying, "My daughter never accepts a mouthful unless it is shared with the others."[70] Drana trained Gonxhe to care deeply about the poor. The first laboratory of Christian mercy for Gonxhe was her native house and her mother. Many poor people of Skopje knew the way to the Bojaxhius door. "Never did anyone return empty-handed. Every day at the table something was left for the poor. Once, Lazër remembered asking his mother, 'who are they?' She replied: Some are relatives; the others are our people. When I grew up, I understood that these were the poor people who had nothing, but whom my mother fed."[71] She would do the same thing, all her life: she would pick people from the street, hungry people, those who were facing death just for lack of a piece of bread, for lack of a glass of water.[72] This was love in action and mercy in action, which Gonxhe learned from her mother, Drana, in the Balkan periphery. Very often, Mother Teresa uses "piece of bread" in her writing, which for an Albanian means more than bodily feeding or sustenance—it means compassion and care. There is a special Albanian expression of hospitality: bread, salt, and heart—which means bread and the salt to nurture the body and a compassionate heart totally given to the neighbor. "The house of the Albanian belongs to God and the guest," which means before the house belongs to the owner, it first belongs to God and the guest.[73]

Thus, Gonxhe grew up practicing an openhearted hospitality—one of the qualities of the Albanian national character. Even the most reviled foes would be the dearest guests while visiting an Albanian household. Early in her life, Gonxhe understood that she had a vocation to provide bread, salt, and heart to the poor, following in the footsteps of Drana. She was only twelve and gave her word of honor, making a pledge to Jesus and, through him, to the poor and the destitute. One's *word of honor* is sacred to Albanians and obviously to Gonxhe. All her life, she abided by the word of honor she promised to Jesus and to her mother to serve Jesus. She promised to protect and feed the poor with bread, salt, and heart and to relieve their thirst. She took the world's poor under her particular care, as Drana her mother had done with the poor of Skopje. She would rather die than break her word of honor, even at the price of her life.[74]

SURVIVING FAMILY TRAGEDY— LOSS OF NIKOLLË BOJAXHIU

In August 1919, tragedy struck the Bojaxhiu family. Nikollë Bojaxhiu, an advocate for the Albanian cause and a political activist, had traveled to Belgrade, which at that time was the capital of the Kingdom of the Serbs, Croats, and Slovenes, to negotiate the rights of the Albanians,[75] who had been marginalized after the new borders of the Balkans were drawn. He died as soon as he returned home from Belgrade at the youthful age of forty-five. Nikollë was buried the next day on August 2, 1919, on the Catholic side of the Skopje cemetery, with a vast number of people participating in the funeral including an official delegation, since he was a city council member.[76] The family still maintains that his death was politically motivated and an orchestrated conspiracy—most probably he was poisoned by Serbian political adversaries.[77] After his trip to Belgrade, Nikollë returned home to Skopje vomiting blood, which turned out to be fatal despite medical intervention and hospitalization.[78] Shortly before Nikollë's death, Gonxhe rushed to the church to bring the parish priest to give the last rites to her dying father. The parish priest was nowhere to be found. Gonxhe remembered that on the way back she began to pray fervently and near the railroad station she ran across an unknown priest, whom she implored to follow her home and assist her dying father. The priest had agreed to pray at Nikollë's deathbed and administer the last rites and then departed. She never encountered the priest again, and Gonxhe never learned who the railway priest really was. Later in life, when Mother Teresa remembered the episode and that unknown, unnamed, and mysterious priest coming from nowhere, she considered that encounter and the priest "God-sent," saying, "It was God's love who made this gift [happen]" to the Bojaxhius, and it was from that moment she started to experiment in her own life with the help of Divine Providence.[79]

Nikollë Bojaxhiu died, leaving behind his young bride, Drana, and his three children, Age (13), Lazër (11), and Gonxhe (9). This was devastating for the family and especially for Drana, who was now a widow in her thirties. Gonxhe cherished all her life the relationship between her parents, and she used to laugh about the way her mother and father overcame differences:

> My mother used to look at the clock, as she knew the time when my father was coming home, and [she would] run upstairs to make herself up every day. We used to play tricks on her. It was so beautiful. They could disagree, but they used to come back together as if nothing had happened, day after day. You see this is something we have to learn from our parents, their care for each other.[80]

Mother always believed "that great love, that comes, or should come from our heart, should start at home: with my family."[81]

For a brief time after Nikollë Bojaxhiu's death, the family received income from his business. However, Nikollë's Italian partner, Mr. Morton, severed his commercial relationship with the family.[82] Drana, through arduous labor in the embroidery-tailor shop, making wedding dresses and elaborate Albanian folk costumes, managed to provide for the family as a single parent and main bread-winner. Drana knew how to unite suffering with love for her family and neighbor. Heroically, she was able to raise and provide for her family literally with her own hands. Drana and Age partnered and opened a sewing-tailoring shop. Lazër remembered his "valiant" mother who worked very hard so her orphans would "still enjoy a peaceful childhood"[83] and pursue an education, which was not common, especially for women (Age and Gonxhe) within the Albanian patriarchal family structures. Gonxhe attended the Albanian-language Catholic elementary school in her home parish in Skopje. After completing her elementary education, Gonxhe enrolled in the public high school, where the education language was Serbo-Croatian. She graduated from high school in Skopje and was awarded a diploma and proficiency in Serbo-Croatian languages besides her native Albanian. Her sister, Age, after finishing both elementary and high school in Skopje, pursued her studies in Austria and became a journalist with professional knowledge of German, Serbo-Croatian, and Turkish languages.[84] Nikollë Bojaxhiu had left behind a strong and faithful woman who knew how to grieve, treasuring the memory of Nikollë and keeping it alive with her three children. Drana learned to embrace grief and heal. The ingenuity of Drana to teach her children values through simple good-housekeeping and commonsense aptitudes such as saving electricity and saving them from bad-mouthing people showed her wisdom. Mother Teresa remembered, "One day the three of us were [saying] not nice things about the teacher. It was night. [My mother] got up and [turned] off the main switch. She said, 'I am a widow…I have no money to spend on electricity for you to talk evil'" about other people.[85]

There is an expression that faithful Christians who have lost loved ones say: "With faith, you do not need to grieve," which is probably taken from "We do not want you to be unaware, brothers, about those who have fallen asleep, so that you may not grieve like the rest, who have no hope" (1 Thess 4:13). This was not the case with Drana; she grieved while keeping her faith, accepting loss and suffering with and through faith. An already strong faith became even stronger for the Bojaxhius. Gonxhe learned how to grieve for a lost parent firsthand and accepted suffering and loss of a parent with stronger faith. Later in life she would reflect that suffering is indeed part of life, but by accepting it with faith we are given the opportunity "to share the passion of Jesus and show him [our] love,"[86] which is the core of the Catholic theology of redemptive suffering that future Mother Teresa embraced from an early age in Skopje. It was what St. Paul told the Corinthians: "For as Christ's sufferings overflow to us, so through Christ does our encouragement also overflow" (2 Cor 1:5). Young Gonxhe and Drana—her role model— accepted the loss, fully realizing that it was his will, or better, "Not my will, but thy will was [be] done." This is the foundation of the theology of suffering for the faithful. This theological understanding of suffering became and remained the foundation for a closer union of the future Mother Teresa with God. Like St. Thérèse of Lisieux, Mother Teresa learned early in life that if one wants to follow the crucified Christ, he or she is given by Christ two companions that lead to sanctification or divinization: suffering and sorrow. She experienced both in the Balkan periphery. Thus, personal loss, suffering, and sorrow became her life's companions, and through them she experienced the kingdom of God. Mother Teresa found love in suffering because it was through "suffering and death that God ransomed the world."[87]

Even in the face of personal tragedy, Drana gave until it hurt— actually, she never stopped giving and sharing, even after her husband died and the family had lost the family's breadwinner and was dependent on Drana and Age's sewing shop. Lazër remembered a Skopjan widow and her six children: "She [the widow] had to work day and night despite her poor health. Our mother took care of her also. When she had no time to go in person, she would send Gonxhe. After the woman died her six children grew up with us as if they had been our brothers and sisters."[88] Bathing a leper would probably be Mother Teresa's legacy. But she learned to dress the wounds of the destitute in the Balkan peripheries. Drana helped an alcoholic woman whose body was covered in sores. Drana bathed her and dressed her sores, and Gonxhe accompanied her.[89] Mother and daughter gave until it hurt; they did ordinary things with extraordinary love, which would later be Mother Teresa's theology of mission, following in the footsteps of St. Thérèse of Lisieux and the prototype Jesus. This giving until it hurts is God's love in action, soothing the body's and soul's hunger, practicing the mother of all virtues, the virtue of the virtues—humility. The virtues practiced in the Balkan periphery fostered a religious vocation in Gonxhe from the early age of twelve, in 1922, when she was still in the family and attending school. As she herself said, "During these years I began to feel a great love for God and a strong desire to dedicate myself completely to Him."[90] The Drana-Gonxhe duo was powerful and capable to show the genius of women: two tiny women reaching out to the society's existential peripheries, helping those who were condemned to the trash heap of humankind. They were indeed ordinary-extraordinary Balkan women. The Bojaxhius family sanctity Gonxhe grew up with was homemade sanctity.

CHAPTER 2

IMPELLED TOWARD MISSION

THE SCHOOL OF THE PERIPHERY

TO JESUS THROUGH MARY: IN THE SCHOOL OF OUR LADY

In the afternoon of August 15, 1922, when twelve-year-old Gonxhe was immersed in prayer and kneeling in front of the statue of Madonna and Child, she felt for the first time in her life that the Lord was calling her in a special way. She was called to be consecrated to him.[1] So in Letnica, in the vicinity of Skopje while praying fervently in the sanctuary of Our Lady, Jesus was calling her. There the religious journey started for the future St. Mother Teresa, who followed Jesus through Mary, the Son through the mother.

What was so special about the Black Madonna of Letnica?

The Catholic families of Skopje, including the Bojaxhius, had a special devotion to Our Lady of Letnica in Kosovo. In August, for the Feast of the Assumption, the Bojaxhius made yearly pilgrimages to the shrine of Our Lady of Letnica, an imposing whitewashed church amid the mountains in the tiny hamlet of Letnica. The pilgrims went on foot, in groups, praying and singing along the way. According to local tradition, the seven-hundred-year-old statue of the Black Madonna of Letnica had miraculously traveled from Skopje, crossed

42

the Karadak Mountains, and arrived at the church in Letnica, where it is still located. This explains the deep connection and devotion to the Black Madonna among the Catholic faithful of Skopje, who believed in miracles and her healing powers while making the same geographic pilgrimage the Madonna once did. The legend goes that the statue was found by locals, hidden under a big tree, and saved from being profaned by the Muslims. So great was the veneration to the Black Madonna, that no one—not even the Muslims who ruled the country for almost five hundred years—could touch her or take away the gifts people brought to her sanctuary, which was built from the end of the sixteenth to the beginning of the seventeenth century. Our Lady had appeared three times in Letnica, urging the faithful to build a shrine. Orthodox, Muslims, Serbs, Croats, Albanians, and Roma "mixed pilgrims" have venerated the Black Madonna of Letnica over the centuries, and the shrine continues to be a bridge builder and unity forger—a place of encounter and dialogue among people of different ethnicities and religions in the Balkans—and is actively helping overcoming religious and ethnic boundaries.[2] Over the years, this sanctuary has acquired and still retains an ecumenical and interreligious value in the lives of pilgrims.

Moreover, the Black Madonna of Letnica is the only one of its kind in Albania, while there are more than 450 Black Virgins venerated in churches in France, Croatia, Slovenia, Austria, Poland, Ecuador, Lithuania, Spain, and beyond. However, the Black Madonna of Letnica still has not made it to the list of the world's images of the Black Madonna and Child. It is still peripheral, although it was the favorite shrine of one of the most celebrated modern Catholic saints—Mother Teresa. Women with infertility problems often have special devotions to Black Madonnas. The most zealous faithful, including Drana, would make the pilgrimage to Letnica on foot. Instead, Age and Gonxhe arrived in Letnica six weeks before the Feast of the Assumption, usually by horse cart, to spend their summer vacation. The sisters enjoyed the healthy climate in the mountains and the thermal waters, which were beneficial to Gonxhe's frail and fragile health—especially her lungs, as she suffered from coughs and malaria. But Letnica had more to offer to Gonxhe than good climate and physical health. The time Gonxhe spent in Letnica would influence her future religious vocation and special calling to religious life, as well as her lifelong dedication to the Blessed Virgin Mary.

In fact, Gonxhe's dedication to Mary ran deep. In Skopje, she was a member of the Congregation or Sodality of Mary from an early age, a youth group in her parish established by the Croatian Jesuits and named after the Sacred Heart of Jesus. The sodality encouraged its members to model themselves after Our Blessed Mother. This entailed trust and character building, steadfastness, humility, and prayer, to never question, never object, and never run away from difficulties, following in the footsteps of Mary, who stood firm near her Son's cross at Calvary. So, Gonxhe's "covenant" with Mary started in the Balkan periphery, in her home parish, and was nourished during her yearly pilgrimages to Letnica to celebrate the Feast of the Assumption. It was natural that her life, which was molded in the "school of Mary," would be later consecrated to Mary. Her vocational call led her to Mary; to Mary she turned continually with great love and affection like a child would do to a mother.[3] As a teenager, she would choose to join the Irish order of the Sisters of Loreto, in memory of the town of Loreto in Italy, where, according to tradition, the Holy House of Nazareth was, having been lifted from its foundations in Nazareth and transported by angels across the Mediterranean—from Palestine to Dalmatia, across the Adriatic Sea and to Loreto. Additionally, Gonxhe took for her religious name Sister Mary Teresa of the Child Jesus, after St. Thérèse of Lisieux, so we can see that the spiritual intimacy with Mary was a lifelong commitment for Gonxhe. She was indeed a Mary-hearted and Mary-guided woman.

Gonxhe's spiritual closeness with Mary was a combination of adoration, devoutness, and total trust in Our Lady's charisma and her succor. It brought Gonxhe to experience the love and power of God through the Mediatrix—Mary. Even the intimacy and unity of

Gonxhe with Jesus's crucifix can be credited to Mary and her intercession. Be all for Jesus through Mary—this was Mother Teresa's theology of redemption, like St. Louis de Montfort's devotion "to Christ through the hands of Mary," with solid foundations in both Scripture and tradition. Never in her life did Mother Teresa experience any difficulty talking to Mary. Mary's spirit and her Immaculate Heart became the heart and the spirit of the Missionaries of Charity Society, the order Mother Teresa founded—but this relationship started in the periphery. Mother Teresa's dictum "to Jesus through Mary" was divided into three developing states of soul: loving trust, loving surrender, and loving cheerfulness. She saw these three spiritual stages as an extension and participation in Our Lady's Spirit. "Love her as He loved her; be a cause of joy to her as He was; keep close to her as He kept; share with her everything, even the Cross, as He did when she stood near the Cross on Calvary," Mother Teresa would write in the Constitutions of Sisters of Charity later in her life.[4] The same dedication to Mary she had experienced since her days in the periphery of Skopje, and especially at the sanctuary of the Black Madonna of Letnica, led her to her lifelong vocation, following in the path trodden by Mary that leads to Jesus. In the case of Gonxhe, Mary led her to Ireland and India—geographical peripheries when she found and served Jesus through the poor.

AN UNTRADITIONAL TRADITIONAL FAMILY

In 1924, Lazër had left the family—or better, the women in his family—to pursue studies for one year in the military academy of Graz in Austria on a full scholarship. After his first military training in Austria, he returned and settled in Tirana, the capital of Albania, where he continued his training at the military academy and graduated in 1928, becoming an equerry of King Zog I of Albania and later a lieutenant in the same army. The same year, Gonxhe would leave Skopje for good to pursue her religious calling. Mother Teresa would recall later how she had responded to her brother when she was about to leave her hometown, comparing the military service her brother was rendering to King Zog of Albania, who had only two million subjects, with her service to the king of the universe, who had many more soldiers.[5] The second was the "military" service she liked best.

Nevertheless, the departure of Lazër from the family seems atypical for the traditional patriarchal Albanian family, as Lazër was the firstborn son in the household, whose "dominion of the household upon the death of the father" was expected.[6] Again, as it was with Bojaxhiu women running family business, none of this was either conventional or common in Albania at that time: partnering with men, beginning with Gonxhe's grandmother Cecilia; Gonxhe and Age pursuing an education unusual for women; or Drana being an emancipated widow and the household's main breadwinner, who partnered with Age in running the family business. Moreover, Gonxhe left for Ireland to pursue her religious calling while Age left Skopje in 1932 to go to Tirana and join her brother, leaving Drana alone to run the business—an atypical move for an unmarried woman living within a patriarchal society and traditional family structures. Drana, alone in Skopje, initially did not want to move and leave Skopje. She was later convinced to join Age and Lazër in Albania in 1934.[7] Most probably Drana wanted to spend the rest of her life near her firstborn son, following Albanian traditional family expectations, which hold deeply ingrained social meaning: parents and especially widowed mothers like Drana who are taken care of by their sons acquire enhanced social prestige in the local community. Therefore, older parents envisage this life and making home together wherever their children (son) might be. In following her son to Tirana, Drana was in line with tradition. Lazër recalls that when Drana joined him in Albania, she was happy that the family was reunited and that Gonxhe was a religious sister who wrote constantly to her family.[8] However, the newfound family unity was short-lived, as the Bojaxhiu family was again separated. After Italy invaded Albania from April 7 to 12, 1939, and Albania became part of the Kingdom of Italy, the Albanian army was folded into the Italian army. Consequently, Lazër was transferred to serve in Turin (Italy) and later remained in Italy because the communist government of Enver Hoxha in his homeland Albania had condemned him to death for treason, with no possibility of returning to Albania. Age and Drana remained in Albania, which became hermetically closed from the rest of the world.

For all the reasons explained above, the Bojaxhiu family—and especially its women—were traditional and nontraditional, typical and atypical. Gender roles in Mother Teresa's family were not necessarily predetermined. There was no dominance of males over females, much less a male superiority or supremacy. The Bojaxhiu women were educated and economically independent, which was a rarity during the beginning of the twentieth century in the Balkans. This breaking of the patriarchal or traditional family structures, laws, customs, and social roles is an almost unexpected contribution of the Balkan periphery to the future Mother Teresa. This first-hand living experience helped her in her new chosen periphery in India. Mother understood the closely knit and traditional Indian family structures, which, in many ways, were not different from what she had left behind in her homeland. Mother, being part of the merchant-educated and elite class, could understand the caste systems, the customs and traditions of India, which would become her new country by choice.

THE PERSECUTED

During Mother Teresa's life and since her death, most people have associated her and her ministry with Kolkata. The Indian periphery that she adopted as her own certainly held a special place in her heart and in her vocation, but she truly never forgot her peripheral homeland. While her ministry was focused on India, she often looked back—though not publicly—to the conditions in Albania. For this reason, it is important that before we follow Mother Teresa on her mission to India, we spend some time reflecting on the roles that her experiences with persecution and poverty had in forming her to be ready for her wider mission.

Of special concern to her were the conditions in which her mother and sister were living. She longed to return home to visit her mother, but civil authorities were determined to prevent this dream—which Mother Teresa and Drana shared—from coming to fruition.

"Well, the communist dictatorship, which isolated Albania from the rest of the world for decades, also prevented one of its most famous citizens, Mother Teresa of Calcutta, from returning to her homeland. But since communism collapsed, Mother Teresa's missionaries of charity organization has moved swiftly to help Europe's most impoverished country. Mother Teresa was particularly moved."[9] This is how the anchor started *BBC Breakfast News*, a popular morning program on BBC One in April 1993, announcing a special interview with Mother Teresa, her first television interview in ten years. Why was a woman who for a lifetime had radiated God's love across the globe not allowed to enter her country and denied a visa to visit her mother, on her deathbed, or her sister, Age? Why was the most celebrated humanitarian of the twentieth century denied entry to provide solace to her people? Why was the periphery denying her own daughter?

"Amen, I say to you, no prophet is accepted in his own native place" (Luke 4:24), wrote the evangelist, telling the story of Jesus who was preaching in a synagogue in the periphery of Nazareth, the city in which he had grown up. Following local tradition, Jesus went to the synagogue, and people were amazed at his gracious words but also found his preaching and teaching about prophets Elijah and Elisha highly objectionable. People were in disbelief that their townsman could speak so wisely. "Isn't this the son of Joseph?" (Luke 4:22), people who recognized him began to ask. It was probably familiarity with him that had blinded people and that led them to reject him: "they…drove him out of the town, and led him to the brow of the hill on which their town had been built, to hurl him down headlong" (Luke 4:29). This story of rejection of Jesus by his own people, the Nazarenes, was not a surprise for Jesus. It might have been no surprise for Mother Teresa either. For more than two decades, Mother tried to visit Albania and was not successful. She was longing to see her mother, whom she had seen last in 1928, when Mother left Skopje for Ireland and then India. "The night is dark, and I am far from home"[10]—this is what Mother Teresa wrote in the second day of her notes from her spiritual retreat held from March 29 to April 12, 1959. Mother was suffering, her heart was empty, her soul was going through darkness, and she felt lonely and in continual pain. The last she had heard from her mother was in 1948. She was missing home and "her" people, her mother and sister, who were suffering unspeakable persecution and economic and political destitution under the communist dictatorship.

Around 1965, Mother Teresa wrote to the Albanian embassy in Rome, asking that her mother be granted permission to travel to Italy for medical treatment, accompanied by her sister, Age. She explained that she had not seen her mother for over thirty years, and this was probably the last chance to see and serve her aging mother. Her requests were turned down. The communist dictator Enver Hoxha wanted to keep her away from Albania and obliterate her Albanian identity. In his eyes, Mother was a Western Vatican agent, coming with an agenda to spread confusion and poisoning people with backward religious ideology. This was followed by a second attempt on the part of Mother Teresa in 1968. Jacques-Maurice Couve de Murville, a French diplomat and politician who was France's minister of foreign affairs from 1958 to 1968 and prime minister from 1968 to 1969 under the presidency of General de Gaulle, knew Mother Teresa personally and presented her request to Javer Malo, the then Albanian ambassador to France. Malo informed Enver Hoxha that Mother Teresa's issue had been brought to the attention of various

Albanian embassies in the West over the past couple of years. This time, too, the response from the Albanian government in Tirana was negative, arguing lamely that the health conditions of Drana Bojaxhiu would not permit her to travel outside the country, and most importantly, that the hospitals and medical care in Albania could provide the needed expertise and care for her condition, and that the son (Lazër) and daughter (Mother Teresa) who had chosen to leave the country should have thought about missing their mother before they abandoned her. The logic behind the government decision is as follows: if both Drana and Age Bojaxhiu were granted permission to travel to Italy, they would probably not return to Albania, as the family would be reunited, since Lazër had made a new life and family in Palermo, Italy. That was enough reason for the government to deny permission to leave Albania. In the eyes of the government, the Bojaxhius were a family with "bad biography" and were not to be trusted.

Additionally, in 1967, Albania had proclaimed itself atheist—the world's only atheistic country—and banned any form of religion in the country, including Christianity and Islam. Religion was considered reactionary, backward, and an opium for the people. Clergy who had served in the country before the establishment of the Hoxha regime were executed, imprisoned in labor or "reeducation" camps, or expelled from Albania. Religion in general, and any personal religious leaning and activity, were banned and severely persecuted. Mother Teresa, being a Catholic religious sister, was immediately classified as an enemy of the people and in a country of bunkers—estimated to number up to 500,000[11]—closed to the rest of the world, Mother Teresa had no chance of being granted an Albanian entry visa. The greatest humanitarian who was caring for the world's poor and destitute was denied the right to visit her family and her people in the periphery who were suffering. She did not give up, and made another attempt, requesting a visa so she could visit her family for only a week. The Albanian authorities were unmoved by Mother Teresa's pleas and by the pressure from foreign diplomats. Thus was her fate in cosharing even in Jesus's denial by his own people, the Nazarenes.

Mother Teresa suffered from the repudiations, and this might have added to her dark night of the soul—carrying Christ's sufferings. This time, they were the sufferings of a different periphery—her family and her people in Albania. On July 12, 1972, she received a telegram from her sister, Age, from Albania announcing, "July 12, at 5:00. Mother died—Agi."[12] Mother Teresa wrote to her cousin File in Albanian to announce her mother's death: "Mommy has returned home to the Lord. Now we have mommy to pray for us.... You have loved Mommy...her sacrifices have helped me, and now she (Mommy) certainly will help more."[13] Mother Teresa ends her letter saying that she is doing well and is in good health but she has a lot of work. The government denied Mother's visa even to participate in Drana's funeral.[14]

"Amen, I say to you, no prophet is accepted in his own native place" (Luke 4:24). Mother receiving the Nobel Peace Prize was never mentioned in the Albanian media, and the Albanian diplomats abroad, her townsmen, treated her as persona non grata following the central party line and policy.

Two years later, in 1974,[15] her sister, Age, died. According to a close family friend, Prof. Inis Kraja, daughter of Marie Kraja, a famous Albanian opera singer and long-time family friend of the Bojaxhiu family, Age was an astute intellectual with broad culture. When Drana and Age moved to Tirana, Age first started working at the Tirana Radio Foreign Programs. She was hired right away as a journalist in the Serbo-Croatian program, due to her talent in languages and her broad culture and knowledge. She worked for the Tirana Radio until 1955 or 1956, when the persecution of religion and especially of Catholics was taking place.[16] After Age lost her job, the lives of Drana and Age became very challenging economically, and the fact that Mother Teresa was a religious sister was an additional major cause for distrust and persecution on the part of the communist government against the Bojaxhiu family.

Their deaths and the impossibility to physically be near them and carry their sufferings might have been devasting to Mother Teresa. Christ was in the persecuted suffering, the marginalized people in Albania who were denied the most basic human rights and who were victims of economic poverty that the communist system failed to eradicate. Mother Teresa did not make any public announcements or media appearances to express her discontent or revolt against the Albanian government for all the denials and injustices her family endured beyond the Iron Curtain. She kept her distance from the Albanian communist politics and believed that it was not her calling to criticize governments or change political systems. Surely, "her" suffering people of Albania were in her constant prayers, and she was carrying their crosses and participating in their labors, spiritually. She would be able to enter her country in 1989 as a prophet bringing freedom to people and the fall of communism in the last bastion of the communist-bloc countries. It was only after the first "private" visit—as this was advertised by the government—of Mother Teresa to Albania, that the communist system days were counted, and Albania was redeemed. After her 1991 visit to Albania, Mother wrote to her sisters, "I feel Jesus and Mary want me here at this time of opening of churches in the country of Albania where God's love has been so rejected for many years and people were starving spiritually."[17] She was going to satiate people's thirst. Mother was back in the Balkan periphery.

POVERTY: THE ULTIMATE PERIPHERY

"We must do as Christ, who loved everyone, but privilege the poor with an intense love"—this is what Pope John Paul I, or Papa Luciani, wrote in his letter to St. Luke the evangelist.[18] This captures Mother Teresa's trajectory from the Balkan periphery to the Indian periphery and her love for those on society's margins. While she identified and felt kinship with those who suffered because of their political peripherality, Mother Teresa understood poverty—and all that comes with it—as the ultimate periphery. Identifying with the poor, seeing Christ in the poor, suffering for the poor: this marked Mother's ministry and vocation to those living in the gutters in India and continues to be the trademark of the ministry of the Missionaries of Charity serving throughout the world. Mother Teresa's dedication to the poor was not motivated by an academic or cerebral understanding of her knowledge of their kinship with Christ; instead, she felt viscerally—from her senses to her soul—that those most in need of care presented her with opportunities to love Christ himself. "To those who say they admire my courage, I have to tell them that I would not have any if I were not convinced that each time I touch the body of a leper, a body that reeks with a foul stench, I touch Christ's body, the same Christ I receive in the Eucharist,"[19] as Mother Teresa said. Society's periphery allowed Mother Teresa and her order to witness the unitive aspect of the Eucharist in action and her life mission to serve the poorest of the poor. Besides their eucharistic focus, Mother and her order identified with the poor even through another important aspect of their experience: the renunciation and the vow of poverty. Her order was consecrated to poverty. This entailed "a life which is poor in reality and in spirit, sober and industrious, and a stranger to earthly riches. It also involves dependence and limitation in the use and disposition of goods."[20] Mother's identification with the poor constitutes her social ethics and the application of Catholic Social Teaching. Besides the theological-christological-eucharistic understanding of seeing Christ in the poor, and the poor as an extension of the Eucharist, Mother cared a great deal for the human touch and the human presence in serving the poor. This was part of her two-way theology of identification: with Jesus and with the poor. St. Ignatius of Loyola, whose spirituality Mother Teresa had appropriated, identified with the poor. Jesuits' poverty was an actual and real poverty, which had kept Jesuits ready to God's service with no attachments, but instead practicing the virtues of solidness and detachment. Thus, no hardships would be insurmountable for a Jesuit. Ignatius achieved his identification with the condition of a certain class of people—the poor—through renunciation of the basics. Mother's identification with the poor was total and radical since the first moment of the foundation of her order. Freedom and poverty went hand in hand for her; it was poverty that guaranteed freedom, as Jesus had instructed Mother in one of his locutions: "I want free nuns covered with my poverty of the cross."[21] As Christ on the cross was stripped of his garments, of everything, he became one and identified with the poor and the outcast. This was the model of an "absolute" or "perfect" poverty Mother Teresa and her order identified with, by making the poverty of Jesus and the poverty of the poor their own.

Poverty can come in many forms. It is an accumulation of many poverties that build upon each other and make a "compound" poverty—this type of poverty is difficult to escape. Poverty in all its steps and complications is an identification mark of the periphery and the peripherals Mother Teresa was serving and suffering for. The peripherals experienced compounded suffering caused by a compounded poverty, including inner or spiritual destitution and exclusion from society's care because of disease. In them, Mother Teresa saw the suffering Christ. Mother identified with any form of suffering, including suffering caused by addiction, AIDS, and disease. This is what she wrote to drug addicts on July 22 (1948 or 1949):

> My dear drug addict: The God who loves you dearly will leave 99 other sheep and look just for you. Please let him find you. He can make you far happier than the passing pleasure of any drug! God loves you—you are precious to Him. No drug can love you wherever you are. God loves you, so do I because you are God's child. God blesses you. Mother Teresa MC.[22]

The spiritually or inwardly destitute people who, although economically and materially rich, were peripheral and abandoned by what Cardinal Ratzinger called "the dictatorship of relativism… whose ultimate goal consists solely of one's own ego and desires"[23] were also part of the contingent of the peripherals Mother Teresa was suffering with and serving. Mother was with this contingent of poor, too, in person, providing them with a human touch, a human presence imitating Christ—the divine physician of body and soul and more generally of humanity in its state of sickness. Jesus most often chose to heal through touching, "stretch[ing] out his hand" (Mark 1:41) to people. Touch and healing go hand in hand in Jesus's philosophy of healing. In the healing of leprosy in Mark 1:41–42, Jesus acts bravely, touching the leper. People who touched lepers would become unclean according to Jewish law, by treating and healing such people living literally in the geographic and social peripheries of the cities. Jesus modeled healing via presence and prayer when he visited Peter's (Simon's) house to care for his mother-in-law: "He approached, grasped her hand, and helped her up" (Mark 1:31).

Mother Teresa and her religious order have been accused of not finding the causes of poverty or finding ways to eradicate poverty. During all her life in service of the poor, Mother kept a distance from political debates over the socioeconomic-political causes of poverty. Mother Teresa, as she herself said, was disinterested in politics. She never got involved in the intellectual debates on poverty, either; she did not feel it was her calling. Her focus was on charity and serving the poor—carrying their sufferings. And for this she never shied away from talking to world leaders to secure their permission so she could have her sisters help the poor in their respective countries. Christopher Hitchens, her unbending critic, writing in *Slate* on October 20, 2003, on the occasion of Mother's beatification, asserted, "MT [Mother Teresa] was not a friend of the poor. She was a friend of poverty. She said that suffering was a gift from God."[24] If one analyzes her life and her lifelong mission, Mother was indeed a friend of both: the poor and poverty—these were the crux of her life-mission. She knew that neither she nor her religious order could change the world's poverty or the economic distress of nations, or even put a dent in poverty. This was not her mission. Her mission and indeed what she and her order have accomplished was individualizing poverty, putting a name and a face to poverty, in all its manifestations, which included the poor and the destitute of society's peripheries, including the poor and poverty in the rich and well-to-do nations. Her poor were personalized and were cared for. Her care for the most peripheral—the poor—brought them to the center. Mother brought the world's attention to world poverty and the poor—to "her" poor, as she called them via her celebrity status: "The physical situation of my poor left in the streets unwanted, unloved, unclaimed."[25] "Many speak of the poor, but they do not speak to the poor,"[26] she wrote in her diary on March 29 (either 1948 or 1949). Listening to and living with the poor is at the core of Mother Teresa's understanding of the Church's social and moral teaching.

She realized that the periphery was to be found everywhere in the world, in the rich and in the poor nations. Her message was credible because she was seeing the poor, touching the poor, and living with the poor—and she and her order were consecrated to poverty. Her speech of acceptance of the Nobel Peace Prize was dedicated to the poor, the unwanted, and the unloved. She realized that her winning of the Nobel Peace Prize had "helped many people to find the way to the Poor,"[27] as she wrote to her spiritual director, Fr. Neuner, on January 9, 1980, a month after she received the Nobel Peace Prize December 11, 1979.

A question can be asked: Can politics be divorced from charity? Or can charity and politics be two opposite approaches to facing social problems? Although Mother maintained her distance from politics, she understood charity and politics, and social institutions of the city and society, as working together to alleviate poverty and social problems, thus working toward and building the common good. Pope Benedict XVI in the encyclical letter *Caritas in Veritate* (no. 7) wrote that the "complex of institutions that give structure to the life of society, juridically, civilly, politically and culturally, mak[e] it the *pólis*, or 'city.'"[28] But there is also the institutional or the political path to charity, which is equally efficient in promoting the common good. According to Pope Benedict XVI, "Every Christian is called to practice this charity, in a manner corresponding to his vocation and according to the degree of influence he wields in the *pólis*. This is the institutional path—we might also call it the political path—of charity, no less excellent and effective than the kind of charity which encounters the neighbour directly, outside the institutional mediation of the *pólis*."[29] This was Mother's political theology, or the political avenue to charity—on one hand keeping a distance from the politics of the nations, but on the other hand through her charity serving and building on the common good of the nation. She could not fathom eradicating poverty without first personalizing and touching poverty firsthand. How can one uproot poverty without seeing and living with the poor? In her view, the politics and politician who were divorced from charity cannot reach to the root or understand the causes of poverty, so she viewed the government and the government social programs as complementary to her charity work, which, unlike government social programs, was a charity centered on Christ:

> I don't worry about orchestrating politics. Better said, I don't have time for worrying about these things. This is something everybody knows. Am I not mistaken? I prefer, in any case, if I make a mistake, to do it out of charity.[30]

But Mother never considered her charitable work serving the peripheries as social service or herself a social worker, or an NGO, divorced from Christ's mission or the Church's mission. Her work and the work of the Missionaries of Charity is an extension of the presence of Jesus, who made himself present and in flesh in the world, in the hungry, the poor, and the discarded. Mother's work, as we have discovered, was an extension of the Eucharist, and she never shied away from making this clear to people: "We are not social workers. We are contemplatives in the heart of the world. We are 24 hours a day with Jesus,"[31] she said in her speech at Regina Mundi

Institute in Rome on December 20, 1979. Mother's mission was centered on Christ. It was both christological and eschatological. Her mission proclaimed the eternal Truth and, in that sense, it was dogmatic and not situational or relativistic. In 2014, in his address to the bishops of the Episcopal Conference of Switzerland on their *ad limina* visit to Rome, Pope Francis, focusing on the social dimension of the gospel and the Catholic Social Teaching, warned that

> the Gospel has its own original strength to make proposals. It is up to us to present it in its entirety, to render it accessible without clouding its beauty or weakening its attractiveness, in order to reach the people facing the difficulties of everyday life, who are searching for the meaning of their life or who have fallen away from the Church. The testimony of Christians and parish communities can truly enlighten their path and support their aspiration for happiness. In this way the Church in Switzerland can more clearly be herself, the Body of Christ and the People of God, and not just a fine organization, another NGO.[32]

This was exactly Mother's understanding of the social and political aspect of the gospel.

Mother sought and found the poor, the peripherals, the persecuted in every corner of the world. They were people in need of material, moral, and spiritual accompaniment. In serving the poor, Mother Teresa had made her own the Jesuit motto *magis*, which entailed greater devotion, greater denial, and greater generosity in the service of Christ. Mother Teresa had brought from the Balkan periphery her dedication to the poor and the marginalized. Since she was young, her family—and especially her mother—had trained her in how to make service and the poor a priority. She witnessed poverty, touched and served poverty, and lived among the poor in her native city of Skopje. She was applying the blueprint from the Balkan periphery in the Indian periphery. From her correspondence with her family, which continued up to 1948, when Albania was sealed off from the rest of the world and closed behind the Iron Curtain, her mother had heard that Mother Teresa had left the Loreto Sisters. Drana was content with Mother Teresa's new mission in the slums of India. Mother Teresa was continuing in the Bojaxhiu family tradition of serving the poor and the neighbor, although Mother had shifted peripheries and continents—material and spiritual poverty and human suffering were the same throughout the world.

Malcolm Muggeridge asked Mother Teresa about her religious calling: When did the feeling that you must dedicate yourself to the poor people come to you? Mother Teresa responded with the usual humility and gratitude: "It was many years ago when I was at home with my people."[33] She said it all. She brought what she had learned in the laboratory of the periphery to the world, from the homemade sanctity of Mother Drana. Despite being away from home—as far away as India—Mother Teresa continued to learn from the periphery of her homeland and from the peripheral experience of her family, bringing this firsthand current experience with her into her work among the poorest of the poor. The school of the periphery was not a peripheral school for Mother Teresa to start a lifelong religious vocation to the poorest of the poor. Instead the school of the periphery was life giving and life itself. In the school of the periphery Mother Teresa learned and lived by the transformative Christian virtues and values she then took with her to the next periphery in Kolkata. From her early life in what many would consider to be a provincial place, Mother Teresa learned universal truths about human nature and the practice of charity. In Shakespeare's main character shipwrecked on the coast of Illyria and in the life of the future St. Mother Teresa, the Albanian periphery proved to be much more resourceful and transformative than expected. Much good came from the school of the Balkan periphery, which trained the saint of the gutters—the face of mercy in Kolkata's gutters.

CHAPTER 3

INDIA

To Steamy Bengal go
To a Distant Shore[1]

MOTHER TERESA—INDIA'S "CROWN JEWEL"

India is a complex country. On the one hand, it includes the erudite and well-educated, globalized, and urbanized elites, and on the other hand, it is home to some of the most isolated people living in primitive conditions. The population of India is very dense throughout most the country. Most of the population is centered in the north along the banks of the Ganges River, with other river valleys and southern coastal areas also having large population concentrations.[2] Kolkata, Mother Teresa's adopted home, ranks third in population density. Moreover, the Anthropological Survey of India (A.S.I.)[3] under the Ministry of Culture—Government of India—which studies the communities that make up the population of India, has identified at least 4,635 different community groups, including a large tribal population of about ten million people referred to as "original inhabitants" of India in official records. India also has the caste system: high caste and low caste, the majority Hindu (79.8%) followed by Muslim (14.2%), Christian (2.3%), Sikh (1.7%), and unspecified others.

Where Would the Balkan Gonxhe Bojaxhiu Fit in India?

With her move, Mother Teresa's trajectory from periphery to periphery had started: destination—Kolkata. She was bringing eighteen years of peripheral experience, firsthand experience of three wars (World War I and the Balkan Wars), and her lifetime of living among diverse ethnic and religious communities to her new periphery, which would become her country of citizenship. She was well prepared in the school of the Balkan periphery to understand Indian society: its hierarchy and patriarchy; its social fabric and social interdependence; its family structure of several generations sharing living space and worshiping together; its authority and harmony in the family; the role of women and seclusion and veiling of women—indeed, it was not much different from the Balkan traditions Mother Teresa grew up with. Additionally, she would be at home with a fight for independence, political-religious unrest, famine, starvation, and the resulting human suffering.

Nonetheless, she went to India as a foreign European-Christian missionary who made the people of India and the streets of Kolkata her own. She became a proud citizen and daughter of India. The eighteen-year-old missionary discovered much to be done in the slums of India, much more than others even dared to imagine. Through her foreignness she discovered ordinariness; through unconventionality, conventionality; through strangeness of a new land, normality and beauty. She would eventually become part of her new country by choice. Mother Teresa applied the advice of Kolkata's native, one of India's most cherished renaissance poets, Rabindranath Tagore (1861–1941), a fellow Nobel Prize winner, when he wrote in *My Reminiscences*, "In the streets of Calcutta I sometimes imagine myself a foreigner, and only then do I discover how much is to be seen."[4]

Mother was indeed a foreigner: she observed, learned, and discovered. Initial foreignness was beneficial. She dedicated her entire life to her beloved Indian periphery and Indian people, and India loved her back. India, which was referred to as the "Jewel in the Crown of the British Empire," made Mother Teresa her "crown jewel." In November 1992, she was presented with the "Bharat ki Mahan Suptri" (the great daughter of India) award, and President Shankar Dayal Sharma named her "Bharat Shiromani" (India's crown jewel). Mother Teresa loved India and the Indians until it hurt because for love to be true it must hurt, as she would say.[5]

WHY A MISSION TO A DISTANT LAND?

Why did Gonxhe choose to go to India? Why Kolkata? What attracted Gonxhe to serve in this distant land that was peripheral to Christianity and the Church? Couldn't Gonxhe find Kolkata in the Balkans, as she herself would advise people to stay where they are? Why wasn't Albania, her land and her people, which Rome considered a mission territory, a good enough option for Gonxhe's love of mission? Albania had all "the benefits" of the periphery that she knew and grew up with. Additionally, she knew the language, culture, and people, and her message would have been credible and authentic to locals. Why was Gonxhe opting for the extreme? Indeed, all the likelihoods were not in her favor in going to foreign missions: Gonxhe was of frail health, which was a family concern. She had suffered from lung disease, coughs, and malaria. And as a rule, the congregations are careful not to send candidates with health problems to foreign and difficult missions.

Gonxhe the missionary was not in search of adventures in mysterious lands or in exploring new and unexplored cultures. In fact, one of the benefits of growing up in the Balkan periphery was that she was not monocultural or monolingual. She left the Balkan periphery as a teenager with proficiency in four languages—Serbo-Croatian,

Macedonian, a little French, and her native Albanian—an uncommon ability among the missionaries of her age. She was not in search of a new community or building a religious community that she had never experienced in her homeland. As explained in the first chapter, she grew up in a religious household, learned Scripture from an early age, and experienced the privilege of an active parish community that made her faith grounded and meaningful. Gonxhe felt fulfilled: she came from a happy and supportive household that included support in her faith formation and education. Still, her mother did not accept her vocation to become a religious sister and her calling to go to a far-away mission easily. She had trouble understanding if Gonxhe's call was authentic and questioned if she knew what would come after the call—normal for any mother to question. How can a mother know if it's God's will that her daughter become a religious sister? Drana did not know, but she let Gonxhe discern that call, and she accepted and respected her decision, although Gonxhe was in her teens and maybe too young to know what she was doing. Many thoughts might have occurred to Drana: I am losing my youngest daughter forever, I will have no grandchildren, I will miss her terribly, will I ever see her? Even in this, respecting Gonxhe's decision to enter religious life and go to missions, Drana was acting counterculturally. The traditional periphery was acting untraditionally.

Under the spiritual guidance of the Jesuit Fr. Jambrenković, it took Gonxhe Bojaxhiu almost six years to discern and join the religious sisters with the goal to go to the missions. On June 28, 1928, Gonxhe wrote an application letter to the Mother Superior of the Loreto Sisters asking to be accepted in the Loreto Order, with the intention to become a missionary. This is what Mother wrote in her application:

> I want to join your Society, so that one day I may become
> a missionary sister, and work for Jesus who died for all of
> us....I don't have any special conditions, I only want to be

in the missions, and for everything else I surrender myself completely to the good God's disposal.[6]

Drana signed her agreement for Gonxhe to become a missionary only on July 11, 1928, a few months before her departure, in the parish office, witnessed by the parish priest Fr. Anton Buković.[7] She had been aware of Gonxhe's special calling for missions for a few years. She wrote,

> I found out that Gonxhja has a calling from God to become a missionary. I do not want to go against God's will. By this [letter] I give her full freedom to follow God's call. I expect nothing of her, except she prays for me. Especially, I give her permission to go to India, a country she has chosen. I entrust her to her [religious] superiors, to safeguard her, so I may see her happy in the company of God in heaven.[8]

How was Gonxhe going to leave her widowed mother and family behind when they most needed her? What Drana and Gonxhe did and the lifelong journey they embarked on was countercultural and countertraditional to the Albanian patriarchal family structure. How can an Albanian woman leave her home when the *Code of Lekë Dukagjini* and the societal expectations demand that she get married and procreate? Marriage was ordered for the common good of society and childbearing, a communal responsibility equally contributing to society's common good. The *Code* defines woman as "a sack, made to endure" for childbearing functions.[9] So the Albanian tradition in which Mother Teresa was born and grew up took for granted that women marry and have children.

Moreover, Gonxhe's choice of a distant mission was not an escape from real-world problems for the tranquil convent life. It was neither detachment nor distraction from the Balkan reality or from family problems. Neither was Gonxhe looking for me-only time.

Gonxhe was not escaping from life in the Balkan periphery. She was leaving behind a culture of relative comfort for one with less. She was indeed opting for an unfamiliar, harder Indian periphery. This was Mother's radical acceptance of a new periphery. She was going against the tide in a part of the world that has little stomach for Christianity.[10] As her life from periphery to periphery demonstrates, Gonxhe embraced the new Indian periphery just the way it was. Through her radical embrace, she was following in the footsteps of the first missionary and imitating Jesus, who did not sit by passively in the comfort of his culture and let people who were interested come to him. It was he who went out and sought the sick and those in sorrow—not the other way around. John Paul I, otherwise known as Papa Luciani, reflecting on the Catholic theology of mission, wrote to the people of his diocese about Jesus as the first missionary to be emulated,

> The history of the Catholic missions is by now a long road: at the beginning of that road is the Father of Mercy, who holds out his arms to all his children. All those who encounter the missionaries encounter the Father. And they also encounter the Son, the first missionary, who, obeying the Father, comes to the earth, becomes flesh in human nature, is one of us, in solidarity with our misery (except for sin) and ends up dying for us in order to then return to heaven, carrying on his shoulders the human race he has won back.[11]

Far less was Gonxhe escaping to find God in a distant land. On the contrary, she went to India because of God, to follow in the footsteps of the first missionary. One cannot impart on others what one does not possess. Missionaries fulfill the call to mission: "what you heard from me through many witnesses entrust to faithful people who will have the ability to teach others as well" (2 Tim 2:2), imitating Christ, the prototype, as Paul "the missionary par excellence" exhorted the churches where he ministered: "Be imitators of me, as I am of Christ"(1 Cor 11:1). In her work and mission in the periphery, Mother Teresa was, in her way, following the universal Christian call to mission.

Mother's call to missions in India and her family's support of her missionary work can be understood only through appreciation of the Christian view of missionary activity. This view involves elements of theology—bringing Christ to the world and furthering his saving work by imitation of his life's trajectory. Missions and missionary activity are eschatological because "the gospel must first be preached to all nations" (Mark 13:10). Thus, missionary activity is nothing other than a manifestation, an Epiphany, a realization of the divine plan in the world and in history: with missionary activity and through missionaries, God clearly leads to conclusion the history of salvation. Thanks to missionary activity, God's people multiply, as it was prophesied:

> Enlarge the space for your tent,
> > spread out your tent cloths unsparingly;
> > lengthen your ropes and make firm your pegs. (Isa 54:2)

The mystical body grows "until we all attain to the unity of faith and knowledge of the Son of God, to mature manhood, to the extent of the full stature of Christ" (Eph 4:13); thanks to the missionary activity the spiritual temple, in which God is worshiped "in Spirit and truth" (John 4:23), is "built on the foundation of the apostles and prophets, with Christ Jesus himself as the capstone" (Eph 2:20).[12]

Mother Teresa found her Kolkata continents away from Skopje. Her calling was extreme, and God worked through her in the Kolkatan periphery to reach the hearts and minds of the entire world. Probably, if asked where is "your Kolkata," her answer might have been, "In Kolkata among the poorest of the poor Kolkatans." If Christ is present in the poor, then the heart of Christ must be in

Kolkata. All her life, Mother went for the extreme and the supreme: she loved until it hurt. In a way, Mother found Kolkata and Kolkata found Mother.

She went to India for the love of Jesus and to fulfill his extreme calling.

TO INDIA FOR THE LOVE OF
MISSIONS AND TO HELP SOULS

Fr. Nikollë Mini, in an article "Misionaret Tona" (Our missionaries) in *Zani I Zojës Cernagore* (Voice of Our Lady of Montenegro) magazine, wrote about the two Skopjen missionaries who were serving in India: "Two young Albanian girls are working as missionaries in far-away India, Sister Teresa and Sister Gabriela, both from Skopjen families. Since 1928, Gonxha Bojaxhis and Nasta [short for Anastasia] Mihillit,[13] as they were previously called [their lay names] left their country and with much zeal began their work in a foreign land, or better in a new homeland."[14] The article explains that not only the religious leaders but the government and especially the people express their deep gratitude to the missionary efforts of the sisters, "who do not spare their efforts and their health to help the neighbor, especially those who needed their help the most."[15]

According to the diary of Gonxhe's cousin Lorenc Antoni, family members had gathered in the Bojaxhiu home the day before (September 25) Gonxhe's departure to bid her farewell,[16] which was an Albanian tradition. The next day, Gonxhe, accompanied by her mother, Drana, and sister, Age, took the train for Zagreb, Croatia. The Bojaxhiu women were guests of an Albanian family of Zagreb until the day their paths separated—Gonxhe to India and Drana and Age returned to Skopje and later to Tirana, Albania's capital. Never did Gonxhe think that this was the last time she would see her mother and sister. "Put your hand in His [Jesus's] hand and walk along with Him. Walk ahead, because if you look back you will go back"[17]—these were Drana's prophetic words to her daughter before her departure from the Balkan periphery. Drana did not want Gonxhe to waste time and look back, but to focus on her future vocation: "Remember not the events of the past, the things of long ago consider not" (Isa 43:18). Apostle Paul handled his past the same way: "Forgetting what lies behind but straining forward to what lies ahead" (Phil 3:13). Paul knew that if he was going to focus on the purpose for which Christ laid hold of him, he needed to look forward and focus on the future. Drana's final farewell words to her might be the reason why Mother Teresa was not keen to speak about her past—the past was not important to her.[18]

September 26, 1928, started the long journey to India for Gonxhe and Nasta Mëhilli, an Albanian Catholic from Skopje, who like Gonxhe wanted to join the Congregation of the Sisters of Loreto.[19] According to most recent research, as well as pictures the two young missionaries mailed to their families in Skopje, and reports published by the *Zani I Zojës Cernagore* magazine, Nasta and Gonxhe traveled together in India and served in an orphanage in Kolkata.[20] Moreover, an article published in *Blagovijest* magazine dated December 1932, a few years after the two Skopjen missionaries were settled in Kolkata, confirms Nasta as Gonxhe's friend and companion from Skopje. In fact, the magazine publishes an impressive picture of the two female missionaries from Skopje (Gonxhe on the right and Nasta on the left) among a collage of photos from India depicting various activities of the young Skopjen missionaries. The picture is a tribute to the two female missionaries who hold on their shoulders the burden of distant missions.

Since the beginnings of Christianity, women missionaries have effectively collaborated with preachers in spreading the gospel. "These virgins consecrated to God are especially worthy of a well-deserved praise."[21] The missionary reports from distant missions published in Catholic religious magazines in Skopje confirm that the Balkan periphery was contributing its share of missionaries, females and males, to foreign mission, responding to the Church's call for missions and evangelization. This was especially important, since the number of missionaries had decreased significantly since the World War I: "it has been so reduced that many areas of the Lord's vineyard are without laborers. We appeal to you, Venerable Brethren, for a particularly vigorous approach to this problem,"[22] Pope Benedict XV wrote in his apostolic letter *Maximum Illud* on the activity of missionaries in the world, issued on November 30, 1919.

With her prophetic farewell to her daughter, Drana was also reaffirming her blessing of Gonxhe's religious vocation and desire for distant missions. The focus of Gonxhe's future life would be Jesus: this should be her pursuit "toward the goal, the prize of God's upward calling, in Christ Jesus" (Phil 3:14). From a cultural perspective, Drana was also giving her daughter peace of mind, not to worry about her (a widow), but instead to lay hold of God's new things and remain focused on the goals ahead.

From Zagreb, the next leg of the trip was much longer than the first. She had to travel by train through Austria, Switzerland, and France and then by sea toward London and Dublin, journeying more than one thousand miles. The first stop was France—Paris, in the convent of Auteuil, for an interview with Mother Eugene McAvin, the mother superior in charge of the Loreto Sisters in France. It seems that Fr. Jambrenković, from Gonxhe's home parish in Skopje, who had discovered and fostered Gonxhe's religious vocation, had arranged for an interview with Mother Eugene. After the interview Mother Eugene was expected to write a letter stating whether she would recommend the Skopjen aspirants to Mother Raphael Deasy, mother general of the Loreto Institute in Rathfarnham, Dublin, at that time. The interview centered on vocation and the motivations why she wanted to become a religious sister and a missionary despite all difficulties of a missionary life in a distant land. After the long interview, in the presence of a translator from the Yugoslavian embassy of France,[23] who was asked by the mother superior to translate into Albanian and Serbo-Croatian for them,[24]

Mother McAvin gave a letter of recommendation to Gonxhe to bring to Mother Raphael Deasy in Ireland. Obviously, Gonxhe was recommended and endorsed by Mother Eugene.

WHY DID MOTHER TERESA JOIN THE IRISH SISTERS OF LORETO?

There is a Jesuit link to the Irish connection: the Croatian Fr. Franjo Jambrenković, SJ, Gonxhe's parish priest, who noticed, nurtured, and directed her religious vocation. Fr. Jambrenković was her spiritual director and confessor and had a profound influence on Gonxhe. She consulted Fr. Jambrenković about her religious vocation to go to faraway India, and it was Fr. Jambrenković who helped her discern her vocation to become a missionary. In a way, there would be no St. Mother Teresa without Fr. Jambrenković and other Jesuits in her life, and the Ignatian spirituality that she knew how to make her own. Fr. Jambrenković and Mother remained spiritually connected: even when she was in India, she corresponded regularly with him, seeking his advice and spiritual guidance.

Gonxhe had known Fr. Jambrenković since she was fifteen, through her work with the Congregation or Sodality of Mary, which he had established in Skopje in 1925.[25] Gonxhe's devotion to the Blessed Virgin Mary was crucial in starting her spiritual journey and in igniting her missionary vocation. The Sodalities of Mary were Jesuit enterprises beginning in 1563. Students who were studying under the Jesuits in the Roman College gathered to practice piety and devotion to Mary. The practice followed in the tradition of the founder of the Jesuits. St. Ignatius of Loyola had a lifelong devotion to Blessed Mary. Not May—the Lady's Month—but every month of the year was Mary's month for Ignatius. Mary played a vital role in Ignatius's religious vocation, his conversion, and the beginning of the Society of Jesus. After Pope Paul III approved the Society of Jesus in 1540, the first Jesuits pronounced their religious vows as members of the Society of Jesus before Mary's image at the Basilica of St. Paul Outside the Wall in Rome. Over time, Sodalities of Blessed Virgin Mary directed by the Jesuits spread all over the world and became powerful congregations of lay apostleship. The sodalities were closely modeled after the Spiritual Exercises of Ignatius of Loyola, emphasizing frequent examination of conscience, prayer, meditation, confession, and communion, with the Blessed Virgin as the center of their devotion.[26] So, Gonxhe since a young age, under the guidance of Fr. Jambrenković, read and practiced the spiritual exercises with her sodality community.

However, the Skopje sodality directed by Fr. Jambrenković offered more than Marian devotion to its members. During the 1920s and 1930s, significant numbers of young Catholics were moving beyond local piety and devotion into social action, defending human dignity and common good in society, social justice, the poor, and the marginalized. A true sodalist was expected to be "an apostle of charity in aiding the needy," as the *Manual of the Sodality* prescribed.[27] So Mother Teresa knew all these principles, and most importantly she had firsthand experience in practicing the sodality "best practices" in her native Skopje.

Additionally, there was a call and heightened sensitivity for foreign missions coming from Rome. Besides the 1919 apostolic letter *Maximum Illud* of Pope Benedict XV, in 1926, Pope Pius XI issued the encyclical *Rerum Ecclesiae*, which focused on Catholic missions and the importance of missions for the Church, emphasizing the formation of new Christians by training the native clergy. Fr. Jambrenković would make these two important documents and the Church's call for missions known to the members of the sodality of Skopje that Gonxhe and her sister, Age, were part of. He organized special prayer services for missions and gathered funds destined for missions. He tried to ignite the love of mission in the hearts and minds of the Skopjen youth, so that they were receptive to and appreciative of missions and missionaries. According to Lorenc Antoni, Mother Teresa's cousin, Fr. Jambrenković spoke to us [students] of missions. He also read to us on missions, the poor, the lepers. He distributed the Catholic press, especially *Katoliecke Misije*. Gonxhe read this magazine very willingly. There were many articles from Croatian and Slovenian [missionaries] in India and from the region of Calcutta where they labored. I can confirm that this particular magazine ignited Gonxhe's desire for missions and helped her develop her religious and missionary vocation.[28]

Again, it was Fr. Jambrenković who first introduced Gonxhe to the distant land India and the work of the Jesuit missionaries who had dedicated their lives to missions and to India. The Society of Jesus had a long history with India, beginning with St. Francis Xavier, the first Jesuit missionary to India (Goa) in 1542, who himself was mentored by St. Ignatius Loyola. St. Francis Xavier contributed much to evangelizing and catechizing the people of India. He was followed by the Italian Jesuit Fr. Alessandro Valignano, who came to be known as the foremost organizer of the Indian missions of his day, Fr. Thomas Stephens, Fr. Roberto de Nobili, and many other illustrious Jesuits who have left their imprint there.[29] Locally, the Jesuits of Scutari had a long tradition of visiting the Archdiocese of Skopje since the times of the great missionary Fr. Domenico Pasi. Gonxhe might have heard stories about and probably met with the Jesuits of the Misioni Shëtitës Shqiptar (Jesuit Traveling Mission), which proved to be one of the most effective and successful Jesuit apostolates founded in Scutari, northern Albania, to serve the Albanian Catholic population and prevent conversions to Islam.[30] The Jesuit missionaries of the Traveling Missions visited and served regularly in parishes in the Archdiocese of Skopje, and especially in the villages with crypto-Christians, called *laraman* (motley) in Albania, people who feared to declare their Christian faith in front of their Muslim compatriots. Although they were baptized Catholics, in public, for fear of repercussions, these individuals practiced Islam. The crypto-Catholics were in an exceedingly difficult pastoral situation, as they were completely neglected by ecclesiastical authorities and their numbers diminished every year because of conversions to Islam.[31]

Besides the missionaries of the Jesuit Traveling Mission, there were local Jesuits who had gone to missions in Bengal whose stories might have fascinated young Gonxhe. In 1927, the Croatian Jesuit Fr. Anton Vizjak was a missionary in Bengal and successfully organized the Bengali missionary province.[32] It was due to his missionary efforts that Bengal and India were made known in the Balkans, although he was called back to Zagreb near his superiors due to health issues related to snake bites. Letters written by Jesuit missionaries in India published in the local *Katoliecke Misije* and *Blagovijest* described the difficulties of missionary life, the burning Indian heat, fights with wild animals and snakes biting out of nowhere—experiences Mother Teresa would personally have when she was there. So Gonxhe was enthused about and ignited for missions by the missions and the missionary stories she was reading, but she also was fully aware of the labors of the missionary and the life her vocation would lead her into. She knew from the start that the life of a missionary is not strewn with roses, but, more accurately, it is covered in thorns.[33] Nonetheless, a missionary's life is full of happiness and joy as they emulate the prototype, Jesus, as she wrote in 1932 in a letter to the editor of *Blagovijest* about the Indian mission. The Ignatian-Jesuit school of mission had taught young Gonxhe the core values of how to become an effective missionary: total confidence in God's providential care and a shared experience of discernment.

In sum, devotion to the Blessed Virgin Mary, love of missions, and the Ignatian spiritual accompaniment and discernment built the foundation of Gonxhe's spiritual life, cultivated and directed by the Jesuits. Gonxhe practiced the Jesuit values: *magis* (more/greater)—her radical decision to do more for Christ by going in mission to India and her utmost concern for people in the existential and social periphery of Skopje; *cura personalis*—she took care of the poor and marginalized in her parish and in her neighborhood, seeing them as people; and God in action. These qualities led to the goal *ad majorem Dei gloriam* (For the greater glory of God).

A Shift in Charism? From Jesuit Charism to Loreto Charism

Mother Teresa did not change much in charism, moving from her native Skopje guided by the Jesuits, to a female congregation based on the spirituality of St. Ignatius of Loyola, contemplative-active sisters, or sisters who are contemplatives in action and active in missions. In 1611, Mary Ward (1585–1645), founder of the congregation Mother Teresa joined, had a revelation that directed to her to "take the same of the society," meaning take the same constitution as the Society of Jesus. Mary believed that God was directing her toward a female order modeled on the Society of Jesus, Ignatian spirituality, and Ignatian charism. The apostolic letter *Regimini Militantis Ecclesiae* (The governance of the Church militant), dated September 27, 1540, described the Ignatius institution as follows:

> Whoever wishes to serve as a soldier of God beneath the banner of the cross in our Society, which we desire to be designated by the name of Jesus, and to serve the Lord alone and his vicar on earth, should keep in mind that once he has made a solemn vow of perpetual chastity he is a member of a community founded chiefly for this purpose: to strive especially for the progress of souls in Christian life and doctrine and for the propagation of the faith by the ministry of the word, by spiritual exercises and works of charity, and specifically by the education of children and unlettered persons in Christianity.[34]

One can notice the striking similarities between the Constitutions of the Society of Jesus and the constitutions of the congregation founded by Mary Ward:

Whoever wishes to serve beneath the banner of the cross as a soldier of God in our Society, which we desire to be designated by the name of Jesus…is a member of a Society founded primarily for this purpose: to strive for the defense and propagation of the faith and for the progress of souls in Christian life and doctrine, leading them back from heresy and evil ways to the faith, to a Christian manner of life, and to special obedience to the Holy See.[35]

To work at the perfection of our own souls and to devote ourselves to the salvation of our neighbor by the education of girls, or any means that are congruous to the times, or in which is judged that we can by our labors promote the greater glory of God and in any place further the propagation of our Holy Mother, The Catholic Church.[36]

Mary Ward is strikingly Jesuitical and her spirituality strikingly Ignatian. She and her order are the feminine way of living out the Ignatius Loyola constitutions: women soldiers of God. As the Society of Jesus, the religious institute that Mary Ward founded (*Congregatio Jesu*) came into being for the glory of God and the good of the universal Church—focusing on women, their growth and maturity in intimacy with Christ. Mary stood her ground in the face of severe persecution and rejection, without resentment and in obedience to the Church as she and her order were viewed suspiciously. After Mary's death her institution was recognized by Pope Benedict XIII in 1713, and later Pope Pius XII spoke of her as "that incomparable woman, given to the Church by Catholic England in her darkest and bloodiest hour."[37] Mary Ward's charism was inherited by the Institute of the Blessed Virgin Mary (IBVM), Loreto branch, which was founded by Teresa (Frances) Ball in Dublin in 1821 and expanded during the nineteenth and twentieth centuries through missionary activity in various parts of the world, including India. Since 1841, the Loreto Sisters of Dublin had a presence in Kolkata—a school for young girls.

It is pure speculation to assume that Mother Teresa joined the Loreto Sisters to rebel against the Church. We are not sure how much Mother Teresa knew about the history of the order she was joining or Mary Ward. But, what comes from documents and Mother Teresa's correspondence is that she knew and had practiced Ignatian spirituality; had a fervent devotion to the Blessed Virgin Mary's spirituality; and saw God in action, through contemplation, and within her desire to be a missionary in India. All these Gonxhe had read about. Consequently, common ground and the same Jesuit charism are what attracted Gonxhe to join the Loreto Sisters in India.

Furthermore, Fr. Jambrenković had a special connection with the sisters of Loreto, given their similar spirituality and view on missions, so he made all possible contacts for Gonxhe to make the big leap forward joining the sisters, which included an initial interview with Mother Eugene McAvin in Paris. Theologically, spiritually, and from a missiological perspective, it was not a shift of charism for Gonxhe. Instead, joining the Jesuit-influenced sisters was the fulfillment of the Ignatian charism in women-led apostolate with the same dictum—for the greater glory of God. Young Gonxhe found herself in *terra cognita*, with the familiar spirituality and charism she had practiced in the laboratory of the periphery. This explains the Jesuit connection to the Irish connection or the extension of the Jesuit Charism to Loreto Charism.

Loreto Abbey of Rathfarnham, Dublin

"The people of the world are my people, but I will always have a special place in my heart for Ireland," Mother Teresa said.[38] In an interview with Nodlaig McCarthy for *This Week*, broadcast on September 15, 1974, by Irish television, Mother Teresa spoke about her vocation, remembering her days at Rathfarnham in 1928. Mother had visited the abbey after forty-six years and had this to say to the interviewer about the visit, which evidently had brought back fond memories of Rathfarnham: "I saw the places where I have been as a young postulant, remembered the community room, the chapel. It brought back what was happening at that time."[39] She and her compatriot from Skopje stayed for two months at the Loreto Abbey of Rathfarnham, located a few miles from Dublin. The two young postulants studied English language under the guidance of Mother Maria Borgia Irwin, but most importantly they received full immersion in the life of a religious sister in community. At Rathfarnham, the young postulants experienced a period of intense prayer and discernment of the religious vocation. There is not a set of rules determining how long one should be a postulant—or a candidate, as the Loreto Sisters call this initial stage—before entering a novitiate. This all depended on the religious community. Thus, postulancy can last from six months to a year, and the candidate may or may not be called *Sister*.

It must not have been difficult for Gonxhe to learn English at Rathfarnham, as she already knew and had studied several other languages and had practiced her linguistic skills when she was in Skopje, translating for Fr. Jambrenković from Serbo-Croatian into Albanian. Usually, people who speak more than one language find it easier to learn another, and then another language. This in fact happened to Mother Teresa, who, after learning English, learned Bengali and Hindi to be deservingly known the "Bengali Teresa."[40]

However, Mother Irwin taught Gonxhe much more than the English language—she gave her a crash course in missiology and monasticism, as she herself had spent many years as a missionary in India. Moreover, Mother Irwin had a lot to explain about St. Patrick, Ireland's great spiritual shepherd who started "life as a more humble one."[41] Probably this was Gonxhe's first exposure to the great saint of the Irish. "I was interested" about St. Patrick, "that despite his missionary activity Patrick also had a contemplative side,"[42] a balance between active and contemplative lifestyles, like that of Martha and that of Mary, that she later applied in her future religious order.

Loreto Sisters from Ireland were established in India in the 1840s with the focus of educating the children of the British Army. Besides this, the sisters directed free schools and orphanages for the disadvantaged Indian children of all faiths—but there was more to be done, especially with the poorest of the poor, the radical periphery, that the Loreto Sisters were not serving. In a sense, Mother Teresa complemented what the Loreto Sisters were doing and was going to India for *magis*—more, touching the untouchable as they were called—people who were born, lived, and died on the streets of Kolkata.[43]

The Little Way That Unites Thérèse and Teresa

In Holy Scripture, when God changed a person's name it meant a new identity. "No longer will you be called Abram; your name will be Abraham, for I am making you the father of a multitude of nations" (Gen 17:5); Abraham's wife's name was changed: "Do not call her Sarai; her name will be Sarah" (Gen 17:15). In the New Testament, Jesus changed Simon's name, "You are Simon the son of John; you will be called Cephas [Peter]" (John 1:42). On the other hand, Peter declared of Jesus, "You are the Messiah, the Son of the living God" (Matt 16:16). Scripture does not provide reasons for the name changes, but perhaps changing the name meant that they were destined to start anew, a new mission in life. In the Scriptures, the new name was a revelation of a divine plan and an assurance that God's plan would be fulfilled in them via their new mission.

At the Abbey of Rathfarnham, Gonxhe Bojaxhiu received the name of Sister Mary Teresa of the Child Jesus after St. Thérèse of Lisieux. How much did Sister Mary Teresa know about St. Thérèse of Lisieux? What united the little flower to the bud flower (Gonxhe)? As is customary in religious orders and monasteries, sisters would read passages from the lives of the saints during dinner or on their own during recreation. Maybe one of the lives read in the abbey was that of St. Thérèse of Lisieux. Moreover, young Gonxhe knew a "little French,"[44] so could probably read St. Thérèse of Lisieux's autobiography and her poems, which the abbey's library might have had in the original language.

Thérèse of Lisieux had an impressive trajectory to sainthood, later being declared doctor of the Church by Pope John Paul II in 1997, the year Mother Teresa died. But there is more in the life of the Little Flower that might have attracted Mother Teresa: on April 30, 1923, Thérèse of Lisieux was beatified and declared Patroness of the Carmelite Missions by Pope Pius XI, known as the pope of the missions. Two years later, on May 17, 1925, she was canonized by the same pontiff.[45] An important, and probably the initial attractive trait of St. Thérèse of Lisieux for Gonxhe might have been Pope Pius XI's decision on December 14, 1927, to proclaim her universal copatron saint of missionaries, together with the famous Jesuit missionary St. Francis Xavier. But there was more recognition of Thérèse of Lisieux related to missions, to which in fact she never went but intensely desired to go. On July 29, 1926, Pope Pius XI declared her to be the Patroness of the Indigenous Clergy of the Papal Missionary Work of St. Peter the Apostle. These are all extraordinary recognitions for a religious sister who at the age of fifteen entered Carmel and never left the cloister until her death.

The Church has paid equal attention and reverence to two lifestyles: first, contemplation and prayer, and second, active life. Both are equally important for missionaries and missions so that, as the Second Vatican Council emphasized, "the entire world may become the People of God, the Body of the Lord and the Temple of the Holy Spirit" (*Lumen Gentium*).[46] Thérèse of Lisieux's "I thirst: These words ignited within me an unknown and very living fire"[47] in mission theology means thirst for souls, nothing more than acting on Jesus's command: "Go, therefore, and make disciples of all nations, baptizing them in the name of the Father, and of the Son, and of the holy Spirit, teaching them to observe all that I have commanded you. And behold, I am with you always, until the end of the age" (Matt 28:19–20). From Carmel, Thérèse of Lisieux bore witness in a direct, intimate, and simple way to Jesus's command to go on mission. She engaged in spiritual warfare for souls and prayed for active missionaries who labored in the missions. For all this, her missionary charism is equally valid and the same as that of St. Francis Xavier. Gonxhe might have been ignited by the dual validity and the multiple application of the "I thirst" command in missions, which she later made the badge of her religious order. In Thérèse of Lisieux, Gonxhe might have found a female model to emulate, thirsty for souls and with "a great desire for the conversion of sinners,"[48] a woman who incarnated the life of contemplation, who saved the same number of sinners as the active missionaries. Gonxhe had found a woman saint and spiritual companion she could count on, a saint who is also the Universal Co-patron of Missions.

But there is more than mission theology that urged Gonxhe to take her name. What St. Thérèse and Sister Teresa had in common was holy simplicity and humility, which are virtues very closely linked with each other. St. Thérèse and Sister Maria Teresa through their lives showed that to be humble and simple means to avoid vainglory, instead seeking the glory that comes from God. "'The Mighty One has done great things for me,' and the greatest of these is to have shown me my littleness, my incapability of all good," wrote St. Thérèse.[49]

The fact that both women lost a parent (mother and father, respectively) during childhood, and both developed a desire to become religious sisters at a very early age, must have provided more reasons for Gonxhe to become Sister Teresa by adopting the "little way"—doing ordinary things with extraordinary love, and depending on God with childlike trust. The little way united Thérèse and Teresa even more intimately.

Farewell to Ireland

On December 1, 1928, Sister Teresa, her conational from Skopje, and three Franciscan missionary sisters embarked on the long journey to India on the ship *Marcha*. This was the first Christmas Sister Teresa would celebrate on board a ship, sailing toward the mission destination. Together with the Franciscan sisters, they improvised a paper nativity scene and at midnight sang *Gloria in Excelsis Deo*, accompanied by the rosary and *Adeste Fideles*. The New Year, 1929, was also celebrated on the ship: "Our New Year was solemn, but nonetheless in our hearts we sang *Te Deum*. Thank God we began the New Year well. We had a sung Mass (*in cantu*), which seemed more majestic [there were no priests or deacons on the ship who could celebrate],"[50] Sister Teresa wrote back home.

While sailing toward India, Sister Teresa wrote the "Farewell" poem, which speaks about her pain of leaving everything behind to start a new life, a new mission of serving Christ. It is a thoughtful poem that reflects Sister Teresa's state of mind. It is theologically profound and a missionary manifesto. The poem dwells into her deepest thoughts of forsaking family and home. She regrets and feels the pain of leaving mother Drana behind but is conscious that a higher power compels her to go to India. It is interesting that she refers to herself in diminutive, like "Christ's happy little one, His new Bride to be,"[51] similar to St. Thérèse of Lisieux's language in the play *The Divine Little Beggar-Boy of Christmas* she wrote in 1895, where Thérèse refers to herself as "a little flower, a flower that in the grasses blows: to be besides your Spouse, beside The King of Heav'n, the Christmas Rose."[52] The use of the diminutive is not uncommon in Christian literature. Mary, the greatest of all saints, was also referred to with such diminutives as the lowly little maiden, "the most lowly Virgin taking the lowest place at the feet of Elizabeth,"[53] though, eventually, Elizabeth did not let this happen and placed Mary by her side.

> In return, I only ask of Thee,
> O most kind Father of us all:
> Let me save at least one soul
> One you already know.[54]

This poem, written on December 9, 1928, is a mirror of what Sister Teresa is and of the future, waiting for the future Mother Teresa. All that she has imagined until now with the eyes of the spirit would be real once the ship reached the harbor. She was ready to take the challenge.

It took almost a month for the ship to reach Port of Chennai (the former Madras), going across the Mediterranean Sea, Suez Canal, Red Sea, Indian Ocean, Arabian Sea, Gulf of Mannar, reaching to the Bay of Bengal, stopping in Port Said in northeast Egypt, Colombo in Sri Lanka (the former Ceylon), and finally stopping in Chennai.

Sister Teresa wrote to the editors of *Katoliecke Misije* back home in Skopje about her first impressions of the trip:

> On December 27, we arrived at Colombo....One could easily notice the profound poverty among the people. We felt especially sorry for those who pulled rickshaws like horses through the streets. We unanimously decided that we would never use the hand pulled rickshaws again as a means of transportation....We were all filled with consternation....All we could do was to pray that the load would be light for them....Here, nature is marvelous. The whole city seems like a big garden.[55]

Mark Twain, when he visited India in 1890, had the same impression of humans carrying humans or the number of what he called "cab-substitutes—open coffins, in which you sit, and are then borne on men's shoulders up the steep roads in time"[56] as a way of transportation in India.

"This was India! the land of...fabulous wealth and fabulous poverty, of splendor and rags, of palaces and hovels," as Mark Twain wrote during his visit there.[57] Sister Teresa wrote her first impressions of Chennai:

> When we visited the city [Madras] we were deeply struck by
> the indescribable poverty of the people. In the streets, along
> the walled city's periphery...live a large number of families.
> They live day and night in the open, on mats woven out of
> palm leaves, or, in many cases on the floor. All were almost
> completely nude....On their foreheads they bear some
> marks, which have some religious meaning.[58]

The periphery-to-periphery trajectory of Sister Teresa was decided
since the first days she spent in India. She was convinced that if
people back home in Skopje would see the extreme poverty and
deprivation that existed in India, they would not complain about
poverty at home; instead, they would thank the Lord who has
blessed them with much abundance. She ended the letter pleading
for prayers: "Pray much for us, that we may become good and
courageous missionaries."[59]

On January 6, 1929, the day of the Epiphany, Sister Teresa
and other missionaries left the sea and took a new route via River
Ganges to Kolkata, which was to become as dear to her as the city of
her birth, Skopje. As it was the Feast of the Epiphany, Sister Teresa
jokingly would say to the sisters that "she and the sisters were the gift
of the Magi."[60] She continued the connections and correspondence
with people at home, providing detailed accounts of her trip:

> On January 6th, in the morning, we sailed from the sea to
> the river Ganges, also called the "Holy River." Travelling
> by this route we could take a good look at our new home-
> land, Bengal. The nature is marvelous. In some places
> there are beautiful small houses but for the rest, only huts
> lined up under the trees. Seeing all this we desired that we
> might, as soon as possible, enter among them. We came
> to know that here are very few Catholics....Our Indian
> sisters waited for us there, with whom, with indescribable
> happiness, we stepped for the first time on Bengal's soil.

In the convent chapel, we first thanked our dear Savior for this great grace that He had so safely brought us to the goal for which we had been longing. Here we will remain one week and then we are leaving for Darjeeling, where we will remain during our novitiate.[61]

Sister Teresa was happy to have reached her new homeland and what she had been longing for. The first encounter with the new world would become the field of mission for the future Mother Teresa. She was prepared with what to expect in the Balkan periphery. Sister Teresa and other missionaries were foreigners. They did not need to imagine themselves as such (foreigners), and they "discover[ed] how much is to be seen,"[62] to use the words of Rabindranath Tagore. Besides "seeing," Sister Teresa understood how much the missionaries were called to do in the new Indian existential periphery.

When Sister Teresa and other missionaries arrived in India, the country was going through what historians define as India's crisis of colonial order, which had begun in 1919 and continued until 1939. It was the beginnings of Indian nationalism and India's movement for self-determination and freedom from British Raj. Indian popular sentiment testified to a deeply rooted animosity toward British colonialism. The factors aiding the growth of Indian nationalism in the nineteenth century were many. Some were related and a result of the British innovations in administration, and some came in the form of reaction to the Christian missionary challenge,[63] which Sister Teresa and missionaries before her were part of. Liberal Western-style education and the birth of the universities of Bombay, Chennai, and Kolkata gave new impetus to the national movement. The response of the Hindus—who were a religious majority—to the Christian missionary challenge came full circle from open resistance to the proud self-confidence under the Ramakrishna Mission[64] and Ramakrishna Movement, a Hindu religious and spiritual organization that, like Western schools, offered educational and philanthropic work. Moreover, it was the advent of Gandhi, not only as a principal architect of India's independence from Britain, but as one of the most original and influential thinkers of the twentieth century.[65] Nationalism and the nationalistic movement, the fall of empires, religious frictions among Hindus and Muslims, and religious minorities (as was the case of Catholics): these Sister Teresa had witnessed in the Balkans. The initial Balkan periphery had prepared her to face the new periphery and the same nationalist aspirations for self-determination and freedom she witnessed and had suffered in the Balkans.

After a few days spent at the convent of Loreto in Kolkata, Sister Teresa took the train for the Loreto Convent in Darjeeling in the Indian state of West Bengal, in the foothills of the impressive Himalayas. The convent was founded in 1846 by Mother M. Teresa Mons, one of the three pioneering Irish ladies who labored in the cause of education in this distant land.[66] For many foreigners, Darjeeling (Dorji Ling) is a city of dreams, romances, intrigues, and delicious tea. But the city is deeply mysterious. For Sister Teresa, Darjeeling would be the city of novitiate and where she heard another call— the call within the call, where Jesus came to talk to her. It was a city of two beginnings for Sister and later Mother Teresa. It couldn't be a better location for an initiation and a new start: in Darjeeling, the place where the precious stone emblematic of the thunderbolt of Indra (the god) rested.[67] The spot where it landed is known as Observatory Hill. In the late eighteenth century, Nepalese troops destroyed the Buddhist monastery that stood atop it, and today a complex of shrines and small temples mark the location that is holy for Buddhists and Hindus.[68] Moreover, Darjeeling district is the place where three international borders meet—Nepal, Bhutan, and Bangladesh. Its boundary also touches the northeastern state of Sikkim and the Jalpaiguri district of West Bengal, a district where different people and religions have met. For Sister Teresa, Darjeeling was the town of three beginnings: novitiate, first, and final vows.

SISTER TERESA'S THREE BEGINNINGS: NOVITIATE, FIRST, AND FINAL VOWS

On May 23, 1929, in the month of Mary, Sister Teresa started her two-year novitiate in Darjeeling under the spiritual guidance of the Mistress of Novices, Mother Baptista Murphy, an experienced and highly devout Loreto Sister. For Loreto Sisters, novitiate is a time of intense spiritual discernment and spiritual growth, which laid the foundations for a total and unreserved dedication to the gospel. It was a regimented two years that required practicing the virtues; silence and punctuality; early morning prayer routine; Mass, meditation, and participation in the life of the community; and a disciplined regimen of reading the Scripture and the lives of saints— especially the life of Thérèse of Lisieux. As we have noted already, the Loreto Sisters foundress Mary Ward's vision for her sisters was to respond to mission, to love and serve the poor, and to go out and find God in all things—the core of Ignatian spirituality. Preparing to live a profound Ignatian spirituality, about halfway through the first year of the novitiate, the Loreto novices made a thirty-day retreat devoted to the Spiritual Exercises of St. Ignatius of Loyola— practices Sister Teresa knew about and had practiced under the guidance of Fr. Jambrenković in Skopje. In sum, knowledge of Loreto spirituality, history, and constitutions were focuses of the first-year novitiate.

Following the second year of novitiate, the candidates had the opportunity for apostolic work among the poor, the infirm, and the needy or in fields appropriate for their gifts and talents. Sister Teresa also started teaching at the elementary school of Darjeeling run by the sisters, so she could have the necessary preparation for the teaching license the sisters ought to pursue after the profession of the first vows. Moreover, each novice had to sew her own religious habit she would wear when she would profess her vows.[69] Sister Teresa was used to obedience, order, and prayer—these were practices she grew up with in her family, so she felt at home with the new routine. She kept her family in Skopje informed of the milestones in her religious vocation. She was happy to share the news of entering the Darjeeling novitiate with her aunt Mary, sending a beautiful picture of her all dressed in black. On the back of the card she wrote in Albanian,

> I am doing well and in good health. I am sending you this picture as a remembrance of the most beautiful day of my life, when I dedicated all my life to Christ. Pray much for me. Regards from your Gonxhe—signed: Tereza e Vogël Krishtit Fëmi (Little Teresa of Child Jesus). Darjeeling February 22, 1929[70]

After exactly two years, on May 25, 1931, in the Church of the Immaculate Conception of Loreto Convent, twenty-one-year-old Sister Teresa completed her novitiate and was ready to take her first vows—vows of poverty, chastity, and obedience—otherwise known as temporary profession, which usually lasts between six and nine years. By the vow of poverty, she gave up her possessions; by the vow of chastity, she gave her heart's love to God alone; by the vow of obedience, she promised to do his will for her, as directed by her lawful superiors.[71] The vows were taken for one year, as was the custom in Loreto. Subsequently she renewed her vows every year for three years and then once for three years before being admitted to final profession.[72] During this period the Loreto Sister may be assigned to various ministries within the order or undertake further studies in theology, liturgy, or a related field. In the case of Sister Teresa, she was assigned to teaching at St. Mary's Bengali School for girls in the Kolkata suburb of Entally, one of the two schools run by the Loreto Sisters in the Loreto Convent.[73]

When Sister Teresa entered her new home, the Loreto Convent in Entally, the sister superior of the Loreto Entally Congregation assigned Sister Teresa to teach history and geography, two subjects she was passionate about. Loreto Entally was a British-style school for wealthy Indian and British girls and the teaching language was

English.[74] In contrast, St. Mary's was run jointly by the Loreto Sisters and the Daughters of St. Anne, a diocesan community of Indian sisters, founded in answer to the situation and needs of the contemporary local Church.[75] The Daughters of St. Anne were a branch of the Loreto Sisters made up exclusively of Bengali sisters, dressed in local costume—blue saris in winter and white saris in summer. St. Mary's middle school was for Bengali girls of various economic backgrounds.[76] The teaching language at St. Mary's was Bengali, a language in which, thanks to her linguistic gifts, Sister Teresa was very proficient. Since there were no language barriers, she was asked to help the Daughters of St. Anne. At Entally, she taught for seventeen years, first as a teacher and later, beginning in 1937, as the school's principal or headmistress.

The assignments at St. Mary's marked the beginning of Sister Teresa's teaching vocation, which for her was a vocation within a vocation, or a vocation that would lead to her life's vocation and the foundation of the Missionaries of Charity. The students Sister Teresa was teaching at Entally were poor, coming from broken families, and the major part of them were orphans and had no social status. Through her students, Sister Teresa was touching the peripheries of the Indian society. The nineteenth century had seen class division, or better, the consolidation of social classes in society.[77] This social stratification or class division, manifested in the difference between schools on the same campus, had entered Loreto education in Ireland and elsewhere, including India. The students who were studying in English were living in another edifice, near the main Loreto House school where the privileged girls came from the middle-class or more elevated castes. The poor students were dependent on benefactors and sisters begging. The differences between the two schools, and the fact that money could buy a better education, might have bothered Sister Teresa a great deal, as "she was for everybody,"[78] treating everybody equally. That explains why teaching students coming from the existential and social peripheries of Indian society became Sister Teresa's mission. She taught catechism, a life of prayer and living the sacraments and saving souls, the mission she had been dreaming about. Life at the school was rewarding for the young Sister Teresa. "When it is hardest, I console myself with the thought that souls are saved in this way and that dear Jesus has suffered much more for them."[79] Life was not easy in India but Sister Teresa was happy "when she thinks that she is doing the same work which Jesus was doing when He was on earth, and that she is fulfilling Jesus' commandment: 'Go and teach all nations!'"[80] she wrote to *Blagovijest*, in November 1932. Sister Teresa knew how to connect her love of teaching with the love of serving the poor: for her these were two sides of the same coin, because teaching is in fact a Christian vocation, a work of mercy—since lack of knowledge is a type of poverty greater than purely material poverty.[81]

Sister Teresa understood how to address the two poverties: the intellectual and material poverty, the apostolate of teaching with the apostolate of serving. In keeping with the Loreto foundress's dictum to "love the Poor"—a dictum Mary Ward modeled during her life with the poor patient in the hospital,[82] opening a school for the poor children of the town, or showing rare affability to the poor and the little ones she met on the road[83]—Sister Teresa dedicated time to the poor and the orphans at the sisters' orphanage. Between the school and the orphanage, the sisters served some five hundred children.[84] She also served at an ambulatory hospital, directed by the sisters in the city's peripheries, a simple, one-room ambulatory to succor people who were sick and miserable. People traveled for miles to come for help. The lines of people waiting to be seen by the sister in charge must have impressed Sister Teresa. She was touching the heart of the Indian periphery and absorbing it.

Moreover, the periphery of the untouchables—the Dalits (literally meaning broken people), who were socially ostracized in Kolkata—were calling young Sister Teresa to "touch" them. From the window of the Loreto Convent, on the second floor, one could see beyond the high walls surrounding the convent to the misery of the poor periphery of Motijhil (Pearl Lake), which, unlike what the name suggests, was a vast "lake" of an overpopulated neighborhood, with poor and starving people on the streets sleeping in the open, open sewers, and disease.

Sister Teresa paid careful attention to St. Mary's students, and their lives and poverty beyond the school. Hers was a holistic education pedagogy that included the social, emotional cultural, and religious dimension of her students' growth, besides academic advancement. Sister Teresa had learned and was applying the vision of the foundress Mary Ward in her work in education. Cardinal Ratzinger preached on this vision at a Mass held in honor of the four hundredth anniversary of Ward's birth: "And with her charism she understood that one cannot teach the faith without forming the whole person, a totally human culture. On the other hand, she understood that every good teaching must be directed toward the art of being human and that the heart of this art is faith."[85]

On May 24, 1937, on the Feast of Mary Help of Christians, in Darjeeling, after nine years, following the Loreto constitution, Sister Teresa took her final vows, proclaiming her final yes and life-long commitment to God with Archbishop Ferdinand Périer, SJ, presiding. She was committed and at peace with her choice and was more than ready to roll up the sleeves and work harder for the glory of God and souls. "What a great grace!" she wrote to Fr. Jambrenković, her former spiritual director and confessor in Skopje, adding, "I really cannot thank God enough for all that He has done for me. His for all eternity! Now I rejoice with my whole heart that I have joyfully carried my cross with Jesus."[86]

The choice of the Marian month to make the landmarks in her religious vocation (novitiate on May 23, 1929; first vows on May 25, 1931, and final vows on May 24, 1937) is striking. She was May and Mary bound. As had her patron St. Thérèse of Lisieux, Mother Teresa had pledged a life under Mary—to live and work under her guidance and intercession, learning to be little by living the little way, and suffering with joy for Jesus.

In the words of Mary Ward, Sister Teresa was going to be "wholly His…giving God what is his due, me my desert," as her sister Barbara Ward wrote in February 1619.[87] Final vows also meant that Sister Teresa would become Mother Teresa according to the constitutions of Loreto Order. This is what she wrote to Fr. Jambrenković, confessing about her final vows:

> Do not think that my spiritual life is strewn with roses—that is the flower which I hardly ever find on my way. Quite the contrary, I have more often as my companion "darkness." And when the night becomes very thick—and it seems to me as if I will end up in hell—then I simply offer myself to Jesus. If He wants me to go there—I am ready—but only under the condition that it really makes Him happy. I need much grace, much of Christ's strength to persevere in trust, in that blind love which leads only to Jesus Crucified. But I am happy—yes happier than ever. And I would not wish at any price to give up my sufferings.[88]

Drink the Chalice to the Last Drop

> Do you remember once you told me in Skopje: "Gonda, you want to drink the chalice to the last drop?" I do not know if at that time, I thought as I do now, but now yes, and that joyfully even without a tear….It does not go so easily when a person has to be on one's feet from morning till evening. But still, everything is for Jesus; so, like that everything is beautiful, even though it is difficult.[89]

The yes Gonxhe gave to Fr. Jambrenković in Skopje was probably not as informed as the firm yes she gave when she professed her final vows. Every suffering was worth suffering for Jesus. "Can you drink the cup that I am going to drink?" (Matt 20:22), Jesus asked in Matthew's Gospel. Can you endure the suffering that I am going to endure? Can you drink from the cup of suffering?—that was exactly what Jesus was asking. The sons of Zebedee, James and John, responded the same way Mother Teresa responded: Yes, "we can" (Matt 20:22). James was the first of the twelve apostles to be martyred, and John willingly offered himself for martyrdom—to suffer and die for Christ—but was spared by a miracle. Modern martyrdom for Christ—giving witness to Christ—was the meaning of the yes Mother Teresa pronounced when she took her perpetual vows.

War followed Mother Teresa in her newfound periphery, her new homeland of India. Two years after her final vows, in 1939, the Second World War broke out, and India was dragged into war by the British government, without any consultation or consensus from the Indian leaders and the Indian National Congress. Large nationalist protests ensued, culminating in the 1942 Quit India Resolution—a resolution passed by Congress demanding the withdrawal of the British Power from India.[90] Gandhi reinforced his demands for independence via a nonviolent movement for India's independence from Britain that resulted in his arrest together with other members of the Indian National Congress. Gandhi's arrest caused national unrest and public protests all over India. 1946 saw the rise of Muslim League nationalism, Muslim-Hindu violence, the partition of India, and creation of a separate state—modern Pakistan, with a Muslim majority, established on August 14, 1947, was a price India paid to gain independence from the British Empire. Partition caused riots, unrest, and an enormous wave of migration for safe havens—Muslims going to Pakistan and Hindus and Sikhs toward India. Between 14 and 16 million people were displaced; refugees flocked to Kolkata. World War II was unfolding in Mother Teresa's convent's backyard: Japan occupied Burma, and Kolkata became a theater of war. The war had literally entered the Loreto Convent as the convent was transformed into a hospital. Students and sisters were moved to another temporary location in the village of Morapai, where Mother Teresa visited the houses of the poor.[91]

As if war were not enough, there was the Great Famine of 1942–43, which was related to the Second World War but also to administrative failure.[92] War and famine combined were disastrous for people in Kolkata: people were starving and dying on the streets. Cholera and malaria epidemics struck the population, causing more than two million people to perish according to conservative government estimates. Black marketeers and moneylenders multiplied all over Kolkata. Mother Teresa lived the horror that was unfolding beyond the walls of the convent. She learned in the Balkan periphery the devastation war can bring to the lives of people including partition, ethnic and religious hatred, strife, famine, and death. What she was witnessing was bringing back the old periphery in the new. She realized that Skopje and Kolkata were inherently connected in human suffering. Witnessing the Great Famine made her take an additional personal vow in April 1942, that she kept secret in her heart: "I made a vow to God, binding under [pain of] mortal sin, to give to God anything that He may ask, 'Not to refuse Him anything,'"[93] as she confessed to Archbishop Périer, September 1, 1959. This was confirming her life-long commitment of witnessing to Christ. It was a deeper reflection and fulfillment of drinking the chalice to the last drop.

Mother Teresa was absorbing what was unfolding beyond the doors of the Loreto Convent. She could not be immune to the periphery and the peripherals, which had penetrated her convent via her students. She understood that Christ will never abandon humanity—he is not disconnected from human suffering but is perfectly and permanently in the middle of human suffering and was using her, the little Mother Teresa, to bring some hope to the peripherals. Mother Teresa had learned how to respond to suffering in the Balkan periphery. She knew Drana's hands-on and active approach to suffering. Those who suffer are not looking for someone to theorize or theologize suffering. Instead those who suffer need action and attention, solidarity and charity. She took to the streets: in 1946, three hundred girls in the boarding school she was teaching at St. Mary's had nothing to eat.[94] Due to the unrest and bloodshed in the streets of Kolkata, the communication with the outside world had stopped along with food supplies and transportation connections. She stepped out into the streets, although she was not supposed to step out. "Then I saw the bodies on the streets, stabbed, beaten, lying there in strange positions in their dried blood...when I went out on the street—only then I saw the death that was following them."[95] Mother Teresa considered suffering of the people in India, being those Hindus or Muslims, her suffering too. Suffering is indeed communal; one cannot face suffering alone: "Bear one another's burdens" (Gal 6:2), wrote St. Paul to the Galatians. And that was exactly what Mother Teresa was doing. It happened that while in the streets, she encountered a lorry full of soldiers, who stopped when seeing the nun among the cadavers and told her to return to the convent. They returned Mother Teresa to the convent together with bags of rice they had in the lorry.[96]

With those terrible images of devastation and immense human suffering ingrained in her memory, on September 10, 1946, Mother Teresa took the train and left Kolkata for her annual spiritual retreat at Darjeeling. It was the journey of a lifetime, and of new beginning, that transformed her life forever. The drinking of the chalice to the last drop was becoming more real. It was what she would call the call within a call, the vocation within a vocation, and speaking of Darjeeling—a beginning within a beginning—the beginning of the Missionaries of Charity. It was the train ride of a lifetime: Mother Teresa had an intimate encounter with Christ. It was a sweet voice, speaking softly, heart to heart.

Initially, she did not want to reveal the details—it was too intimate, personal, and precious, but this is what she wrote:

[It] was a call within my vocation. It was a second calling. It was a vocation to give up even Loreto where I was very happy and to go out in the streets to serve the poorest of the poor. It was in that train, I heard the call to give up

94

all and follow Him into the slums—to serve Him in the poorest of the poor....I knew it was His will and that I had to follow Him. There was no doubt that it was going to be His work.[97]

She was called to quench God's thirst. She had been thirsting to quench God's thirst for quite a while. The two thirsts had met in her in a manner described by St. Augustine: God thirsts that we may thirst for him.[98] "Will you do this for Me?" Jesus asked Mother Teresa, and her response was yes. Her hope to bring light to those in darkness would be fulfilled, but in a way, she could not have anticipated as she traveled to her chosen mission land. The call within a call was yet a new beginning for Mother Teresa while she was traveling to Darjeeling. It was a beginning to go even deeper into the periphery. She was gifted to the periphery by her special calling and through that calling she became a gift from the periphery to the entire world.

CHAPTER 4

SPIRITUAL DARKNESS

With me the sunshine of darkness is bright.[1]

A TAINTED SAINT?

On the tenth anniversary of Mother Teresa's death, a new book edited by Fr. Brian Kolodiejchuk, a member of the Missionary of Charity Fathers, a male religious order founded by Mother Teresa, and postulator of Mother Teresa's canonization, published a book including her personal and very intimate letters indicating her doubts of faith, her "atheism," and, most importantly, Mother's prolonged utter darkness, spiritual warfare, loneliness, and feeling of the absence of God. The book—a must read for any spiritual director for the religious and lay, for the Christian and the non-Christian, for the atheist, the nonbeliever, the Marxist, the communist, the doubter and the doubting—sent out shock waves all over the world. Mother's almost fifty years of doubting and dark night of the soul caught the media and publicity glare. She had been a media celebrity—she did not want or seek celebrity status, but the media sought her. She was genuine, a fresh voice and extreme in loving— her actions sent a message modern society needed to hear. In return, Mother touched millions through the media with her extraordinary, simple, and unassuming charisma. So, when Fr. Kolodiejchuk's book was published, the media jumped on the unexpected and very surprising story and Mother was making headlines again, this time from beyond the grave.

The same *Chicago Tribune* that in 1997 wrote "Mother Teresa Left Us Great, Deep Love" realized that besides great and deep love, Mother Teresa had left behind a legacy of doubt and disbelief. Still, the *Tribune* writer asserted that nonetheless the publishing of the book "will not hamper her path to sainthood."[2] At the same time, Geneviève Chénard, writing for the *New York Times*, used the news to state that she was not "convinced we should be so quick to canonize Mother Teresa,"[3] raising issues about saint-to-be miracles, her relations to dictators, political choices, mental health, schizophrenia, psychosis, and anxiety disorders[4] or clinical depression, which had started early in Mother Teresa's life due to the tragic death of her father.[5] Others, including Mother Teresa's harsh arch-critic Christopher Hitchens, jumped at the opportunity and used Mother's dark night of the soul as a weapon against a confused old lady who had ceased to believe[6] and more generally against religion and faith as a pure human construction. This is how Hitchens ends his August 28, 2007, *Newsweek* article: "I say it as calmly as I can—the Church should have had the elementary decency to let the earth lie lightly on this troubled and miserable lady, and not to invoke her long anguish to recruit the credulous to a blind faith in which she herself had long ceased to believe."[7] Catholics and non-Catholics wondered why the Vatican would allow the publishing of a book of doubts by none other than Mother's postulator at a time when her case was in the process for canonization. The publication of this book of letters by her cause's postulator would seem to go against reason: it made no sense. Would that be beneficial to the Church, the faithful Catholic or non-Catholic who had thought that Mother had an intimate relationship with Jesus and was carrying out his mission among the poor? Was Mother a fake Catholic, an imposter—a fraud? What about the most recent Roman pontiffs starting with Paul VI, John Paul II, Benedict XVI, and Francis: How and why did they support and promote her order, mission, beatification, and canonization when the Church knew of her doubts and her dark night of the soul? In the end, why was the Church encouraging questions about the orthodoxy of the people's saint?

There is much more to the publication of these letters and diary about the dark night of the soul. The reality is quite different from what the critics and uninformed Catholics and non-Catholics thought or jumped to conclude. Mother and her mission to serve the poorest of the poor cannot be understood without a mystical-ascetical theological framework. Mother, through her letters, was taking a stand to enlighten people's ways, including the minds and the paths of her critics from beyond the grave. After all, trials are human, but how she stands the trial, including the trial of faith, is the key to understanding Mother Teresa's dark night of doubt and darkness. She endured the trial and never gave up—in the words of poet Alfred Lord Tennyson (1809–92), she "cleave[d] ever to the sunnier side of doubt, and cl[u]ng to Faith beyond the forms of Faith."[8] For Mother, doubts never became unbelief. She did not feel ashamed discussing her doubts with her spiritual advisors. In fact, for those who have doubts about the very possibility of faith, Mother's experience might be enlightening, leading them to a path she walked before them. Additionally, the dark night of the soul, which is a well-known state in Christian mystical-ascetic tradition, never overwhelmed Mother. She was not "sunder'd in the night of fear."[9] Mother's dark night of the soul was well known to her, her spiritual directors, and Church leaders, but remained unknown to her most intimate sisters and collaborators. Her smile is profound, which is captured in iconography; hers was a darkness that was invisible to the outside world. Mother's case of the dark night of the soul was a special case in the history of mysticism. Mother was peripheral even in her darkness among the Christian saints and especially women mystics like St. Teresa of Avila, St. Thérèse of Lisieux, and St. Gemma Galgani who experienced the dark night of the soul but not as long and as intensely as St. Mother Teresa. Was she a tainted saint? As this chapter will explain, one thing that she was "tainted" with was contagious holiness, which ended up lifting others to holiness.

RECENT PONTIFFS ON DOUBT AND DARKNESS

Most recent pontiffs have reflected on doubt, belief and non-belief, and the blurred line separating believers from nonbelievers. Joseph Cardinal Ratzinger, in his classic *Introduction to Christianity*, explores doubt versus belief, or the doubt versus faith dichotomy. Even when the individual faithful has discovered God in the presence of Jesus Christ, there is need for reflection and questioning, which does not exclude questioning, "Are you really He?"[10]—a question asked anxiously in the dark hour even by John the Baptist. The future pontiff admits the legitimacy of doubt as a reality in the life of the faithful: "The believer will repeatedly experience the darkness in which the negation of unbelief surrounds him like a gloomy prison from which there is no escape, and the indifference of the world, which goes its way unchanged as if nothing had happened."[11] What the believer and the unbeliever have in common is doubt; the unbeliever is also surrounded by doubt and questions about the "faith" of his nonbelieving or lack of faith in God. Neither believer nor nonbeliever is immune to doubt. Consequently, the dark night of the soul of Mother Teresa will serve both: the believer and the nonbeliever of Ratzinger's dichotomy. In the end, and if appropriately understood, Mother and her dark night of the soul will be an encouragement for all those who are in doubt, estranged, or in opposition to everything ecclesiastical and religious, including Christianity, as Paul Tillich, a Lutheran philosopher and theologian wrote. In a way, it seems as though Mother and her recorded dark night of the soul would say to anyone experiencing doubt, come and ask questions, "I am here."[12]

Since the first homily inaugurating his pontificate on October 22, 1978, Pope John Paul II extended an invitation to dialogue to

Thomas's doubters, those tormented by doubts, thus acknowledging the belief and doubt or light and obscurity that are part and parcel of the mystery of faith.[13] The pope invited people to listen once again, to give faith a fresh chance so that doubt does not turn it into despair,[14] which was never the case for Mother Teresa. Besides dealing with the "doubters," Pope John Paul II provides a key to understanding the philosophical and theological framework of the dark night of the soul, something young Karol Wojtyła had studied. The future pope wrote his doctoral dissertation on St. John of the Cross under the guidance of the distinguished Dominican theologian Fr. Garrigou-Lagrange,[15] titling the dissertation "The Doctrine of Faith according to St. John of the Cross" and focusing, as he himself explained, "on the subject of Faith according to St. John of the Cross."[16] Wojtyła's dissertation director was an eminent scholar on ascetic and mystical theology in the history of the Church who had written and researched in depth the three stages of spiritual life on the lives of saints as they transitioned to holiness and union with God. Fr. Garrigou-Lagrange defined the three stages of spiritual maturation that result in union or spiritual marriage with Christ as the beginning of grace, the illuminative way, and the unitive way. The conclusion Wojtyła arrived at in his dissertation is crucial in understanding Mother Teresa's mystical experience through her unprecedented and prolonged dark night of the soul: by encountering God, one comes to live within God. In this way, God lives in his people and his people become God-like, without each—God and humans—losing their essence. This process in Eastern Christianity is called *theosis*—union with God, becoming *like* God: "I in them and you in me, that they may be brought to perfection as one" (John 17:23). Wojtyła's interpretation of St. John of the Cross's mysticism is that the goal of the Christian life is to become *God by participation*.[17] As with doubters, Wojtyła's understanding of mysticism was neither reserved to or practiced by a few elect people. Instead, the way to encounter God *by participation* was wide open to all—a "social" mysticism in dialogue with the world, which includes dialogue with atheists or unbelievers. Consequently, the dark night of the soul is an experience that is typically human and Christian because even in darkness one can find the loving hand of the Divine Teacher and hang on to faith ever more strongly. "He is silent and hides Himself sometimes because He has already spoken and manifested Himself with sufficient clarity. Even the experience of His absence can communicate faith, love, and hope to one who humbly and meekly opens himself to God,"[18] as he would write in his apostolic letter to Fr. Felipe Sainz De Baranda, Superior General of the Order of The Discalced Brothers of the Blessed Virgin Mary of Mount Carmel, on the occasion of the fourth centenary of the death of Saint John of the Cross, on December 14, 1990.

In a shift from the tone of his predecessors, Pope Francis gets more personal on the topic of doubt: in the general audience of November 23, 2016, Pope Francis spoke about healthy doubts people in general and religious faithful experience through life. Francis connected doubt and doubting with what academics call the process of critical thinking or critical inquiry into the subject matter: when one asks questions and analyzes the information in order to answer the questions accurately based on the evidence. By employing critical thinking and "doubting," greater knowledge on the subject matter is achieved, which leads one to sound conclusions. Additionally, Francis dwelt with the doubts related to faith in God. He made this crucial, faith-related question very personal by saying, "I think that some of you might ask me: 'Father, but I have many doubts about the faith; what should I do? Don't you ever have doubts?' I have many....Of course, everyone has doubts at times! Doubts which touch the faith, in a positive way, are a sign that we want to know better and more fully God, Jesus, and the mystery of his love for us."[19] The argument Francis was making is that doubts are normal, even healthy! In fact, doubts and questions about faith open the door to a greater study and catechesis, an entry to spiritual growth and spiritual maturity. Doubts are an indicator that faith is alive and vibrant, as faith that is unquestioned and untried becomes a weak faith. But the question remains: How can a person keep a balance between faith and doubt, or be a faithful faithful and a doubting doubter? Doubt is healthy until it becomes denial or unbelief, or when a person is overwhelmed by negative doubts that lead to unbelief and ultimately to a progressive separation from God. By believing in doubting as a stage in spiritual maturation and the significance of the dark night of the soul for the faithful, John Paul II, Benedict XVI, and Pope Francis supported the evidence for Mother Teresa to become St. Mother Teresa of Kolkata.

FIFTY YEARS OF *VIA DOLOROSA*: MOTHER TERESA'S JOURNEY THROUGH DARKNESS

Darjeeling, the town of three beginnings—novitiate, first, and final vows—would mark two more fresh beginnings for Mother Teresa. Here she would hear Jesus's voice, or *the Voice* as she would refer to it in her letters, and write the constitutions of her new order in 1947.

During the train journey to Darjeeling, on September 10, 1946, something extraordinary happened to Mother Teresa, more breathtaking than taking in the view of the Himalayas, valleys, woodlands, tea gardens, and little villages that impress passengers. This train ride was a life-changing journey. During the ride to Darjeeling the train must climb. From Sukna station—at an altitude of 533 feet—the train proceeds to an ascending path. The train must climb almost 900 feet in approximately 4 miles to reach to the next station of Rongtong (1,404 feet), followed by additional steep rises, quite unusual for a train ride. The train trip to Darjeeling with sharp turns, inclines, bends, and curves resembles the spiritual journey of Mother Teresa. In the Sacred Scripture, mountains are meeting places where God encounters people, changes lives, makes pronouncements, and sends people back down to the world with a prophetic message to deliver. God delivered the Ten Commandments to Moses on Mount Sinai, when

"Moses was speaking and God was answering him with thunder" (Exod 19:19). Centuries later, God spoke to the prophet Elijah on the same mountain and ordered, "Go out and stand on the mountain before the LORD; the LORD will pass by" (1 Kgs 19:11). The same experience was happening for Mother Teresa—she was hearing the Voice calling her to change the course of her life. During this prophetic train ride to Darjeeling for an eight-day spiritual retreat, on September 10, 1946, the thirty-six-year-old Mother Teresa heard the Voice and had an intimate spiritual encounter with Christ. The Voice called her to change the course of her life and leave the Loreto Sisters and the Loreto Convent, leave teaching at St. Mary's, and go deeper into the far-away peripheries of Kolkata:

> [It] is a call within my vocation. It was a second calling. It was a vocation to give up even Loreto where I was very happy and to go out in the streets to serve the poorest of the poor. It was in that train, I heard the call to give up all and follow Him into the slums—to serve Him in the poorest of the poor....I knew it was His will and that I had to follow Him. There was no doubt that it was going to be His work.[20]

As he calls everyone individually, Mother Teresa was called by name: she was his (Isa 43:1). Mother would later describe it as a deeply personal, inward, and spiritual call, a voice heard in faith and by faith. Fr. Lush Gjergji, an Albanian priest who was a friend and confidant of Mother Teresa, asked Mother to describe her call within the call, or the second call, as she often called it. "Was it a vision or something else?" Fr. Gjergji asked. Mother Teresa responded, smiling, "I was sure that was the voice of God. I was sure that He was calling me....This was an order, an assignment, a certainty. I understood what I had to do it, but I did not know how."[21] Beginning in September 10, 1946, Mother Teresa experienced specific revelations or locutions. Christian tradition abounds with private revelations that include hearing audible voices. The prophet Elijah heard

> a voice [who] said to him, Why are you here, Elijah?... The LORD said to him: Go back! Take the desert road to Damascus. When you arrive, you shall anoint Hazael as King of Aram....Elijah set out, and came upon Elisha, son of Shaphat, as he was plowing with twelve yoke of oxen; he was following the twelfth. Elijah went over to him and threw his cloak on him. (1 Kgs 19:13, 15, 19)

The prophet followed God's revelation and command. Peter the apostle had a revelation from God: "As Peter was pondering the vision, the Spirit said [to him], 'There are three men here looking for you. So get up, go downstairs, and accompany them without hesitation, because I have sent them.'" (Acts 10:19–20).

Similar to other mystics like St. Teresa of Avila, St. Thérèse of Lisieux, and St. Catherine of Siena, who at the age of six had her first vision of Christ seated in glory with the apostles Peter, Paul, and John that changed her life forever, Mother Teresa had intimate spiritual conversations with Jesus, who called her to start a fresh mission. The Voice implored Mother Teresa, "Come, come, carry Me into the holes of the poor. Come, be My light."[22] Mother Teresa related the train ride experience to Fr. Celeste Van Exem, SJ, her trusted spiritual director. She also shared with him her personal notes she had written during the retreat. By so doing, Mother was following the vows of obedience to God and to her superiors that she had taken in Darjeeling and within the Church's established structure and procedure in the case of personal revelations. Mother did not act immediately on the revelations without first discerning them. Moreover, Mother knew that structure and Church approval would give voice and structure to the Voice, permanency and organization to a new-indigenous religious community that the Voice was calling her to establish in order to serve the poorest of the poor. Between the months of September 1946 and mid-January 1947, Mother Teresa asked Fr. Van Exem for his permission to talk to the archbishop of Kolkata about her extraordinary experiences, but she was not allowed to do so. Mother Teresa had no doubt that the revelation was authentic. Probably, Fr. Van Exem was following the steps of Ignatian Spirituality in discerning God's will: he was employing the analytical approach, gathering detailed information, reasoning about complexities, and analyzing pros and cons. He might have consulted with Jesuit friends and other individuals who might be affected by the new revelations of Mother Teresa. In his reasoning heart, he knew that Mother Teresa's revelation was clear and genuine, and that Mother had no doubt in her mind that it was a special call—a second vocation. Mother's confidence might have helped Fr. Van Exem in his evaluation.

Only after four months of discernment did Fr. Van Exem finally give Mother Teresa permission to write to Archbishop Périer, SJ, describing her encounter and call in detail, as he instructed her:

> You will write to His Grace as a daughter to her father, in perfect trust and sincerity, without any fear or anxiety, telling him how it all went, adding that you talked to me and that now I think I cannot in conscience prevent you from exposing everything to him.[23]

In her letter to Archbishop Périer, Mother Teresa made clear that she was marking yet another periphery, a new trajectory in her religious vocation. It seems that working as a teacher inside the Loreto Convent, or being a Loreto religious sister teaching in Kolkata, was not peripheral enough for Mother; she had a calling for the radical periphery, be this the material, social, or spiritual periphery. Who wants to leave comfort for discomfort, the known for the unknown, security for insecurity, and a radical and apostolic poverty, all for Jesus, as she wrote to Archbishop Périer: "To leave that what I love and expose myself to new labours and sufferings which will be great, to be the laughing stock of so many—religious—to cling and choose deliberately the hard things of an Indian life—to [cling and choose] loneliness and ignominy—uncertainty—and all because of Jesus."[24] The change of habit was also a move further into the periphery— she exchanged the classic black and white habit of the Loreto order for the white and blue sari worn by the commoners of the Indian periphery. The changes she was now making, and about which she was consulting Archbishop Périer, were animated by the same desire and thirst for the radical periphery that in the past had led Gonxhe from her native Skopje to Kolkata. Mother's letter to Archbishop Périer was long and impassioned and laid out in minute detail her supernatural experience and intimate communications with Jesus.[25] Mother Teresa had read the life of Mother Cabrini and was determined to do in India what Mother Cabrini had accomplished in America. Mother Teresa's letter showed that she understood that the key to missionary success was identifying with the locals, adaptation, and making her adopted periphery her own, following in the footsteps of Mother Cabrini. She was not going against her nature by subtracting or diminishing her identity. Instead, she was adding a new identity via adaptation to the Indian culture, that she would be totally immersed in and make her own. The Voice had dictated that it wanted distinctly "Indian nuns, Victims of my love, who would be Mary and Martha."[26] Mother had enough experience with and appreciation of India and the Indian culture—by then she had almost two decades of service in India—and was ready to take the missionary challenge of further adaptation with the locals a step further, presaging Pope Pius XII's encyclical *Evangelii Praecones* (1951): "whatever there is in the native customs that is not inseparably bound up with superstition and error will always receive kindly consideration and, when possible, will be preserved intact."[27]

The Voice had practically dictated the constitutions and the mission of the new religious order Mother Teresa was going to found. How could Mother Teresa refuse what she had been asked to do? The thirst she had for souls brought her so far in the deep periphery of India—now she had been asked to go even farther and satiate the same thirst even deeper. Would she refuse the call? Would she refuse to obey or not humble herself before God? How could she not obey Christ's urgent plea?

The ongoing communication between Mother Teresa and Jesus continued from September 10, 1946, to approximately December 3, 1947. The end of 1947, however, marked the beginning of Mother Teresa's mystical journey of interior darkness and suffering. Darkness had come to stay and became her permanent interior state of the soul for fifty years, one she became used to and ended up loving as a special gift from God, as a way of participating in his suffering. In fact, Mother Teresa's spiritual darkness, or *via dolorosa*, was a three-way-unitive darkness: with Christ, the poor, and the people of every walk of life—believers and nonbelievers, Christian and non-Christian, the skeptic and the atheist, the pessimist, the prejudiced, and the persecuted. Her doubts and darkness were not symptoms of a crisis of faith; instead, it was Mother's strong faith that led her through darkness, making friendship with darkness and ending up loving darkness. While going through the dark night of the soul, Mother Teresa relied more than ever on her faith. In fact, her reliance on faith was increased through darkness. Although the experience of the dark night of the soul and the crisis of faith may seem similar experiences because they might be connected with or caused by crisis in faith, these two spiritual experiences are totally different. Crisis of faith is a crisis of prolonged doubt about faith or having a hard time agreeing with the articles of faith, which is not a healthy doubt. Faith cannot be based on empirical evidence 100 percent, nor can it be measured; instead, faith is based on the teaching authority of the Church (magisterium). Mother Teresa was not going through a crisis of faith. She was not indecisive about accepting or rejecting Christianity, Christ as Savior, or the main tenets of the faith. On the contrary, her faith was strong and became even stronger through the dark night of the soul. She remembered not to fear because he had

promised to remain in and with her: "I shall be with you always....
Trust Me lovingly—trust Me blindly."[28]

Furthermore, Mother, who had been exposed to trials since
her youth in the Balkan periphery, knew that trials are human and
part of the human journey. She overcame the trial of losing a parent, moving to a distant land, and living away from her family and
her people. However, she knew that she was not going to be tried
"beyond your [her] strength...with the trial he will also provide a
way out, so that you [she] may be able to bear it" (1 Cor 10:13).

Speaking of trials, Mother endured even the trials of misunderstanding. By mid-January 1947, her Loreto superiors decided to
transfer Mother Teresa to the Loreto community of Asansol, a city
in the Indian state of West Bengal and the second largest and second
most populated city of West Bengal after Kolkata. She was going
to teach Hindi, Bengali, hygiene, and geography. Mother Teresa
accepted the move with joy as part of his plan, although the move
was a form of punishment. "Some sisters of her community had
noticed Mother Teresa's frequent and long conversations in confession with Father Van Exem in the months following her retreat in
Darjeeling."[29] The sisters did not know why she was having long
conversations with Fr. Van Exem, her spiritual director, and they
considered these conversations inappropriate for a religious sister,
so they brought the issue of Mother Teresa's misbehavior to the
attention of the religious superiors, who reacted swiftly by "separating" Mother Teresa from Fr. Van Exem. Fortunately, Mother had
the Voice, and the intense spiritual conversations between Mother
Teresa and Jesus continued until May 1947, when she left Asansol
for Darjeeling for the yearly spiritual retreat that took place from
May 8 to June 14, 1947. According to a letter from Fr. Van Exem
to Archbishop Périer on June 14, 1947, Mother Teresa had passed
through some rough times and doubts or, as he wrote, awful desolation, and the idea of the work seemed to be a stupidity to her. But
this passed, as the Voice was there to assure her: "Our Lord told her
that her great fear had hurt Him."[30]

The doubt and the darkness were making an entrance into the spiritual journey of Mother Teresa. The Voice was giving her neither sign nor voice. She felt lost and conflicted. She was mourning the six months of close interaction with Christ and realized that "the sweetness and consolation and union of those 6 months—passed but too soon."[31] Christ had come unmasked to her but had left. However, she was confident in one thing: the voices and visions had helped her to be more trustful and draw closer to God,[32] and the faith had not perished; instead, it had become stronger, as she wrote in a letter to Archbishop Périer on June 5, 1947. The letter to the archbishop turned out to be the founding document and the rough draft of the constitutions for her new religious order the Missionaries of Charity. In the message to the archbishop, Mother explained her theology of mission, which consisted in adopting and making Indian culture her own. Her Missionaries of Charity would have to become Indians. However, little did Mother Teresa know that darkness was going to be her life companion and had come to stay in and with her until her death in 1997.

It is puzzling that the dark night of Mother Teresa started as soon as she began her new order and her new mission in Kolkata's deep periphery. By August 15, 1948, Mother had realized that darkness was there to stay. She was in tears but following to the letter the vows of obedience to her superiors, which she considered to be a blessing. In fact, Mother Teresa lived the vow of obedience freely and joyfully during all her life. It was her free choice she made in Darjeeling in 1929 and renewed when she started her new order. Darkness is a mystery—and a multitude of things can happen in the darkness, including new and longed-for and fervently prayed-for births. Indeed, light comes through and penetrates darkness. Mother Teresa's spiritual journey through darkness provides a valuable pathway, a model of how to act upon, or even enjoy its benefits. Probably a spirituality of darkness is in order, as most people do not know what they mean by "darkness," but they want to stay away from it.[33] Darkness is not only negative, after all. Didn't God promise Cyrus, the anointed Persian king, to give him treasures of darkness (Isa 45:3)? After all, God created everything—forming light and darkness (Isa 45:7), order and chaos. In Genesis, God worked in darkness to create light, and met Abraham in the darkness when "a great, dark dread descended upon him" (Gen 15:12). The Missionaries of Charity religious order had its start when Mother Teresa, the founder, was going through darkness, so in this case darkness had hidden treasures, the new life of a new order—in darkness, God creates anew. There is hope in darkness; the light shines in it (John 1:5). As Sister Gertrude Gomes, MC, would describe Mother Teresa's mission in the Indian periphery, using the dark-light dichotomy: "a Light has dawned in the darkness of the slums."[34] In the case of the religious congregation of the Missionaries of Charity, which is dedicated to the people in the dark slums, its birth was when Mother was going through the *via dolorosa* of darkness. Mother and her new congregation made darkness and the poverty of the dark slums their own to bring light to.

After several years of spiritual suffering in silence and obedience, in March 1953 Mother Teresa disclosed the interior suffering and darkness to Archbishop Périer. She referred to it as terrible darkness and felt that everything was dead inside her. She also confessed that this state of the soul had been present in her since she started the new religious congregation. The archbishop counseled her, writing a positive note saying that probably her darkness was not as dark as she thought it to be. From the correspondence, the archbishop seemed to be afraid of the dark and advised her to pray for light to come. He also considered her spiritual darkness superficial, more in the realm of feelings and unclarity than deeply rooted in her soul. His advice and counsel did not prove very helpful to Mother.

Gradually, Mother's interior darkness became even more challenging for her, but the progress of her order was a living sign of God's blessings and her firm yes to acting on what the Voice had dictated to her in 1947. While her soul remained in deep darkness and desolation, she continually reminded herself that she was nothing but a little pencil in God's hand, a little dispenser of his love: "No

I don't complain—let Him do with me whatever He wants."[35] In January 1955, according to a letter she wrote to Archbishop Périer, Mother Teresa felt a sense of solitude and alienation, a sense of void and abandonment from God and from the people she loved and trusted. Archbishop Périer probably misunderstood the spiritual state, the dark night of the soul Mother Teresa was going through. He seemed to believe that Mother was suffering the dark night of the passive purification of the soul.[36] Although Mother was gracious and kind with the archbishop, his spiritual advice was again unhelpful. He blamed her impulsiveness, overburdening, or the devil's temptation for her spiritual darkness.

Mother had a strong longing for the Voice to return. How long would Our Lord stay away? she asked Archbishop Périer.[37] She could not find the answer to this daunting question. She was probably missing Drana, her mother, and the rest of her family back home in Skopje. It had been almost three decades since she had last seen her family in 1928. Additionally, she had not talked to Fr. Van Exem for several months, although she found "no help" in his spiritual direction to guide her through her spiritual darkness. Nonetheless, she obeyed him and his advice "blindly."[38]

The early Church fathers called the state of suffering and desolation Mother Teresa was going through a spiritual martyrdom, or white martyrdom—to distinguish it from blood, or red, martyrdom. Mother Teresa gave witness to Christ through her darkness and by serving the poorest of the poor in the periphery. It was through darkness that she was entering into the mystery of the suffering Christ, the mystery of the redemptive cross—or, as John Paul II said, becoming Christ by participation.[39] She embodied the service of "a dedicated soul [who] is also a martyr and a daily one,"[40] daily martyrdom as witness in the time of peace. St. Augustine challenged the Christians of his time regarding martyrdom as witness. The Christian call to martyrdom is perpetual. Trials, including the dark night of the soul, are permanent. He wrote, "Let no one say: I cannot be a martyr, because there is now no persecution. Trials are never lacking....The

Christian soul is tried and, with the help of God, it conquers and wins a great victory....It fights in its heart, it is crowned in its heart, but by Him who sees into the heart."[41]

On February 9, 1956, Archbishop Périer answered Mother Teresa's letter with a comforting message explaining the perils of white martyrdom and mysticism without mentioning specifically St. John of the Cross or the two Teresas (of Avila and of Lisieux) who went through spiritual darkness. The archbishop wrote,

> In what you reveal there is nothing which is not known in the mystical life. It is a grace God grants you, the longing to be His entirely without return on self or creatures, to live by Him and in Him but that longing which comes from God can never be satisfied in this world, simply because He is infinite and we finite.[42]

Fr. Joseph Neuner, SJ, her new spiritual director, captured the patterns of darkness, and what was really happening in her soul was most helpful to Mother Teresa's state of spiritual darkness. After reading a long confession of Mother Teresa, in his testimony, Fr. Neuner would conclude that there was no reason for Mother Teresa to blame herself, because what she was experiencing "was simply the dark night of which all masters of spiritual life know,"[43] adding that Mother's was a deep and prolonged darkness that he had not noticed in other cases of Christian mysticism. The only response to the trials Mother Teresa was going through, according to Fr. Neuner's confession, was "[her] total surrender to God and the acceptance of the darkness in union with Jesus."[44] This conclusion proved most beneficial and useful to Mother.

As she was progressing in her spiritual ascent, Mother Teresa made a deal with darkness—darkness had become her permanent companion. "My darkness is a very small part of Jesus's darkness and pain he endured when he was on earth."[45] She had fallen in love with darkness, as she explained to Fr. Neuner:

For the first time in this 11 years—I have come to love the darkness.—For I believe now that it is a part, a very, very small part of Jesus' darkness & pain on earth. You have taught me to accept it [as] a "spiritual side of 'your work'" as you wrote.—Today really I felt a deep joy—that Jesus can't go anymore through the agony—but that He wants to go through it in me.—More than ever I surrender myself to Him.—Yes—more than ever I will be at His disposal.[46]

Darkness was brought by God, so she had accepted it as a gift. She thanked Fr. Neuner in her diary for teaching her "to accept darkness as a spiritual part of [her] work."[47] What was really happening in Mother's soul was that the night of passive purification of the soul had transitioned to a night of reparation for other souls.[48] Mother's trials at this point of her spiritual journey had reached a breakthrough, or solace—she had accepted darkness as part of her soul. Given Mother was not a beginner in her spiritual journey, her trial was not one of purification, but rather of a reparatory nature. She was following the prototype: the passion of the Christ on the cross; and she was working by the same means as he did for a greater spiritual cause—the foundation of a new religious order, the Missionaries of Charity. Given the highly dedicated religious and playful life Mother had led since her youth in the periphery of Skopje, to the Indian periphery, Mother might have moved into unity with Christ early in her spiritual journey, perhaps even shortly after the dark night began for her in 1947.[49] In all probability and while looking at key indicators in her spiritual ascent, Mother's purgative way and illuminative way, or dark night of the senses and dark night of the spirit, might have been brief transitions to the perfect unitive Way—spiritual marriage with Christ. In Eastern Orthodox theology, Mother's *kenosis* or self-emptying had led to *theosis* (union or deification),[50] following the example of the prototype:

Rather, he emptied himself,
taking the form of a slave,
coming in human likeness;
and found human in appearance,
he humbled himself,
becoming obedient to death, even death on a cross.
    (Phil 2:7–8)

Christ's *kenosis* reveals the character of God, but also human holiness understood as participation in God's holy, kenotic, cruciform life, which in Eastern Christianity is called *theosis*.[51] What *kenosis* meant for Mother was not only an imitation of Jesus in her self-giving until it hurt, but participating in the first person and acting firsthand in it, a "cocrucifixion," which meant that the suffering of going through the purgative way and illuminative way and "coresurrection" (unitive way) were realized partly in the present life here and now.

The unification or spiritual marriage with Christ that Mother experienced during her lifetime explains her profound two-way identification with the sufferings of Jesus on the cross: her Christ-likeness and cocrucifixion, and the identification with the poor and the world's suffering. Her virtuous works of self-giving, serving the poor and the world's peripheries, proceed flawlessly because her soul was in union with Christ; she had reached *theosis*. Fr. Brian Kolodiejchuk concurs regarding the sublime state of spiritual marriage of Mother Teresa. He thinks that her darkness had been reparative beginning in 1947:

> She came to realize that her darkness was the spiritual side of her work, a sharing in Christ's redemptive suffering. Regardless of how she had understood it, this trial of faith, hope, and love was not a purification from the defects characteristic of beginners in the spiritual life or even from those defects common to those advanced on the path of union with God. At the time of the inspiration, she had

114

frankly stated to Archbishop Périer that she had "not been seeking self for some time now." Moreover, in the months prior to the inspiration of September 10, she was, in the estimation of her confessor, near the state of ecstasy.[52]

Additionally, experiencing the supernatural gift of ecstasy is indicative that the soul has reached the spiritual marriage union with Christ. According to a letter of Fr. Van Exem to Archbishop Périer dated August 8, 1947, Mother Teresa must have reached the state immediately before ecstasy early in her life: "That had been my conviction,"[53] Fr. Van Exem explained. What about darkness after union? Is that an unusual and even peripheral case in mystical theology? The fact that Mother had reached the peak in her spiritual maturation early in her life did not mean that the state of union was the end journey, the end of suffering and darkness, and that she was enjoying glory. Mystical marriage means spiritual fruition and necessitates a return to the world, and an increase of activity[54]— this was exactly the case with the spiritual darkness and mysticism of Mother Teresa. Unlike other mystics, including St. Catherine of Siena or St. Teresa of Avila, who went through the dark night of the soul and withdrew from the world to fight their spiritual warfare, Mother never withdrew from the world. Darkness found her in the darkness in the slums of Kolkata and continued beyond the spiritual marriage. Simultaneously, she was combating spiritually and acting physically to alleviate suffering. This was the original pathway of Mother Teresa through darkness—and because of her unity with Christ and his suffering, Mother was able to fully suffer for others.

Mother Teresa's postunion dark night of reparative suffering is a special state of the soul freely chosen by the mystics. She was sharing in the sufferings of Christ, and her suffering was compensating for the sins and conversion of the others. That is why Mother's mysticism can be called a form of social mysticism. Mother was social even in her mystical darkness: reparation and saving souls was the mission she thirsted for. Moreover, the state of reparation presupposes voluntary exclusion from the joys of the union, so her suffering continued; however, the unitive source of the joys had been accomplished in the soul.[55]

The soul who is going through reparation is believed to be a purged and purified soul, in spiritual marriage with Christ and in union with other souls who are working their way through purification. Angelo Cardinal Comastri, in his book on Mother Teresa, explained that the postunion spiritual darkness Mother experienced was not related to a preparation for union, but rather it was "a loving participation in the redemptive suffering of Christ, who makes the mission of the saints fecund. The soul penetrates/participates far more intimately in the same experience of Christ on the Cross and this co-sharing [of the Cross] with Jesus produces the effect of attracting the others to Christ."[56] Mother Teresa's union with Christ is similar to the union St. Paul of the Cross (1694–1775) experienced. He, like Mother Teresa, suffered a prolonged forty-five years of spiritual darkness and suffering for others during all his long life, even after the spiritual union with Christ—St. Paul of the Cross lived to be eighty-one. However, there are differences in their paths: Mother's night of the soul was slightly longer—fifty years, and she found consolation only once, on the occasion of the requiem Mass for Pope Pius XII, who died on October 9, 1958. Coincidentally, it was the same pontiff who ten years before on August 8, 1948, had granted her permission to leave the Loreto Order and begin her new mission in the slums. After approximately eleven years of darkness Mother felt a very brief joyful solace of the soul from darkness, as she wrote to Archbishop Périer on November 7, 1958:[57]

> You will be very happy to hear the day you offered your Holy Mass for our Holy Father's soul in Cathedral—I prayed to him for a proof that God is pleased with the Society. There & then disappeared that long darkness, that pain of loss—of loneliness—of that strange suffering of ten years.[58]

Atypically, Mother's darkness would remain until the time of her death,[59] unlike the experience of other saints who suffered the dark night of the soul. After forty-five years of trial and darkness, St. Paul of the Cross was able to find spiritual consolation—"from time to time only, the Lord granted him a short respite."[60] Especially during the last five years of his life, when he had an apparition of Our Lady of Sorrows, he seemed to have reached the beatitude of heaven. However, both St. Paul of the Cross and Mother Teresa, who through darkness achieved union with Christ, sought to lift up others or to open the way for others to union or divinization, and this is one of their commonalities, besides creating new religious orders—Mother Teresa, the Missionaries of Charity, and St. Paul of the Cross, the Passionists. Darkness led Mother Teresa to action and more service. Even in darkness she was going for *magis*—more actively helping world's poverty. She did not seclude herself to reflection and prayer alone. Hers was an active prayer, communicating with God through her service. She led a life of active prayer and prayerful action. The first chapter of the Rule of the order founded by St. Paul of the Cross stated that "one of the principal ends of this least Congregation is not only to apply themselves untiringly to holy prayer so as to devote themselves to holy union with God but also to lead others to do the same, teaching them this holy exercise in the best and easiest manner possible."[61] The same approach is shared by Mother Teresa and her order, an additional commonality between the two saints who experienced the mystical experience of the dark night of the soul and founded new religious orders.

What Mother was suffering from was invisible—internal "bleeding" for fifty years. The spiritual suffering is, generally, more painful than the visible, bleeding stigmata. Mother Teresa was bearing the suffering and the marks of Jesus on her spirit (Gal 6:17). She was chosen to be a victim soul, taking upon herself the redemptive power of human suffering. She willingly accepted this unique and difficult mission of offering up her pains for the salvation of others and lifting people up with her example and exemplary obedience.

She was not longing for the joys of heaven. Instead, she envisioned heaven as fresh opportunity to bring light to those in darkness, which contributed to the spirituality and mysticism of darkness. There is a two-way identification and unity in darkness and a two-way journey: God to people and people to God.

Darkness united her to Christ, to the poor, and to suffering humans who were working their way to redemption and divinization. As darkness increased, so did her thirst for God and the redemption of souls. These were the effects of Mother Teresa's dark night of the soul—*magis* for more souls and for the greater glory of God, the motto of the Society of Jesus and the Ignatian spirituality she knew and was experiencing: a greater identification with Jesus, the poor, and the people. Mother Teresa proved that she was radical even in her love of darkness, appropriating and suffering like Christ and the poor she was serving. Her sacrifice of darkness was a price she had to pay to light the fire of love in others and bring them to the light of faith by "repairing" their image, as creatures were before the fall—through her darkness and suffering she was participating in Christ's redemptive mission on earth.

Mother achieved unity/*theosis* with God through his suffering and she became one with the great crowd she had visions about at the beginning of her vocation. It was the same crowd that had called her by name: "Come, come, save us—bring us to Jesus."[62] Greater identification with Jesus, the poor, and the people: this was the outcome of Mother Teresa's unusually long, peripheral, and custom-made darkness of the soul. It was from darkness and through darkness that she was enlightening people.

His work prospered, while Mother suffered. The painful darkness that continued for fifty years united her ever more intimately to Christ, and Christ radiated light through her darkness, transforming the darkness of the world into his light. Mother's was a trial of faith, not a crisis of faith; she was a selected victim soul, not a tormented and disbelieving soul. Her faith was a heroically incarnated faith she lived in the fullness of love for Christ and his people. Mother Teresa lived her faith "face-to-face with darkness,"[63] as St. Elizabeth of the Trinity, one of the greatest twentieth-century mystics, wrote in her letter to Abbé André Chevignard on June 14, 1903. Her darkness was to the end and to eternity. Mother Teresa is a canonized saint, and is probably, as she desired, a saint of darkness, which is highly unusual for a saint to desire, let alone be.

WAS THE UNION WITH CHRIST THE REASON WHY MOTHER WAS JOYFUL AND SMILING?

A radiant smile was constant on Mother Teresa's face, even when she was going through the icy cold darkness, loneliness, desolation, and abandonment. Mother paid special attention to smiling and being joyful and required her sisters to smile abundantly. One of the resolutions she made during the 1956 retreat, and in which she persevered during her entire life lived with spiritual darkness, was to smile at God. Smile more tenderly, pray more fervently, and all the difficulties will disappear[64]—this was Mother Teresa's maxim. "Joy is one of the best defenses against temptations,"[65] she wrote in her diary on April 27 (either 1948 or 1949). She cites St. Francis de Sales, bishop and prince of Geneva (1567–1622), in her diary, who used to say, "A sad saint is a sorry saint," and St. Teresa of Avila who was worried about her sisters only when she saw any of them "lose their joy."[66]

What was in Mother Teresa's smile? To keep smiling for fifty years when one is going through spiritual darkness must have been a challenging and difficult aspect of her spiritual martyrdom. However, Mother's broad smile provides evidence that she indeed was in union with Christ and in control of her spiritual darkness, not the other way around. There is more to a smile than a smile—there is theology and mystery all packed in it, which Mother Teresa understood and acted upon. Pope Benedict XVI, in his 2008 visit to Lourdes, reflected on the theology of smiling as a gateway to mystery.

A simple smile opens the door to the mystery of redemption, which leads to the mystery of the Trinity. As Mary taught Bernadette, to know Mary she had "to know her smile."[67] Today, Mary dwells in the joy and the glory of the resurrection. The tears shed at the foot of the cross have been transformed into a smile nothing can wipe away.[68] What was Mother Teresa's smile? She provides an answer: "The greater the pain and darker the darkness, the sweeter will be my smile at God.—Pray for me that I may love Jesus," she wrote in a letter to Fr. Neuner on October 16, 1961.[69] So was the smile of Mother Teresa, which transformed whoever was in her company, but especially the poor—it was a smile that never faded away. Her dark night of the soul transformed mystically into a radiant smile because of her joy of serving, and this transforming power of a smile is indeed the theology or the mysticism of smiling in Christian tradition.

Mary smiles at all, but her smile has a particular relevance to those who suffer, so that they can find comfort and solace through her smile.[70] The same can be applied to Mother Teresa's smile: she smiled at the poor she served, radiating whose work she was doing, to all people—even her arch-critics. In his 2018 apostolic exhortation, *Gaudete et Exsultate* (Rejoice and Be Glad), Pope Francis wrote about how the saints live lives of joy and good humor: "The benevolent and kind smile on the miseries and contradictions of life is part of the Christian wisdom that is a gift of the Holy Spirit. Far from being timid, morose, acerbic or melancholy, or putting on a dreary face, the saints are joyful and full of good humor."[71] So was Mother Teresa. She was joyful and smiling while she was suffering because she was faithful to Christ and the poor. As she wrote to Fr. Picachy on June 27, 1962, "Pray that I be a cheerful dog."[72]

But there was more in Mother's smile. If one can observe her smiling in action, Mother did not smile with her mouth and face alone, but with her eyes also. Her whole face was involved in a simple smile. Besides her mouth, she communicated with her smiling eyes, which according to experts are the most important indicator of a "sweet soul"—the smiling was happening when Mother was going through the dark night of the soul. According to psychologists Paul Ekman and Wallace Friesen, who study facial expressions and emotions, with particular attention to smiling, a way to detect a false smile is the absence of *orbicularis oculi* (a muscle in the face that closes the eyelids), which as they explain is easy to detect.[73] Until the end of her life, in her public appearances, Mother displayed a smiling mouth, and involved in her smile were her piercing smiling eyes. In an interview she gave to BBC's correspondent Bill Hamilton in May 1993 one month after Pope John Paul II's first visit to Albania, and only four years before her death, Mother speaks about the situation of the people in Albania after the collapse of communism. She is joyful for the newfound freedom and her return to her country. One can see her broad, continuous, and contagious smile on her face, accompanied by smiling eyes, throughout the interview.[74]

Veteran photographer Lance Wagner adds one other thing that differentiates a fake smile from a felt or genuine one: "When you're shooting someone, you can tell when they're doing a forced smile. The mouth will go up but the eyes don't tighten up, like when you laugh a little. With a real smile, you'll see a sparkle in the eyes that you don't get with a fake smile. You don't smile with your mouth alone; the whole face is engaged in a real smile."[75] The sparkle Mother had in her smiling eyes never faded away, during all her life and even through darkness. Angelo Cardinal Comastri explains a personal story with Mother Teresa that has to do with her smile that always accompanied her, which he considered contagious. The cardinal remembers Mother participating in a celebration of profession of new religious sisters in a Roman parish, when a photographer was bothering Mother taking flash pictures right in front of her face. The cardinal intervened, asking the photographer not to bother Mother by taking pictures when she was praying. The photographer responded rather bluntly saying that "Mother Teresa has one of the ugliest faces that I have ever encountered, but her eyes are the happiest that I have ever seen, how is this possible?"[76] Cardinal Comastri was shocked by the comment and at the end of the celebration, he repeated to Mother what the photographer had commented about her eyes. To his great surprise and with her usual simplicity and humility she responded, "My eyes are happy, because my hands have dried many tears. Try it, I can assure you that works like this."[77] Besides theology, the smile and her smiling eyes is another argument that proves that although Mother was going through darkness, she was not clinically depressed or displaying symptoms of smiling depression, which cover depression with a false smile or what psychologists call social smiles. These false smiles are common among people with celebrity status as Mother had, who were constantly haunted by the media. Phyllis Zagano and C. Kevin Gillespie, SJ, in their 2010 study proved that indeed "there is no real evidence of her [Mother Teresa] being clinically depressed."[78]

THE "BENEFITS" OF DARKNESS: UNION WITH CHRIST AND THE PEOPLE

St. Elizabeth of the Trinity (1880–1906) wrote to Abbé André Chevignard in 1903, "It seems to me that nothing better expresses the love in God's Heart than the Eucharist: it is union, consummation, He in us, we in Him, and isn't that Heaven on earth?"[79] The mission and the work of Mother Teresa can be properly understood if one looks at her intense eucharistic life. She found heaven in faith when she communed; the Eucharist was for her second best before seeing God face-to-face. Her "love affair" with the Eucharist started early in her life in the Balkan periphery. She received the first Eucharist at the age of five and a half, and as she herself wrote in her diary, the love for souls entered inside her via the Eucharist—it was love that grew through the years.[80] "Soon Our Lord will be with us.—Everything will be easy then—He will be there personally,"[81] she joyfully wrote to Archbishop Périer, on September 23, 1950. Mother was pleased that the Church had officially approved her new religious community, but she was most pleased that she received permission to have the Blessed Sacrament present in the chapel of her tiny convent. Jesus would be constantly present in their midst.

The center and the source of Mother Teresa's mission was celebrating and living the Eucharist. In Mother's words and her teaching the connection between the two—celebrating and living the Eucharist—becomes clear: "If we feed our lives with the Eucharist, we will not find it difficult to discover Christ, to love him, and to serve him in the poor."[82] The Eucharist, which was celebrated in her tiny convent and which she received every morning, did not end in the chapel; it extended beyond the chapel and the convent—to her mission in the slums. Mother Teresa's was a christological and eucharistic vision of life, and due to this theological understanding of the Eucharist, she could discern the two extensions of the incarnation: the real presence of Christ in the poor and for her to be unconditionally and intimately in union with Jesus in the Eucharist.

Her motto and inspiration were to drink the chalice to the last drop and to be unconditionally all for Jesus—the christological and eucharistic theology behind this maxim was that God had given himself totally in the Eucharist; so she would give herself totally to him through serving others. In so doing, she was mimicking the prototype—Christ. Mother's *wholeness*, or being all his, and total dedication to Jesus and the poor sustained her through her life and through the dark night of the soul. This was the crux of Mother's theology and definition of leading a Christian life. Through her great faith in the Eucharist, Mother Teresa unintentionally left a precious teaching on the Eucharist: without it one cannot understand, let alone love, willfully God and the neighbor. Her life was woven in and with the Eucharist, and that is the reason that Mother would never miss daily holy communion. Additionally, never did Mother Teresa receive holy communion in the hand—she genuflected, sometimes with both knees, in total reverence before the Eucharist and received it on the tongue, and this practice is still the norm with the Missionaries of Charity. Additionally, after each Mass, Mother

Teresa would kiss the priest's hands, saying, "Thank you for bringing Jesus to us."[83]

The eucharistic theology of Mother Teresa is in line with the teachings of the Vatican II constitution *Gaudium et Spes* (22): "For by His Incarnation the Son of God has united Himself in some fashion with every man. He worked with human hands, He thought with a human mind, acted by human choice and loved with a human heart."[84] The Eucharist was the starting point in the spiritual experience of Mother. For her, Eucharist equaled incarnation and incarnation equaled the Eucharist, because the Eucharist contained the mystery of the Word of God becoming human. The incarnation binding and bonding Christ to every human being is a theological synthesis of the life and mission of Mother Teresa, which surpassed boundaries, ethnicities, race, and differences of religion—because for her, every human was God's masterpiece, and in every human she saw Christ and an extension of the incarnation. Additionally, Vatican II teachings are visibly expressed in the life of Mother Teresa in another aspect—Christ loved with a human heart, elevating human love to divine love, making humans capable of loving with the same intensity and profundity with which God himself loves: this is what becomes clear through the life and mission of Mother Teresa. Consequently, for her, all humans are destined for and bound to divinization while remaining profoundly human—preserving the human nature in its totality while striving to become Godlike. The divine-human nature of Christ causes the maturation and transformation of human love to divine love. In summary, love of and great faith in the Eucharist was an "outer form" of Mother's profound love for Jesus that extended to the poor, and her dark night of the soul united her even more with the Eucharist, which was, for her, a pathway to light.

Mother's *via dolorosa* through darkness and her prolonged spiritual martyrdom, which continued even after the spiritual union with the Spouse, was her invisible suffering and her spiritual ascend to Darjeeling, up the Himalayas. It was a spiritual life and a dark night of the soul that took sharp turns, inclines, bends, and curves but it was an ever-ascending journey, and even brought others to ascend. Mother was peripheral even in her darkness, if compared to other saints and especially to women mystics like St. Teresa of Avila, St. Thérèse of Lisieux, and St. Gemma Galgani, who experienced the dark night of the soul but not for as long a period, as persistently, and as intensely as did St. Mother Teresa. Was she a "tainted" saint because of her prolonged darkness? We can say that one thing that she was "tainted" with was holiness, and through her holiness and martyrdom she lifted up others. Mother's unification or spiritual marriage with Christ, early in her life, explains her profound two-way identification with the sufferings of Jesus on the cross: her Christlikeness, and her identification with the poor and the world's suffering. Her darkness was an active participation in the redemptive suffering of Christ. Moreover, her own darkness could bring light to others bearing the same burden. Maybe Christians need a more nuanced spirituality of darkness, as at some point in spiritual maturation many Christians might go through doubt and darkness, and they should know how to search and discern light in the darkness. Mother Teresa's spirituality can be an excellent guide in this element of Christian life: it had the force to turn darkness into light; with Mother, the sunshine of darkness was bright.

PART II

MYSTICAL PERIPHERIES

CHAPTER 5

MAKE ME A CHANNEL OF YOUR PEACE

ST. FRANCIS OF ASSISI AND ST. MOTHER TERESA

ST. FRANCIS OF ASSISI

In 1979, when Mother Teresa gave her acceptance speech for the Nobel Peace Prize, she began with a word of gratitude and a popular prayer known as the *Simple Prayer*:

> Lord, make me a channel of your peace, that where there is hatred, I may bring love; that where there is wrong, I may bring the spirit of forgiveness; that where there is discord, I may bring harmony; that where there is error, I may bring truth; that where there is doubt, I may bring faith; that where there is despair, I may bring hope; that where there are shadows, I may bring light; that where there is sadness, I may bring joy.[1]

St. Francis of Assisi, one of the most celebrated thirteenth-century Christian saints, never wrote this prayer, but what is important is the fact that the celebrated medieval saint abided by and lived his whole life following the principles of this simple but profound prayer composed by an anonymous author. This simple prayer is gospel in action, and that is the reason why Mother Teresa was attracted to it and followed its principles. She probably did not know that the author of the prayer was not St. Francis of Assisi. However, it was an intentional choice on the part of Mother Teresa to recite this prayer, and invite the audience to do the same, in her acceptance speech. This was a smart choice by Mother, as this simple and unpretentious prayer united humankind, transcending religions, nations, divisions, people with different political views, and ethnic particularities. Mother knew perfectly well that the Catholics in Sweden were a minority, and very few Catholics would have been among the illustrious guests at her acceptance speech, which included the king and queen of Sweden, distinguished members of the parliament and the government, and members of the Nobel Prize committee. Nonetheless, she astutely chose what united:

> Let us all together thank God for this beautiful occasion where we can all together proclaim the joy of spreading peace, the joy of loving one another and the joy acknowledging that the poorest of the poor are our brothers and sisters. As we have gathered here to thank God for this gift of peace, I have given you all the prayer for peace that St. Francis of Assisi prayed many years ago, and I wonder he must have felt the need what we feel today to pray for. I think you have all got that paper? We'll say it together.[2]

In essence, the *Simple Prayer* was Mother Teresa's life's mission and vision, as she considered herself a little pencil in the hand of a writing God, who is sending a love letter to the world and, through the letter, bringing peace to everyone's hearts and minds. Mother believed that each could contribute to peace. Peace is a collective enterprise: it neither depends on nor is a result of agreements among the governments and states. Instead, she maintained that peace is a result of a profound conviction coming from below—only people's love will win over the world's evil. She was certain that only by giving anticipated trust to a person and loving that person unconditionally could peace come upon the person, freeing her from evil.[3] So much did Mother Teresa like the message contained in the *Simple Prayer* that every day after holy communion, Mother Teresa and her community would recite it.

But there was more than the *Simple Prayer* that united Mother and St. Francis: in fact, the whole spirituality of the Missionaries of Charity is Francis- and Franciscan-centered in the axiom: "I want to serve and love Jesus in the poor. I want to live like St. Francis of Assisi, a poor life, and serve Him,"[4] Mother Teresa once said. Mother Teresa's sisters do not have worldly riches, they depend on Divine Providence—a principle she strongly believed in and lived by every day of her life. Chapter 8 of Mother Teresa's *Constitutions* speaks of "Consecrated Poverty" and the vow of poverty the nuns take, similar to the vow of poverty Franciscan friars take in imitation of the prototype, Christ, following the example of what Christ said to the scribe who approached him: "Foxes have dens and birds of the sky have nests, but the Son of Man has nowhere to rest his head" (Matt 8:20).

MOTHER TERESA'S FRANCISCAN POVERTY AND BENEDICTINE LABOR: PILLARS OF THE MISSIONARIES OF CHARITY'S ASCETICISM

When Mother Teresa reflected on "the Call" and how everything was fitting together and the future was becoming clear to her, she wrote,

> To be an Indian—to live with them—like them—so as to get at the people's heart. The order would start outside Calcutta—Cossipore—open lonely place or St. John's Sealdah where the Sisters could have a real contemplative life in

their novitiate—where they would complete one full year of true interior life—and one in action. The Sisters are to cling to perfect poverty—Poverty of the Cross—nothing but God.—So as not to have riches enter their heart, they would have nothing of the outside—but they will keep up themselves with the labour of their hands—Franciscan poverty—Benedict's labour.[5]

In founding her new, periphery-bound order, Mother Teresa was revisiting the roots of Christian asceticism, keeping in mind the ascetic principle of fleeing the world. She was envisioning a place outside Kolkata, where the sisters would have a contemplative start into the order, which would prepare them for active, evangelical life. She was thinking of perfect and life-long-perfecting poverty, which for her was not a theological or academic abstraction but a living poverty: the most difficult part of applying the virtue. Poverty, besides being an ideal, a vow, should be a living reality and a guiding principle. The two giants and their *Rules*—St. Benedict of Norcia and St. Francis of Assisi—coming from different centuries and contexts in the history of Christian religious life, became the two pillars of St. Mother Teresa's religious community and the *Constitutions* she wrote for the Missionaries of Charity. She did not see any contradiction between the Benedictine and Franciscan *Rules*, as some traditionally have presented them; instead, both rules regulating religious life were complementary, a complementarity she made a foundation and enriched further. Mother and her *Constitutions* moved a step further in combining Benedictine and Franciscan charisms into a rich synthesis particularly suited to her time and place. It might be safe to say that Mother Teresa and her Missionaries of Charity picked up and complemented where these two traditional and fundamental orders left off, and this is the order's contribution to continuity and progress, while keeping faith with Scripture and the Benedictine and Franciscan traditions alike.

For St. Benedict, according to his *Rule*, fleeing the world, prayer, contemplation; worship; and living a communal, coenobitical life were the pillars of the order. With solemn profession, the Benedictine monks' vows are *stabilitas* (stability), *obedientia* (obedience), and *conversatio morum* (conversion of life). The monk vows fidelity to the Benedictine life and permanence/stability in the community of the monastery to which he is bound. The virtue of obedience is fundamental to the Benedictines. This entails listening closely to God's call and answering it. Additionally, according St. Benedict's *Rule*, obedience is openness to God and to one's neighbor. This obedience, respect, and humility are indispensable virtues of the Benedictine community in the search for God; they allow the monks to focus on the essentials and the constant effort toward self-conversion, personal poverty, and chastity. The Benedictine monk does not take a vow of poverty; however, St. Benedict's *Rule* forbids private property and ownership of any kind. St. Benedict calls private property or private ownership a vice and evil "to be cut out of the monastery by the roots,"[6] so the Benedictine monk has no possessions. The monastery or the community owns the property, so the property is communal and shared by all monks.

In contrast, for St. Francis and the order of friars he founded, living an active Christ-like life in the plenitude of peripheries of his time meant serving outside the monastery, so Benedictine stability, in its original understanding, is not a vow the friars would take. "To observe the holy gospel of our Lord Jesus Christ, living in obedience without anything of our own, and in chastity"[7]—these are in essence the three classical vows the Franciscan friar takes: obedience, poverty, and chastity. However, the Benedictines and the Franciscans have the same understanding of "the yoke of holy obedience," envisioning it as a dual obedience, toward God and the abbot. The same goes for the virtue of chastity: "the diligent custody and continual watching of our bodily and spiritual senses, keeping them pure and spotless before God—that is truly called chastity."[8] The same weight is put on the life of prayer and contemplation in the three orders (Benedictines, Franciscans, and Missionaries of Charity), with one slight difference. The Benedictines and the Sisters of Charity of Mother Teresa emphasize communal prayer and a communal-shared place that constitutes the community, which is not a priority for the Franciscan itinerant way of life, as St. Francis's *Rule* indicates that "wherever brothers meet one another, let them act like members of a common family."[9] As we can see, life in community was not a day-to-day living experience for the Franciscans, but occasional, whenever the brothers happened to meet.

St. Francis and St. Mother Teresa advocated for personal and communal poverty—the order should possess no goods. Given their mobile lifestyles, owning immovable property became an impediment to itinerant life. The holy poverty lived by St. Francis and St. Mother Teresa was literal and radical, and most importantly it was understood as way to perfection and perfect joy. But unlike the Manicheans, St. Francis did not think material property was evil, as for him and the Franciscan Order he founded every created thing is a venue and vehicle to the Creator: "God is above, is within, is without, is beside all created things."[10] Thus, all of God's creation, including the material world, is created good. Consequently, the most perfect way to enjoy God's creation is by nonownership, because creation is something that belongs equally to all, to be shared and held in common by the community. So, with this understanding of the material world and property as created good by God, St. Francis's and St. Mother Teresa's poverty is a healthy or ecological poverty that affirms and focuses more on the common property, the common home created by a benevolent Creator that belongs to all. If this understanding is kept in mind, one can draw parallels and similarities among the Benedictines, Franciscans, and Missionaries of Charity—although the Benedictines do not take an explicit vow of poverty, these three religious orders reject private or personal property in favor of the Christian virtue of detachment from earthly riches. However, theirs is more of a detachment-attachment Christian paradigm. Meister Eckhart, the fourteenth-century Dominican theologian, mystic, and preacher, explains the benefits of Christian detachment. According to Eckhart, the Christian must be attached to things that really matter: divinization and becoming one with God. This is what he writes in sermon twelve: "The eye in which I see God is the same eye in which God sees me; my eye and God's eye are one eye and one seeing, one knowing and one loving."[11]

Mother Teresa founded her order of women and men and of the lay workers, combining the foundations of Benedictine and Franciscan charisms, but her order went a step further: the Missionaries of Charity of Mother Teresa, besides the classical vows of chastity, poverty, and obedience, take an additional vow: consecrated service to the poorest of the poor. Her *Constitutions* explain:

> Our response to the call of Christ is our fourth vow by which we bind ourselves to give wholehearted and free service to the poorest of the poor according to obedience and so to ceaselessly quench the thirst of Jesus. This vow binds us equally to our sisters in the community and the Society as it does to the poorest of the poor outside.[12]

The additional fourth vow is St. Mother Teresa's contribution to modern asceticism and twentieth-century religious life, which continues and contributes anew to the medieval tradition. Mother, although not formally trained in theology, understood that it was imperative to go and revisit the fountain of monastic tradition—the "old" monasticism—following even in this revisiting of tradition a scriptural principle: "Then every scribe who has been instructed in the kingdom of heaven is like the head of a household who brings from his storeroom both the new and the old"(Matt 13:52). Yves Congar's book *Tradition and Traditions* explored how tradition is transmitted, communicated, and is developed. He called the "development" the second sense of tradition, which complements transmission or, as he put it, "tradition is development as well as transmission."[13] Tradition develops in history and responds to new historical situations, by answering new questions. In his 2005 address to the Roman curia, Pope Benedict XVI defined "the hermeneutic continuity."[14] Mother

Teresa's is indeed a hermeneutic continuity: keeping with the tradition (Benedictine and Franciscan traditions) but also contributing and bringing development to the same. Mother, as Vincent of Lérins, the fifth-century ecclesiastical writer, said, was open to polishing what had been received[15] (i.e., the Benedictine and Franciscan traditions), while bringing a new interpretation or adding a new perspective to the body of tradition. This faithfulness and updating help Mother Teresa to better respond to historical circumstances of modernity and the exigencies of a modern order serving the world's poorest of the poor.

Why was Mother Teresa looking to medieval religious life and to a medieval saint, St. Francis of Assisi, as a role model? What united St. Francis of Assisi and St. Teresa of Kolkata, two of the most celebrated saints in Catholicism, who lived under vastly different historical and theological circumstances and centuries apart?

Spiritually, St. Mother Teresa and St. Francis of Assisi have many things in common, including family histories; holiness in littleness and dedication to the world's peripheries; bridge building and peace building; the same "I thirst" for Jesus crucified; striving to be Christlike via imitating Christ; a religious life of combined contemplation and action; the veneration of Mary; and suffering, which for St. Francis was visible and for St. Mother Teresa was invisible. Both enjoyed a saintly grassroot status well before the Church's official canonization, founded religious orders for men and women, and shared their love for Lady Poverty and the Church of the poor. St. Mother Teresa and St. Francis of Assisi further both demonstrated complete dependency—both spiritual and material—on Divine Providence for the needs of their communities, with no worries about tomorrow but with a resolve to live in the present with complete trust in God.[16] Both saints also shared the utmost care for society's discards, peripherals, and sinners, which goes hand in hand with their love for the Creator and creation. There is a mystical and "peripheral" connection between St. Mother Teresa and St. Francis. This chapter will focus on the three **P**s St. Francis of Assisi and

St. Mother Teresa had in common: **p**arents and family; **p**eriphery of prisoners and lepers; **p**eace and joy.

ST. FRANCIS OF ASSISI AND ST. MOTHER TERESA: A SYNERGY IN HOLINESS

Parents and Family: Holiness Starts in Ordinary Families

Holiness starts in the family among ordinary people in their everyday lives. As Mother Teresa said, "Love starts at home and lasts at home.…The home is each one's first field of loving, devotion, and service."[17] The domestic holiness Mother Teresa was talking about is a product of the theology of the family and the relation of the family to the Holy Trinity. A way to understand and interpret the mystery of salvation is through the family, as a sacred place where God revealed himself. From the first moment when God entered into human history through the family,[18] he became part of the normal family, made up of a woman and a man, and then from this married couple, Christ entered the world. The periphery of Nazareth is the place where God became one with us, where he was made flesh. He made his entrance into the world: "'Behold, the virgin shall be with child and bear a son, and they shall name him Emmanuel,' which means 'God is with us'" (Matt 1:23). For Mother Teresa, the Holy Family represents the archetype of the family: as home of the Trinity, but also a place where God lived and shared with others. This made the Nazarene family into which Jesus was born and in which he lived for around thirty years extraordinary and ordinary at the same time. Jesus's family began with a couple: salvation began through a man and a woman. The work of salvation started with the virginal, marital union of Mary and Joseph, and through them the ordinary became extraordinary: the peripheral family of Nazareth became the universal Holy Family.

This is St. Mother Teresa's theology and understanding of the family, which she abided by throughout her life and mission. Chapter 1 of this book analyzed the family and family relations in Mother's home country: the formative years of Mother Teresa in her nuclear family in Skopje, her secure nest in the periphery of the Ottoman Balkans. Mother's childhood, family, and extended family in the city of Skopje, in contemporary North Macedonia, left indelible marks on her character and on the religious order she founded. Mother founded the Missionaries of Charity following the values and virtues of the periphery, the same values and virtues she lived and was formed into. This peripheral family model bore its fruit in the Missionaries of Charity, helping her religious order grow in numbers and establish religious houses all over the world.

Gonxhe Bojaxhiu, before becoming Mother Teresa, followed in her mother Drana Bojaxhiu's footsteps and the family values she learned in her own family in the Balkan periphery and later transplanted in the order she found in another periphery—India. For Mother Teresa, family was the foundational block of human society. "First think of your family then the others"—Agi Bojaxhiu Guttadauro, Mother Teresa's niece, the only surviving member of the Bojaxhiu family, remembers Mother Teresa saying.[19] Mother Teresa remembered with affection her family, how she lived within her family, and the respect and love her parents shared for each other. Mother's father, Nikollë Bojaxhiu, was a merchant always in search of new market opportunities, and quite ingenious in his business affairs besides being a city council member and involved in the politics of the time. Mother Teresa's family belonged to the merchant class of Skopje, which was well-to-do, well traveled, well educated, and among the city's elites. The lives of Mother Teresa and her siblings changed when the family lost the father. However, her mother, Drana, took the driver's seat, becoming mother and father, providing tenderness and the heart of the family but also providing economically for her family through the labor of her hands. Drana embodied what Pope Francis described in his foreword to a book published on the occasion of Mother Teresa's canonization in 2016, *Amiamo chi non e Amato* (Love those who are not loved):

> Mothers are the heart of the household; those are who form the family by accepting, loving and taking loving care to their children....Most of the sufferings of the youth are caused by the family life. It is the mother who makes the household a nest of love. At times being a mother might be an arduous experience, it might be a cross to carry, but we have with us the Madonna, the best among the mothers, who always teaches to be tender with our children.[20]

Young Gonxhe was surrounded by much affection from her family members—especially from her mother. Mother's Balkan family was not perfect; it was ordinary. But the ordinary faith, love, and affection Mother received from her family turned out to be transformative and extraordinary in the impact this tenderness had on the future Balkan saint. During her life in mission, Mother found ordinary ways to solve problems, something she learned in her household— the domestic Church. The same can be said for St. Francis, who learned to be determined and tough in his home, with his parents, Pietro di Bernardone and Pica de Bourlemont.

In medieval Assisi during the time of St. Francis, family constituted the foundation of society; parents provided the nurturing nest and support through which the young achieved personal maturity. The role of the family was central to medieval society, and because of the role played by the family in the medieval societies, the medieval man enjoyed freedoms, which were based on the trust, well-being, and stability of the family. The way the medieval society operated was that the family became the greatest guarantor of freedom for the individual. Catholic Social Teaching recognizes the family as the cornerstone of society and Christian life, and represents a remnant of the medieval conception of the family. Both St. Francis and St. Mother Teresa came from strong families, with parents who were committed to family and children. Both saints' lives, their well-being, and their *extraordinification* were "intimately linked with the healthy condition of that community produced by marriage and family,"[21] in their societies, times, and the historical circumstances in which they lived.

The conversion or stripping of St. Francis of Assisi and his adoption of a life of asceticism cannot be understood apart from his nuclear family—in particular, St. Francis's father, Pietro di Bernardone, and his mother, Pica de Bourlemont. There are similarities between Mother Teresa's father and St. Francis's father. Both men were successful merchants and entrepreneurs; they had strong characters, and both in their way cared a great deal for their families and their children. However, the role of St. Francis's father in the upbringing of the saint is different from that of Nikollë Bojaxhiu in raising his daughter. The role of St. Francis's father has been downplayed and constantly put in contraposition to his son, in both hagiographical literature and scholarship.

However, the sources give a far more complex view of family relations within the nuclear family of St. Francis, which included the relations between his parents and the profound love that both parents had toward Francis. There was an emotional and educational bond lived by Francis within his nuclear family that prepared and made the future St. Francis of Assisi. *Legenda trium sociorum* (The legend of three companions) provides a different portrait of Pietro di Bernardone and his relationship with Francis. He idealized his son and considered Francis the son he wanted.[22]

According to *Legenda trium sociorum*, Francis had a very pleasant character: "He was a merrier man than was his father, and more generous, given into jests and songs, going round the city of Assisi day and night in company with his like, most free-handed in spending."[23] The conflict with his parents started because of Francis's spending habits, excessive carelessness and laxity,[24] and they rebuked him as any parent would do, but "nevertheless…[they] loved him most tenderly, [and] they bore with him in such matters."[25] They

saw the future of their family, family fortune, and business as connected to Francis and his courteous manners and word—Francis
never spoke ill of anyone. Francis's parents might have been proud
of Francis and the possibility that he might become a knight, which
in fact did not happen because of the conversion that made him turn
away from vanities, luxury clothes, and titles, and toward a life of
prayer, dedication to the poor, and almsgiving.

Francis's parents were worried about his new life: his lack of
interest in spending time with friends, leaving the table without
eating, and leaving home. They, in their way, tried to resolve the
situation—his father by taking more severe measures, even impris-
oning his son within the house, and his mother playing the interme-
diary between father and son to resolve the situation, and defending
her son. But Francis did not change his decision to leave home and
dedicate his life to the poor. Pietro di Bernardone reacted firmly and
violently, which caused a rupture in the family and a crisis in relation
to his son, leading to the dramatic public event of Francis stripping
and giving back to his father his worldly clothes, as he was hence-
forth going to be clothed in a different habit and serve a different
father—the Heavenly Father. However, one can see Pietro in Francis, especially in Francis's determination to pursue his ascetic life,
or "his confident temper"[26]—Francis remained as determined as his
father was for him *not* to leave home and join an ascetic life. Unlike
Gonxhe Bojaxhiu, who changed her name to Teresa, Francis never
changed the name his biological father had given him, even when he
founded his order of friars. He always remained and signed his name
as *Frate Francesco*—Brother Francis. So, Francis not only accepted
but honored his father, remaining son of Pietro di Bernardone,[27]
proudly carrying the name given him. This nonchange of name is
indicative of a deeper union between father and son, and the role of
that ordinary, complex, and sometimes violent family. Pietro, in his
stubbornness, angry irruptions, imperfectness, and ordinariness, was
able to form a saint of the stature of Francis. Pietro and Pica worked

out the differences as every husband and wife do, including the parents of Mother Teresa.

It is striking to observe that both St. Mother Teresa and St. Francis of Assisi were raised by faithful women—mothers who taught the future saints piety and faith at home. Both mothers were witnesses of the domestic faith. Pica, as Drana, was a woman of faith. Brother Thomas of Celano presents her as a woman inspired by God, who prophesied the sanctity of her son. Although Francis never speaks directly of his parents in his writings, there are numerous attestations of the centrality of the figure of the mother in his experience: he himself poses as mother to his friars in various passages and indicates her as an ideal. There is a special bond between mother and son, even in almsgiving and help for the poor. When Pietro was not in the house, in the presence of his mother, Francis "covered the table with loaves, as though he were preparing for the whole household, and when his mother asked wherefore he placed much bread on the table, he made answer that he did it as alms to be given unto the poor, for that he was minded to give alms unto every man that did ask it for God's sake."[28] This episode shows a strong bond of tenderness, and even a silent complicity, between Francis and his mother, who witnessed what he was doing, bore with him, and did not stop him from almsgiving—they were partners in charity toward the poor of Assisi. Francis was her favorite—she loved him more than her other sons. As Mother Teresa, Francis does not speak about his parents or his nuclear family. The saint from Assisi did not come from a perfect family, but from an ordinary family, with problems: his father was not a saint; his mother was not a saint either, but an ordinary woman. However, at the end, Francis reconciled with himself and his previous life of laxity and leisure, and eventually with his parents.

The Periphery of Prisoners and Lepers

Both saints had an intense urge to go out to the periphery, to be radicals in their own ways—because of their faith and trust, they became holy fools for Christ:

St. Francis, while yet in the secular habit, albeit he had renounced the world, was wont to go about in meanest guise and so mortified by penance that by many he was held to be a fool and was mocked and hunted as a madman and pelted with stones and filthy mire both by his kinsfolk and by strangers.[29]

The life of Francis and his friars was a life of *minores*—lesser brothers, a fraternity of celibate and poor men who depended on people's generosity and held no personal possessions: living "without anything of our own, and in chastity."[30] Indeed, no man the saint encountered would be poorer than he! Francis wanted to become little and enjoyed the life of littleness. Pope Francis commented on the core of Franciscan life and their literal "littleness": "This [Franciscan life] is a difficult path, because it is opposed to worldly logic, which seeks success at any cost and desires to occupy the first place."[31] During the time of St. Francis, the *minores* were fleeing the city of Assisi, in search of the peripheries and peripherals.

Later, Franciscans, as did other religious orders, moved from the periphery to big friaries, from itinerant-mendicant lifestyle to that inside the walls of the friary and the city. However, the friars of St. Francis still kept the principle of serving the poor a priority, following in the footsteps and model of their founder, who identified with the poor, the marginalized, and the sinner, by joining their ranks—Francis became as poor as the poorest. The complete identification with the periphery opened to Francis and his friars the window to universality. The same is true for St. Mother Teresa and her sisters. As their lives in mission indicate, St. Francis and St. Mother Teresa brought the periphery to the center's attention. They raised attention and alerted the ecclesiastical authorities to the status of the people living in the periphery— the forgotten society within society. Both St. Francis and Mother Teresa became peripherals like those following Christ, the prototype of their mission.

Geographically, Mother Teresa was born, formed, and lived in the Balkan periphery before she transferred to the periphery of India. St. Francis, on the other hand, was born in Assisi in the Umbrian province of Italy, which was initially under the Roman Empire of the West and then a subject of the Papal State and by no means geographically peripheral. Assisi did not represent any of the peripheries Mother was exposed to since her youth. However, just as Mother Teresa witnessed and lived through the decay and the eventual fall of the Ottoman Empire, Balkan wars, genocide, ethnic cleansing, and the rise of nationalisms, Francis of Assisi was born when his native city of Assisi was in turmoil. By the beginning of 1200 Assisi was going through a triple crisis: economic, social, and political. On one side were the internal Assisi conflicts among the bishop (the spiritual leader and a landholder) or the clergy; Assisi's landlords (the wealthy merchant class and the aristocrats who had inherited lands); and artisans, merchants and the people who were demanding better living conditions and more participation in the public life of the city; and on the other hand external conflicts between Assisi and the neighboring city of Perugia, which aimed at enlarging its dominion.

Francis had fought on the side of Assisi against the nobility of Perugia and was imprisoned after Assisi's army lost the battle of Collestrada in November of 1202. Francis was among the prisoners of war and was imprisoned in Perugia for over a year (1202–3), enduring the horrors of imprisonment[32] in medieval prisons. The imprisonment in Perugia was a formative event in the life of St. Francis. His life among the prisoners or society's peripherals put young Francis in direct contact with the oppressed, which also had a direct impact on his conversion. His rite of passage to littleness and holiness, to his dedication to the poor and lepers, went through the prison of Perugia. It was right after the prison experience when the opportunity to go to Apulia to increase the profit and his family prestige (a Count Genile had promised to make him a knight)[33] knocked on his door. But Francis changed his mind—he decided to pursue littleness, poverty, and a life away from vanities:

Which can do the better for thee, the Lord, or the servant? And when he answered: "the lord," that other said again unto him: "wherefore then dost thou leave the lord for the servant, and a rich lord for a poor?" And Francis said: "Lord, what wouldst Thou have me to do?" "Return," said He, "unto thine own country, and it shall be told unto thee what thou shalt do, for the vision that thou hast seen behooveth thee to understand in other wise."[34]

The periphery of the prisoners was a call to conversion for Francis. Thus, it might be safe to say that even before Francis's identification with material and social poverty living literally and existentially in the margins of society of his time, Francis experienced the periphery of the prison and prisoners. He had a personal experience in the Perugian prison and later in his home-made prison, created by his father. In both prisons he did not lose hope—he kept doing works of charity, pacifying prisoners, and trying to elevate their sadness by being merry in his chains.[35]

After his stripping and conversion, which followed his exposure to the social periphery of prison, Francis entered into other areas of society's existential periphery, touching the wounds of the existential and social poverty of his time, because of the love of Christ, who directed men's actions to the good of the others, following St. Paul's motto: "for the love of Christ impels us" (2 Cor 5:14) to go beyond ourselves, to go in search of the periphery. In this conception of existential periphery, by touching with their hands—literally and radically—the poverty of their times, Mother Teresa and Francis followed the same theology of the periphery or, as Pope Francis calls it, the theology of poverty centered in the mystery of Jesus: "Jesus Christ was rich—from the richness of God—but he became poor.... Being poor is letting ourselves be enriched by the poverty of Christ and not wanting to be rich by other means that are not those of Christ."[36] Thus, Jesus acted in and through both saints when they touched the periphery; but Jesus also worked through the peripheral who received help, enriching the one helping.

In fact, the poor saved Francis from his existential crisis; it was the poor who educated him to begin a new life.[37] Francis encountered and fed the poor in his parents' house, preparing alms to be distributed to them. The same with Gonxhe Bojaxhiu. The future Mother Teresa remembered her father saying, "When you do good, do it quietly, as if you were tossing a pebble into the sea."[38] Mother Teresa followed in the footsteps of her parents in helping the poor; the same can be said about Francis and his special relationship with his mother, Pica, in sharing their wealth and helping the poor.

In his dictated *Testament* before his death in October of 1226, St. Francis said that he was writing the testament so that his brothers would continue to follow the *Rule* authentically. Francis did not intend the *Testament* as a substitute for the *Rule*; on the contrary, the *Testament* was intended to enforce the authenticity of the *Rule*. The *Testament* has a meaningful opening, starting with St. Francis's emphasis on the social peripheries of his time: the lepers. This encapsulates the theology of peripheries of St. Francis, which St. Mother Teresa took to heart and to action in serving the modern lepers and leprosy of the twentieth century. The first paragraph of Francis's *Testament* starts where his conversion—new—life started. Lepers are mentioned first, giving them paramount importance in his conversion and his life as a friar:

> The Lord granted me, Brother Francis, to begin to do penance in this way: While I was in sin, it seemed very bitter to me to see lepers. And the Lord Himself led me among them and I had mercy upon them. And when I left them that which seemed bitter to me was changed into sweetness of soul and body; and afterward I lingered a little and left the world.[39]

St. Francis does not seem to have gotten over the leper encounter that changed his life. Centuries later, his encounter with the leper
would have a profound effect on Mother Teresa's life, too. Judging
from the *Testament*, St. Francis was still doing penance and regretted
the way he initially treated the leper. In this episode one notices the
fragility of Francis the sinner.[40] Francis remembers his past life as
immersed in sin and sinning with bitterness. He regrets his miscon-
duct, annoyance, and avoidance of the leper. Francis remembered
the bitterness, disgust, and fear he had felt about leprosy and those
walking corpses, the lepers, affected by the infectious disease. But
his changed life came from the lepers, from the periphery. It was
the event in the leprosarium's periphery and the encounter with the
leper that converted Francis. This event was foundational for him
and the order of *minores* he founded. It was the lepers—the most
peripheral of the peripherals, the most excluded and detested in
St. Francis's society—that converted the saint, or that even made
him a saint. Francis wanted his *minores* to keep the theology of
the peripheries as a centerpiece of their mission and ministry; the
leper encounter was the Jesus encounter and it is exactly here in this
encounter that Jesus and the peripheral (the leper) become identical. It is to this foundational event that his order can return in
time of crisis: here the priorities were set; the periphery was and
remains the well of the Franciscan tradition. When one touches with
one's hands the periphery—cleaning the bodies of the lepers, dress-
ing their wounds—perceptions are changed and priorities are reset.
Francis's embrace of the leper is Francis's embrace of fear: fear of the
disease, but also fear of leaving behind a comfortable life. Reminding his brothers of the identity and the priorities of the order in the
Testament was Francis's last contribution to the order, which during
Francis's last years was going though turmoil. It was thanks to the
fateful encounter with the leper that the young Francis discovered
the truth of his life and of his existence, and practically, his future
mission. Francis came to terms with his mission when he embraced

the leper and the periphery, and "it is only then that Francis's spiritual nightmare was over. He had found peace."[41]

Moreover, the experience lived with the lepers had made Francis discover and choose the life of a pilgrim on this earth, with nothing of his own and in solidarity with those who lived along the road, society's peripherals.[42]

Francis achieved detachment from earthly belongings—renounced his inheritance—by dreaming of becoming even a foreigner to his own order, which chased him away on a cold and rainy day. He speaks of this episode with perfect joy. Where exactly is perfect joy to be found? Brother Leo asked Francis. It is in being Christlike, enduring the same abuse, humiliation, and suffering that Christ endured. And where can one find Christ? In going "unto the lepers and [abiding] among them, with all diligence serving them all for the love of God."[43] And what is the way to encounter Christ? In the periphery of his time, which included the prisoner and the leper. Francis's service was via complete identification with the person or the marginalized group being served, offering them "humble and kindly services in his benevolent goodness."[44] This is Francis's concluding answer to Friar Leo's question.

> Above all the grace and the gifts of the Holy Spirit that Christ giveth to His beloved is that of overcoming self, and for love of Him willingly to bear pain and buffetings and revilings and discomfort; for in none other of God's gifts, save these, may we glory, seeing they are not ours, but of God.[45]

St. Francis's ministering to and total identification with society's peripheries and peripherals, serving the bottom of the periphery—the prisoners and lepers—is what unites St. Francis and Mother Teresa even more in their charisms. Mother Teresa touched the periphery of modern prisoners and lepers and was touched by the peripherals in return. However, unlike St. Francis, Mother Teresa was never imprisoned. Nonetheless, ministering to prisoners was one of her priorities. Mother's approach was to never pass judgement on prisoners who were serving their sentences. She never looked down on prisoners—showing utmost mercy and following Jesus's maxim: "I was…in prison and you visited me" (Matt 25:35–36).

For St. Francis and St. Mother Teresa, prisoners were society's peripherals, living in the societal periphery waiting for a second chance to be integrated into and included in the society. In dealing with prisoners, as St. Francis, St. Mother Teresa was interested in offering a personal touch. She "was always ready to offer someone another chance (and not just a second chance!)."[46] She brought God's mercy to the inmate serving a sentence in high security prison, or to the emperor of Ethiopia who overnight had turned into a prisoner. Cardinal Angelo Comastri,[47] who personally knew Mother Teresa, recalls this noteworthy episode in which Mother Teresa ministered to unconventional prisoners. Mother Teresa, who had just arrived in New York, learned of turmoil in Ethiopia that resulted in the imprisonment of the elderly Haile Selassie (emperor of Ethiopia from 1930 to 1974) and the royal family. The emperor had helped Mother open a house for the poor in Ethiopia in 1973, one year before the coup on September 12, 1974, which resulted in his arrest and imprisonment. Mother decided to go to Ethiopia and visit the emperor in prison. When Mother Teresa arrived in Addis Ababa, the news spread all over Ethiopia of her unusual visit and a grant reception was underway. Mother was brought before the head of state, Mengistu Haile Mariam, the communist leader who took over after the fall Selassie. "Mother, what can I do for you?" Mengistu asked. The response he heard from Mother was as unexpected as her visit: "I want to visit Emperor Haile Selassie in prison," to Mengistu's great disappointment. In her usual direct and succinct way of speaking Mother continued, "Mister president, yesterday the emperor was rich, today he is poor; yesterday you were poor, today you are rich. I want to see the poor Haile Selassie." Mother Teresa was accompanied to the cell where the deposed emperor was held. As soon

149

as the emperor saw her, he said, "Mother, see what has happened? All has changed in an instant." Mother Teresa hugged him and said prophetically, "Emperor, the thrones of this world are worm-eaten; today one was deposed; tomorrow it will be another: have no fear! Cling to the Lord, believe in Him: [he] is the only rock on which we could cling."[48] Mother Teresa was the only person allowed to visit the emperor and his family in prison, where the emperor and the royal family were enduring appalling prison conditions, which probably caused the death of the elderly emperor.[49]

Mother Teresa had read the *Life of St. Francis*, and Francis's first encounter with the leper had made a long-lasting impact on her. As it happened, she would have the same encounter with Indian lepers knocking on her door. Mother remembered, "This is what happened to Saint Francis of Assisi. Once, when he ran into a leper who was completely disfigured, he instinctively backed up. However, he overcame the disgust he felt and kissed the face that was completely disfigured,"[50] questioning, "What was the outcome of this? Francis felt himself filled with tremendous joy."[51]

The periphery inhabited by lepers is another periphery in which St. Francis's and St. Mother Teresa's missions, ministries, and mysticisms meet. Medieval and modern lepers were dead while alive, segregated and insulated from the society. If the leper—the peripheral par excellence—called on and converted Francis the sinner, Mother Teresa was surrounded by a plethora of peripheries in her native Skopje. It was while praying in front of the Black Madonna of Letnica that she was called to go in mission to the far-away peripheries. This first call was followed by what Mother called "the call within the call" that she received on the train ride to Darjeeling. The periphery of the outcasts, the Dalits (literally meaning broken people), and the periphery of Motijhil (Pearl Lake), an overpopulated, starving, and disease-ridden neighborhood, called Mother Teresa a second time.

I heard the call to give up all and follow Him into the slums—to serve Him in the poorest of the poor....I knew

150

it was His will and that I had to follow Him. There was no doubt that it was going to be His work.[52]

Mother's call was to go deeper in the periphery and live with the peripherals, where she was not known by people and her superiors, pleased to do anything and help anyone. She was not afraid to serve and minister to the lepers, who were among the poorest of the poor and the most excluded class of the society, like the lepers living in the peripheries of Assisi that Francis literally touched. As Francis before her, Mother was attracted to the lepers because of the pains of their disease and the greater pain of total rejection by society.

When she was planning to build Shanti Nagar—"City of Peace"—to serve and minister to lepers, she wanted to be "immersed in the pain of rejection, she was extremely sympathetic to the lepers' experience of being rejected, unwanted, and unloved."[53]

Mother Teresa went right into the heart of the twentieth-century periphery of the lepers with a well-thought-out plan to minister and most importantly to provide self-worth and inclusion to them. Her focus was on the lepers' families, whose lives were impacted by the disease. Mother wanted to improve the lives of those who were living at the very bottom of the periphery: giving them a better chance to live; providing them with something meaningful to live for with human dignity; and most importantly, making them feel that they, too, were children of and equally loved by God. Talking to a leper in Kolkata, who was abandoned by society, she was explaining how much Jesus loved the world and his people and he died on the cross "for you and for me and for that leper."[54] The leper wanted to hear this statement once more and asked Mother to repeat: "It did me good. I have always heard that nobody loves us. It is wonderful to know that God loves us. Please say that again!"[55] Her theological approach, like that of St. Francis, was seeing Jesus in the peripheral leper. Following this is the theology of *Christ in distressing disguise*. As she wrote in her personal response to Matthew 16:15, "Who do you say that I am?" and who Jesus was for her, she replied that Jesus is the Leper—her response was to wash his wounds.[56]

Additionally, both St. Francis and Mother Teresa were following in the footsteps of Jesus, who touched, cleaned, and healed the lepers. They asked for help defying a disease considered both incurable and contagious; further, they worked to mitigate the social exclusion and abandonment of lepers in their time. According to the Gospel of Luke, as Jesus was traveling to a village, ten lepers approached him asking for help: "Jesus, Master! Have pity on us!" (Luke 17:13). Jesus "stretched out his hand, touched [one], and said, 'I will do it. Be made clean.' His leprosy was cleansed immediately" (Matt 8:3). St. Francis knew that the disease was detestable, believed to be contagious, and a living death for the person who suffered from it, but nonetheless he touched and ministered to lepers.

In the nineteenth and part of the twentieth centuries, leprosy was still considered a contagious disease. In India, as elsewhere, the lepers were considered cursed and unclean, divinely punished for sinful behavior.[57] Leprosy was predominantly in Asia and Africa, due to the climate and extreme poverty. Approximately thirty thousand people suffering with leprosy lived on the outskirts of Kolkata.[58] Probably since her early days in Kolkata Mother had either encountered or heard about this class of outcasts living in the society's periphery who suffered from the disease, but also from a social stigma due to the severe deformity that had made them disabled. Like the leper who appeared in front of St. Francis, five lepers knocked on the door of the Missionaries of Charity in 1957. Deformed and disabled, they were in desperate need of food and shelter, but mostly, as Mother said, the lepers were more in search of love and acceptance. As St. Francis before her, Mother Teresa was shocked by sight of the lepers' disfigured bodies. In fact, the man crawling across the threshold had no face at all. The infectious disease had eaten it away. Mother Teresa hugged the leper, invited him in, and fed him.[59]

Abandoned by all, including their families, inhabitants of the leper colonies on Kolkata's peripheries could live either through begging for alms or stealing even from their own families. There were lepers coming from the educated and professional classes who, as soon as they discovered a white spot on their skin, were forced to leave their jobs and families.[60] Leprosy was indeed caste-blind. Mother Teresa was interested in learning more about the disease and what the medical field had to offer to either rehabilitate or cure the lepers. She learned that there was a Belgian medical doctor, Frans Hemerijckx, near Madras who had invented a cure for leprosy and developed a method for treating the disease on a large scale via mobile clinics.[61] Mother joined the famous doctor for a few days of training in how to prevent and control the disease. Mother decided to adopt Hemerijckx's method in Kolkata.[62]

In January of 1957, Mother Teresa inaugurated a mobile assistance unit for lepers, following Frans Hemerijckx's method, providing donated drugs or shots to hinder the disease. Due to the success of the Missionaries of Charity Mobile Clinics, the Indian government decided to donate land to the missionaries in Shanti Nagar, two hundred miles away from Kolkata, for lepers.[63] In 1969, Mother Teresa built Shanti Nagar (the city of peace), where families affected by leprosy could lead a normal life and provide for their own sustenance, growing their own food. The main street of the city of peace was called Pope Paul VI Avenue, as a sign of gratitude of the Missionaries of Charity to Paul VI, who had donated to Mother Teresa the Lincoln Continental limousine he had used during his visit to India in December 1964. With this car a lottery was organized to raise the necessary funds for the construction of Shanti Nagar. Mother Teresa explained how the initial money needed to build the facility was collected: "We raffled the car that Pope Paul VI gave me in Bombay. With the money we collected, we created a great center for lepers that we have named City of Peace."[64] This is how the city of peace for the lepers was organized: "While there are spotlessly clean and comfortable small wards for the seriously afflicted, there are also small cottages where families can live together. For children born in Shanti Nagar there is a protective creche, but wondrously there are children living with parents whose disease has been arrested and who are well on their way to recovery."[65]

The activity grew considerably to include new work projects, such as the weaving sheds, where the lepers wove colored fabrics and the distinctive blue-bordered saris used by the sisters of Mother Teresa. Mother sought not only social inclusion for the lepers, but social worth following Catholic Social Teaching on labor and the right of every member of the society to work: "Work is a fundamental right and a good for mankind, a useful good, worthy of man because it is an appropriate way for him to give expression to and enhance his human dignity."[66]

Sister Simon, the superior of the Missionaries of Charity of the Rome province, made quite an important point when asked about the significance of the saris: "In India, women who can afford it spend a lot of money to have a sari made of fine fabrics. However, ours are precious not for the fine fabric but because of those who weave them, the lepers who sometimes do not even have fingers in their hands. This is why they are something sacred to us, a symbol of our commitment."[67] In July 2017, the blue saris worn by the Missionaries of Charity became a registered trademark to be protected and prevent any misuse for commercial purposes. Mother Teresa might have never fathomed registering a trademark when she came about with the simple blue-bordered saris. But the lepers who wove the saris meant the world to Mother Teresa.

Mother Teresa was not a leprosy activist but a Christ activist. It was Jesus in the prisoners and the lepers living in the outskirts of India who constituted her theology of service: "Jesus is the one we take care of, visit, clothe, feed, and comfort every time we do this to the poorest of the poor, to the sick, to the dying, to the lepers, and to the ones who suffer from AIDS."[68]

Unlike the other contemplation-in-action saints, who sought to find God either in the neighbor or in the secret of their hearts, Mother Teresa's theology contemplated the mystery of Christ's redemption incarnated in the peripherals she served. However, for her, contemplating Christ in the peripherals did not simply mean that Christ was in the poor, but that she suffered with Christ in the poor, that she shared his passion and his death via the poor, "bear[ing] pain and buffetings"[69] for the poor. In itself suffering was nothing, but suffering divided or shared with the passion of Christ is a gift and proof of his love, because by giving up his Son, the Father has proved his love for the world.[70] Another way of understanding Mother's theology of the periphery is the Eucharist. In the Eucharist, Christ is present under the appearance of bread and wine. In the slums of Kolkata, he was present in the wounded bodies of the lepers that Mother could directly touch and nurse. It was in the slums that Mother Teresa found St. Francis's perfect joy. Mother Teresa remembered that someone once told her that not even for a million dollars would they touch a leper. Mother's response was quick and cut to the core of her theology: "Neither would I. If it were a case of money, I would not even do it for two million. On the other hand, I do it gladly for love of God"[71]—and this was the source of her sense of perfect joy.

Mother was a realist and had a realistic vision of poverty. She was not sentimental about the periphery and the peripherals, nor did she sentimentalize them; she thought actively and in action and found commonsense solutions to remedy their situation, thus contributing her part to remedy society's poverty and marginality. She was convinced that the peripherals needed Christ and his love for them, so bringing Christ to them was her priority. Mother shared the poverty and the cross of Christ, contemplating in the poor the living and bleeding image of Christ—and because of all these Mother lived in the spirit of St. Francis.

Peace and Good

As previously mentioned, in his early twenties, St. Francis of Assisi took part in the battle of Collestrada, which ended up in defeat for Assisi and caused Francis to spend a year in prison as a hostage to the winning Perugia. The inhuman prison conditions had a life-long effect on Francis—even on his attitude toward building peace. It was in prison and before his conversion that Francis built peace among the desperate prisoners who were fighting over a knight who had done injury to one of them. As a result, all the prisoners wanted to stay aloof from him, but Francis intervened by not refusing company to the problematic knight and building peace between the knight and the other prisoners; he "exhorted the rest to do the same"[72] and accept him.

Francis repented and reordered his life into the practice of virtues. This is confirmed by the crucial moment in Francis's changed life, which came after his dramatic conversion. As Francis confesses in his *Testament*, his repentance is linked to a dramatic act of reconciliation and making peace with himself—body and soul. How did Francis reach his reconciliation and peace? Francis achieved inner peace not only by leaving behind his life of laxity and vainglory but also his hostility toward the lepers—the peripherals. Thus, he won over the selfish inner self. The presence of the Lord was evident in Francis's conversion. Francis's achieved peace was a biblical peace with a triple effect of reconciliation: peace with God, with God's creation, and with self. Peace is a reconciliation between God and humanity, and Francis's peace was through asceticism. This reconciliation was an undeserved gift through Christ's incarnation. What medieval Francis and modern Mother Teresa taught is that authentic peace is achieved first and foremost via reconciliation with the Creator, and this bears fruit in works of mercy and charity.

Both St. Francis and St. Mother Teresa were in friendship with God, and because of this acquired friendship there was a corresponding acquired peace. Their peace was inner and outer, with oneself and with the neighbor. This is exactly Francis's theology of peace as he taught it to his friars. To achieve peace means "to live in peace and concord with God and with men and with their own conscience, and in the love and practice of most holy poverty."[73] Francis's and Mother Teresa's lives and missions were based on self-denial, self-submission, and self-abnegation. They were both radicals and lived the Christian ideal profoundly and authentically, and that was the main reason they radiated inner and outer peace.

During his life as friar and preacher, Francis took charge of the political situation in his native Assisi, showing by example that besides the belligerent way of resolving conflict there was another, more effective and enduring way—building peace. Assisi and its fractured political landscape provided the laboratory for Francis and his friars to build peaceful alternatives. "Peace and good, peace and good"[74]—was Francis's constant salutation in the roads of Assisi. When the bishop of Assisi noticed that the life of the friars was extremely harsh because the *minores* owned nothing, Francis answered frankly following the Scripture maxim:

> My Lord, if we should have possessions, we should need arms to protect ourselves. For thence arise disputes, and law-suits, and for this cause the love of God and of our neighbor is wont ofttimes to be hindered, wherefore we be minded to possess naught of worldly goods in this world.[75]

Francis's mission of peace surpassed religious boundaries. He did not shy away from crossing enemy lines to explain the Christian faith to the sultan. Francis preached the faith of Christ so divinely that for his faith's sake he even would have entered the fire[76]— martyrdom at the hands of the Saracens. How did Francis preach among the Saracens and engage in a multiple-day dialogue with the sultan? Francis and his brothers preached among them "with stead-fastness of mind…with the power of spirit…with eloquence and confidence he answered those who were reviling the Christian law."[77] Francis's purpose in preaching to the Saracens was his testimony of his found peace in Christ, which he wanted to spread beyond Christians. Muslims had no objection to praising Jesus, who was a prophet for them too, as long as the speaker avoided any suggestion that Muhammad's message was false or deluded. Francis himself never spoke ill of Muhammad, just as he never spoke ill of anyone.[78]

St. Francis's christocentric model of peace, beside people, extended to all creation; after all, people are part of creation and deserving of the peace he was bringing. Francis delighted in God's creation, including animals, which were part of the creation. On occasion, Francis pointed to animals as an opportunity to reflect on the Gospels and their message,[79] preaching the word of God even to birds as he said, "My brother birds, much ought ye to praise your Creator, and ever to love Him who has given you feathers for clothing, wings for flight, and all that ye had need of."[80] Through creation Francis praised the one and only Creator: he saw the Creator reflected in the creatures, including animals.

Francis's theology of conversion and dialogue with people was through peace, much as Mother Teresa's was. Only after seeking to build bridges and offering peace to the person would he start the dialogue:

> Whensoever he preached, before setting forth God's word
> to the congregation he besought peace, saying, "The Lord
> give you peace." Peace did he most devoutly proclaim to
> men and women, to those he met and those he overtook.
> Wherefore many who had been haters alike of peace and
> of salvation, embraced peace with their whole heart, the
> lord working with them, and themselves became children
> of peace and zealots of eternal salvation.[81]

Mother Teresa hailed from a multireligious and multiethnic nation in the Balkan periphery, and shared St. Francis's christocentric theology of peace, a theology that had a triple peaceful effect: peace with God, with self, and with the neighbor and creation. Both saints achieved peace through asceticism, cheerful obedience, absolute poverty, angelic chastity, and humility, as Mother Teresa wrote in her vows. Peace was a natural consequence for both saints because of their strong relation with Jesus. At the end, inner peace is authentic when it is relational—with Jesus and in Jesus. St. Francis and St. Mother Teresa's peace was christocentric because it was Jesus—the relation and the service to Jesus that mattered. Additionally, Mother Teresa's christocentric formula of peace was centered on a three-way dispensation of love. She believed that humanity was created out of God's love for creation; it is created to love, and consequently, to be loved. Love in littleness, love that is centered in small projects, in everydayness, in the family, in ordinary things was the love that brought peace for Mother Teresa.

Mother's message of peace was credible because she and her family lived through the political and economic upheavals of the Ottoman Empire as it breathed its last; she witnessed firsthand the struggle for power between the European superpowers fighting to get the biggest piece of the pie and enlarge their territories at the expense of the people of the Balkans, who had been subjects of the Ottoman Empire for almost five centuries. She saw the Balkan Wars, new borders being drawn, ethnic cleansing, genocide—all these side effects of conflicts and wars had left permanent effects on Mother. This eyewitness exposure to war in the Balkan periphery made Mother the most enthusiastic supporter of peace and made her cling to the rock—the nuclear family as the dispenser of love and peace, and as the peace starter. As she herself said, "Peace and war begin at home. If we truly want peace in the world, let us begin by loving one another in our own families."[82]

Although Mother Teresa was hesitant to talk about her nuclear family and her early childhood in the Balkans, she did not shy away from discussing one long-lasting benefit: "Mine was a happy family"[83] full of joy, of love, and of happy children.[84] Her family was close, and the support she received from her parents, siblings, and extended family in Skopje made her strong to cope with loss of a parent and foster a religious vocation. That is the reason why Mother places such an extraordinary importance on the role of the family, which brings peace to children. Her peace was not a contractual peace, a government declaration; instead, it was a personal peace made at the kitchen table among the members of the family. As she said, "Everybody today seems to be in a hurry. No one has any time to give to others: children to their parents, parents to their children, spouses to each other. World peace begins to break down in the homes."[85]

Why does peace start at home? According to Mother Teresa's theology of peace, it is because love starts at home, too. If these two are practiced at home, then it will spread to other homes and society—start little, sow the seeds of peace among your family members, find your Kolkata peace at home. For Mother, love and peace were birthed and nurtured at home, and that is how love transformed into peace—or as she put it, works of love are works of peace.[86]

The integral connection among home, peace, and homemade peace is a contribution of Mother Teresa to the Catholic understanding and theology of peace. This is her genius subsidiarity in peacemaking, as Fr. Daniel Jones, who addressed the conference at the United Nations on the spirituality of Mother Teresa, said.[87] In the preface of the book *Amiamo chi non e Amato* (Love those who are not loved), Pope Francis reflects on St. Mother Teresa's thinking on the family and love among the family members, as dispensers of love and peace:

> In the family, in fact, we learn from mom and dad how to smile, how to forgive, how to welcome, how to sacrifice for one another, give without expecting anything in return, pray and suffer together, rejoice and help each other. In no other life situation, it is possible to live the way one lives in a family. And Mother Teresa, in one of the answers during the meetings reported in this book, tells us: You must become ever more the joy and consolation of God, bringing prayer back into your families. The family needs love, communion and hard work. And this will be the greatest gift you can offer to the Church.[88]

Mother Teresa connects St. Francis's perfect joy with the achievement of peace. She used peace and joy almost interchangeably in her writing, as she knew these two were interdependent and could not be understood separately. It is when one achieves inner peace, peace with God, and peace with neighbor, only when this tripartite peace formula is followed, that Francis's perfect joy is guaranteed. This explains why she and her religious sisters aimed at bringing the peace and joy of Christ to broken homes, or the margins where the peripherals live, by helping the dying to make their peace with God.[89] Expressing her passion for peace, she wrote to Eileen Egan, her biographer, on October 13, 1969: "If you only knew how I long to light the fire of love and peace throughout the world.—Pray for me—that He may use me to the full."[90]

However, Mother Teresa's peace was not an abstract peace; instead, it was a peace that one displays and generously dispenses in how people act—in people's attitudes, faces, gestures, and promptness.[91] For Mother Teresa peace starts with a simple smile. Smiling is contagious and easy to mimic either consciously or unconsciously by humans, and this is scientifically proven and labeled as *sensorimotor simulation*.[92] Humans tend to mimic each other and tend to experience other people's feelings either of joy or sadness. If peace begins with a smile, then according to Mother Teresa people need to smile more and more often. This is her peace formula: "smile five times a day at someone you don't really want to smile at. Do it for peace."[93] Mother knew how to radiate that peace and smile, even when she was going through the trials of the dark night of the soul—she kept smiling despite everything happening inside her. She smiled at everyone and considered smiling a bridge builder and a peace builder. Smile more tenderly, pray more fervently and all the difficulties will disappear—this is how Mother Teresa led her life.[94]

The fruit of Mother's service was peace, she wrote to the Missionary of Charity Sisters on January 31, 1980. Thus, Mother was a peace maker, a peace enactor—putting the promise of peace into action. Moreover, Mother considered works of love to be works of peace and bridge building between people. Love, for Mother Teresa, radiated in two directions: vertically to God and horizontally to one another and the neighbor. She believed that all people are family who belong to one another. Fighting and conflict occur in the world because people have forgotten that they belong to one another. What Mother meant by "works of love are works of peace" was service—and service, for her and her religious order, does not mean a multistep program of building peace. Her service was not an extra bonus point to boost the numbers of her congregation. Her service was her vocation to Jesus; it was service until it hurts. That is Mother Teresa's active peacemaking theology—dispensing God's love among the people she was serving.

The diminutive Mother Teresa was not too shy to bring the suffering of the peripherals affected by war to the attention of world's leaders. She had experienced firsthand the devastation war caused not only to buildings but to people's lives. In her peace-building efforts, Mother kept in mind Pope Pius XII's August 24, 1939, warning on Vatican Radio, just one week before World War II broke out: "Nothing is lost by peace; everything may be lost by war."[95] Mother sought to build fraternity and peace among people. She never hesitated to go in between people and end bloodshed among them. When Mother Teresa heard of unrest and violence between Hindus and Muslims, she always asked someone to take her where the fighting was taking place. She raised her hands, signaling her peaceful intentions to the crowds. Mother Teresa listened and begged both sides to resolve the conflict without bloodshed. Hindus and Muslims stopped fighting and thanked Mother Teresa in the most reverential way they knew: by touching her feet in a sign of respect. Muslims and Hindus, as the sultan did with St. Francis of Assisi in the thirteenth century, saw in Mother Teresa a person of deep, simple, and active faith in pursuit of peace.

On January 6, 1971, Mother Teresa received the John XXIII International Peace Prize, from the hands of Pope Paul VI. It was the first time that this prize was awarded. Paul VI expected people to follow Mother Teresa's example, strengthening solidarity and human fraternity.[96] Mother Teresa, who did not know that she was going to receive the prize, reused an envelope that still has the address of the Missionaries of Charity in Kolkata printed in capital letters in the front, sharing the news with her congregation, writing in English on January 17, 1971,

> My dearest children,
>
> At last Mother is back. I will soon be coming to each one of you. It has been so long since I saw you—but now that the society is growing these are the sacrifices of growth which you and I must make with a smile. The award was most unexpected, so I had no chance to let you know...but I am sure each and everyone of you were at the feet of the Holy Father—to receive his love and gift. It was all so very beautiful. When I come I will bring you...a copy of what was said.[97]

In August of 1982, Mother visited war-torn Lebanon, saving children left behind in a Muslim hospital. The Lebanon War between Israel and the Palestine Liberation Organization had started in June of 1982. Mother Teresa was first in line to lend a helping hand to countries at war. Her approach to war and conflict resolution was simple: "Let us not use bombs and guns to overcome the world but let us radiate the peace of God and extinguish all hatred and love of power in the world and in the hearts of all men."[98]

After she landed in Jounieh, Mother Teresa talked to a priest and an officer. "I feel that the Church must be present at this time," Mother Teresa told the two men sitting in front of her. "Because we are not into politics. This is why we need to be present."[99] When she was told that it was absolutely impossible to cross from East to West Beirut to evacuate and save the disabled children who were trapped in Dar al-Ajaza al-Islamia Mental Hospital, she confidently responded, "Ah, but I asked Our Lady in prayer. I asked for a cease-fire for tomorrow eve of her feast day" (it was the eve of August 15, Feast of the Assumption).[100] Mother did it. One by one, thirty-seven children who were left behind in West Beirut were saved. On August 15, 1982, the *New York Times* reported, "In her blue-fringed white habit, the 72-year-old nun, who won the 1979 Nobel Peace Prize, moved quietly through the knot of children, ranging in age from 7 to 21, giving a handshake to one of the older ones."[101] The disabled children were taken to the Spring School in East Beirut, operated by the Missionaries of Charity. Mission accomplished.[102]

On January 2, 1991, Mother Teresa took an active stance to stop the Persian Gulf War, writing a letter urging Presidents George H. W. Bush and Saddam Hussein to find a peaceful solution to the crisis. She begged these world leaders to save people from the war in the name of the poor and those who would suffer. Mother Teresa held these leaders accountable, saying, "You have the power to bring war into the world or to build peace. Please choose the way to peace."[103] Mother Teresa had the same love for the Christian, Muslim, Hindu, Buddhist, Jainist, and for all people when war broke out, because she viewed humankind as the work of the Creator. She was in love with the human person as reflection of God's creation.

In 1989, Mother Teresa's heart condition was deteriorating. But she found good in her suffering and how it brought people together. In a December 16, 1989, letter she wrote to Brother Roger of Taizé, explaining how her sickness has brought forth prayers from people from different countries and different religions: "One very good thing was the fruit of my sickness—that the whole world prayed to the same God to make me well."[104] Drawing people to God and to each other: these were Mother's ways of peace building.

Theologically, Mother Teresa's attitude toward people of different religions she served is called dialogue of life, and she learned this living in the Balkan periphery when people of different religious faiths coexisted. Mother and her sisters were practicing the dialogue of life via unconditional service and love offered to everybody— especially to the peripherals and the poorest of the poor, who were all created by God. Lack of human peace was lack of a sense of belonging to the same creation. As she said, "If we have no peace, it is because we have forgotten that we belong to each other,"[105] and in fact we cannot do without one another.

Peace with Creation

As St. Francis of Assisi in the thirteenth century shared his love for God's creation, Mother's outspoken voice against abortion should be understood within a christocentric framework of creation—the ecology of creation that ought to be preserved. Her belief in safeguarding creation at any cost was biblical.

> Can a mother forget her infant…?
> Even should she forget,
>   I will never forget you.
> See, upon the palms of my hands I have engraved you.
>   (Isa 49:15–16)

That unborn child has been carved in the hand of God. Second, as with saving the disabled children in the periphery of Beirut, she wanted to save those living in the periphery of the unborn, the peripherals who did not have a voice. Mother connected abortion with lack of peace, saying, "The greatest destroyer of peace today is abortion, because it is a direct war, a direct killing, direct murder by the mother herself."[106] Mother Teresa found common ground with the then first lady Hillary Clinton to fight abortion with adoption. In 1995, the Mother Teresa Home for Infant Children—an adoption center in Washington, D.C., run by the Missionaries of Charity—was opened.

On November 2, 1996, Mother Teresa wrote a letter from Kolkata to Hillary Clinton. It was one month before Mother Teresa's health would take a critical turn for the worse from a heart condition, ultimately leading to her death in 1997. The letter, now displayed in the Clinton Presidential Library and Museum in Little Rock, Arkansas, is a response to a previous communication from Mrs. Clinton. Mother Teresa thanked the first lady for her concern for her health issues: "Thank you very much for your concern and for your prayers for my recovery," wrote Mother Teresa, assuring the first family of her continuous prayers: "I am praying for you and your family especially Mr. Clinton. God has entrusted to your care such an important responsibility as head of a great nation." Mother Teresa considered the leadership of the country as God-given responsibility. Additionally, she might have sensed the need for a dialogue and common ground to protect the lives of the unborn. It is also important to keep in mind that Mother Teresa, as she did with other world leaders, always tried to find goodness in every person. Her religious conviction and Christian hope had taught her that God has put good in the human heart, and it is up to people to search and find it.

The road to the establishment of the Mother Teresa Home for Infant Children and Mother Teresa's ongoing correspondence with Hillary Clinton is worth discussing, as it shows how Mother Teresa took an active role in peace building in the United States, gently but persistently spreading a message of peace in the heart of the First World. In February 1994 Mother Teresa was invited to deliver a speech at the National Prayer Breakfast, an ecumenical interfaith event that takes place every February in Washington, D.C. The title of her speech was "Whatever You Did unto One of the Least, You Did unto Me," which was the core of Mother Teresa's theology of mission to the poorest of the poor. It was the same love and protection for creation that Mother Teresa spoke about in her Nobel Peace Prize acceptance speech on December 10, 1979. Then President Bill Clinton, Hillary Clinton, Al Gore, Tipper Gore, and other dignitaries were among more than three thousand attendees. President Clinton had invited Mother Teresa and, according to her biographer Kathryn Spink, she went reluctantly—Mother was not a fan of big gatherings or public appearances.

Mother Teresa's speech started on common ground, focusing on what people of faith share. She was conscious of different religious faiths of the people in the audience. She raised poignant social issues, including poverty, neglect, and spiritual poverty that affluent countries were especially suffering, thus bringing the periphery to the center's attention. Then she proceeded with her usual humility and strength to the topic that was dear to her heart: love of the child, where love and peace begin. Mother Teresa's strong and straightforward prolife message made national headlines and was not music to the ears of everyone attending. "The greatest destroyer of peace today is abortion, because it is a war against the child, a direct killing of the innocent child….Any country that accepts abortion is not teaching its people to love, but to use any violence to get what they want. This is why the greatest destroyer of love and peace is abortion," said Mother Teresa.[107] She had just pointed the finger to what Catholics consider to be a grave sin and was appealing to the U.S. government, as she had done with other governments in the past. Identifying an issue and appealing for its solution was not enough for Mother Teresa. She was not afraid to offer a solution that she and the Missionaries of Charity were successfully practicing internationally: "I will tell you something beautiful. We are fighting abortion by adoption—by care of the mother and adoption for her baby. We have saved thousands of lives." Mother Teresa's controversial speech received a standing ovation from part of the room. However, Mother Teresa was not done yet. As Hillary Clinton would recall later, Mother Teresa had asked to see her: "And I thought, Oh, dear. And after the breakfast, we went behind that curtain and we sat on folding chairs." This was the first time Hillary Clinton met Mother Teresa in person. Clinton was extremely impressed by this small, simple, direct, and tough woman. She recalled Mother Teresa's "powerful hands," which were somewhat disproportionate to her tiny and hunched body. February is cold in Washington, and Mother Teresa did not fear wearing her sandals in thirty-five-degree weather, Clinton would recall. "We began to talk, and she told me that she knew that we had a shared conviction about adoption being vastly better as a choice for unplanned or unwanted babies." Hillary Clinton admits that Mother Teresa "directed" her to work with her to open a shelter for infants and young children.

Moreover, Hillary Clinton, as a practicing Methodist, knew and studied the Scriptures. The Methodist focus calls on the social gospel, and the sense of obligation to help others resonated with the first lady. She would say that she considered Mother Teresa's request for the home as coming directly from God: "The message was coming not just through this diminutive woman but from someplace far beyond." So this invitation and insistence by Mother Teresa was also a call to Clinton and an opportunity to put her faith into action. She believed that "the most important commandment is to love the Lord with all your might and to love your neighbor as yourself."

To her credit, Hillary Clinton went straight to work making the Mother Teresa Home for Infants project happen. The road was bumpy, even for the first lady. There was red tape and the project took longer than expected. Mother Teresa, for her part, was insistent and did not lose sight of the project. She would call the first lady and ask for the project status from India, Vietnam, and anywhere she was traveling. Moreover, in March 1995, as part of her South Asia tour, Hillary Clinton visited Mother Teresa's orphanage in India to better understand the Missionaries of Charity's approach to adoption. She was impressed with the adoption rates at the missionaries' house. Through Clinton's work and dedication, in June 1995, the Mother Teresa Home for Infant Children was opened. Mother Teresa flew from Kolkata for the inauguration. The *Los Angeles Times* reported Hillary Clinton saying that the shelter "will grow to have meaning in people's lives as lives here are saved and changed," and she repeated her consistent stance that she would do everything she could to help children. Mother Teresa, who was thrilled that the project came to a successful conclusion, said that she and the first lady had made "amends" and found common ground to fight abortion through adoption. Unfortunately, the house did not last for long. It operated until 2002, five years after Mother Teresa's death, and then it closed.

Even with her strong stance of preserving creation and via peace with creation, Mother Teresa brought the periphery, the poor, and those who did not have a voice to the center. As she herself said of meeting the press, "For me it is more difficult than bathing a leper." But, she added, "The press makes people aware of the poor, and that is worth any sacrifice on my part."[108]

CHAPTER 6

TWO MYSTICS IN ACTION

ST. PADRE PIO AND ST. MOTHER TERESA

MYSTICAL COMPANY IN MOSAIC

In February 2016, as part of the Extraordinary Jubilee of Mercy celebrations and upon special request from Pope Francis, the remains of St. Padre Pio were moved from San Giovanni Rotondo in the province of Foggia, in the Puglia region in southern Italy, to Rome for a week-long exposition. For the first time in one hundred years, Padre Pio left his beloved convent of San Giovanni Rotondo, which he entered on September 4, 1916. According to Padre Pio's biographer Fr. Luciano Lotti, Cardinal Bergoglio, the future Pope Francis, had great esteem for and devotion to Padre Pio. On the occasion of the Great Jubilee Year 2000, on special request from Cardinal Bergoglio, a few relics of St. Pio arrived in Buenos Aires.

On March 13, 2015, exactly two years after his election, during a Lenten service in St. Peter's Basilica, without any prior warning, Pope Francis announced the Extraordinary Jubilee of Mercy. It would start on December 8, 2015, the Solemnity of the Immaculate Conception, and end on November 20, 2016, the Solemnity of Christ the King. The year's focus on reconciliation and freeing Catholics to participate fully in the life of the Church caused Pope Francis to enlist the service of clergy he designated as missionaries of mercy. In addition to the first surprise of the announcement of this special year, there was another one: Francis announced that St. Pio and the then Blessed Mother Teresa of Kolkata were his jubilee's patron saints. St. Pio was an example for the missionaries of mercy and Mother Teresa an example of mercy in action. Mother Teresa and Padre Pio never met in life, although there is evidence that Padre Pio might have heard of the Missionaries of Charity and their work and mission in India and obviously about their foundress Mother Teresa of Kolkata. What we know for sure is that Mother Teresa visited and prayed at the tomb of Padre Pio.

When Mother Teresa of Kolkata visited the tomb of Padre Pio on September 13, 1987, she was following in the footsteps of another future saint, Pope John Paul II, who had visited the tomb on May 23, 1987. Among the nine small altars, there is one dedicated to Mother Teresa of Kolkata. A colorful mosaic of a radiant, smiling, and joyful Mother Teresa is mounted on the left part, at the beginning of the central nave of the Sanctuary of St. Mary of the Graces. Mother is smiling with her hands in prayer position, dressed in the white and blue sari, with three friars depicted in the background. At the bottom of the mosaic in red is inscribed a maxim of Mother Teresa, her signature about how she lived her life and mission: "Keep the joy of the God's love in your heart and share this joy with everyone you meet." The mosaic was dedicated on the occasion of the twenty-fifth anniversary of Mother Teresa's visit to Padre Pio in 2012.

On the right side of the same sanctuary is a mosaic depicting a radiant and smiling Pope John Paul II. As is the case with the Mother Teresa mosaic, Pope John Paul II's mosaic commemorates the twenty-fifth anniversary of the pontiff's pastoral visit to San Giovanni Rotondo, which coincided with the one-hundredth anniversary of the birth of Padre Pio. Pope John Paul II had a special devotion to Padre Pio and was the pontiff who beatified (1999) and then canonized the friar in 2002. There was a strong, mystical connection between the two that started after World War II. In 1948, then Fr. Karol Wojtyła was studying in Rome and took a trip to San Giovanni Rotondo. He spent almost a week there and had the opportunity to personally know and converse for lengthy periods with Padre Pio on topics dear to the young priest's heart. Wojtyła must have felt the need to talk to and ask for advice from a mystic—he could not find a better one than Padre Pio. Wojtyła's admiration for Padre Pio continued after the visit; in fact, when Wojtyła became a bishop of Krakow on November 17, 1962, he wrote a letter to Padre Pio asking for his special prayers for forty-year-old mother of four from Krakow, Dr. Wanda Poltawska, who was suffering from cancer. He wrote a second letter to Padre Pio on November 28, 1962, informing him that the patient, just before surgical intervention (on November 21, 1962) had regained health due to his intervention. The prayer of Padre Pio certainly strengthened the faith and resolve of Wojtyła. It is fitting, then, that at the bottom of the St. John Paul mosaic is inscribed in red letters his unforgettable remarks when he was elected pope on October 22, 1978, which he repeated several times during his pontificate: "Do Not Be Afraid! Open, I Say, Open Wide the Doors to Christ!"

On the main altar of the Sanctuary of St. Mary of the Graces is a new mosaic of St. Padre Pio leading the faithful to Mary, Mother of All Graces, while an angel holding a crown of glory is kneeling in front of the stigmatic friar. A crown was offered to St. Padre Pio, who had "finished the race...kept the faith" (2 Tim 4:7). The mosaic was added later when Padre Pio was canonized. The same is true for the mosaics of Sts. Mother Teresa and John Paul II. The Sanctuary of St. Mary of the Graces, Padre Pio's old church, has become a meeting point of the three modern mystics—a mystic (Padre Pio) attracting mystics—Sts. Mother Teresa and John Paul II prayed at the tomb of Padre Pio and kept a close mystical relation with the Franciscan friar during their life.

What do Padre Pio and Mother Teresa have in common? The geographic and mystical periphery; extraordinary-ordinary and objective-subjective mysticism; eucharistic mysticism or profound devotion to the Eucharist; priestly vocation understood *in persona Christi*; evangelical medicine and medicine of mercy as founders of Home for the Relief of Suffering and Home for the Dying—Nirmal Hriday, respectively. Padre Pio and Mother Teresa were witnesses and models in how they lived and served. Witnessing was key to both saints, and that is the reason why their mission, vision, and apostolate continue. Modern humanity listens more willingly to witnesses than to teachers, and if one does listen to teachers, it is because they are witnesses.[1] Padre Pio and Mother Teresa were both witnesses and teachers, and it is the witnessing and teaching—faith in action—that they have in common.

WHERE MYSTICISMS MEET

Geographic and Mystical Periphery

God chose and assigned a special mission and ministry to two individuals coming from the geographical peripheries of the Church—a little town in Pietrelcina in Southern Italy (Padre Pio) and the Balkans/India (Mother Teresa); they were both known for their simplicity, littleness, and sharing a radical call to live the gospel. One thinks of the passage wondering if anything good can come from Nazareth (John 1:46). Indeed, in the case of Sts. Padre Pio and Mother Teresa, the periphery was chosen for a special mission: to announce to the modern world the good that comes from the periphery.

Besides the geographic periphery, what Sts. Padre Pio and Mother Teresa have in common is the mystical periphery. Both saints, because of their mysticism and the dark night of the soul, became both holy and haunted, which is not unusual for mystics in Christian history. Authenticating mystical experiences and supernatural phenomena is not easy, and until 1978 the Church did not have an official procedure to discern presumed apparitions or revelations.[2] Given the mystical complication, a question can be asked: Were Sts. Padre Pio and Mother Teresa part of a spiritual elite in pursuit of a dangerous path of mysticism, or were they authentic modern mystics who were misunderstood and endured trials because of their unusual charism, similar to medieval mystics-saints?[3] Padre Pio carried the sufferings of visible and bleeding stigmata for almost fifty years, which became cause of mistrust and decades of trials and persecution on the part of his superiors and members of his religious order. They also became a cause of shame for Padre Pio himself, who had several times begged Christ to relieve him of the visible stigmata, while keeping the invisible suffering, which he was not afraid to carry. Due to mistrust and gossip, Padre Pio suffered persecution, which led to 750 days of house arrest: he could neither confess, nor celebrate Mass, nor perform any of the duties required by his clergy-religious status.

The stigmata of Padre Pio, besides the physical pains they caused, became a heavy moral suffering and a cause for controversy—both medical and moral. Understanding the stigmata Padre Pio suffered enriches our appreciation of Padre Pio's interior life, and it gives us a window into Mother Teresa's spiritual experience. Padre Pio—the patient—and his stigmata became case studies for medical doctors who were sent by the Holy Office to check the rare phenomenon from a medical and scientific perspective. Prof. Luigi Romanelli was the first medical doctor invited by the superior general of the Capuchin Order, Padre Pio's superior, to conduct a medical examination on Padre Pio. After a meticulous medical exam, Romanelli was unable to provide a scientific explanation of the phenomenon. The same inconclusive remarks were given by a second medical doctor, Prof. Amico Bignami, who added that the pathology of the stigmata perhaps had appeared unconsciously to Padre Pio due to suggestive phenomena, or by using a chemical medium, for example tincture of iodine.[4]

In 1920, Fr. Agostino Gemelli, a Franciscan of the Order of Friars Minor, requested a special visit to Padre Pio. Fr. Gemelli was a reputable physician and psychologist, and he had served as a consultant of the Holy Office in the past. However, Gemelli went to Gargano to examine Padre Pio on his own initiative, not on behalf of the Holy Office to conduct a medical visit. Given the unusual mystic phenomenon of Padre Pio and people's curiosity, the Vatican had prohibited any medical examination of Padre Pio's stigmata without written authorization from the Vatican, which Gemelli did not have. It happened that Padre Pio had a very brief meeting with Gemelli in the sacristy of the church, and no medical examination was conducted on Padre Pio, as testified by two witnesses. Padre Pio, who was acting in full obedience to the Holy See and his superiors, asked Fr. Gemelli to display written authorization to conduct an examination. Fr. Gerardo Di Flumeri, Padre Pio's fellow friar and biographer, suspects that Gemelli wanted to perform hypnosis on Padre Pio, which Padre Pio, due to his unusual and mystical knowledge, might have known.[5] It happened that the very brief encounter between Padre Pio and Gemelli did not end well, and a furious Gemelli wanted to return to Milan immediately. According to Renzo Allegri, who has conducted research on Padre Pio, Gemelli wrote a report to the Holy Office in Rome in fury without being asked specifically by Rome, maliciously reporting that Padre Pio had all the characteristics of a hysteric and psychopath; the wounds on his body were fake, self-inflicted, and fruit of a morbid pathological action. Gemelli concluded that Padre Pio was indeed a sick man with self-inflicted lesions and suffering of hysterical pathology.[6] Padre Pio was condemned, and the Holy Office declared that for the time being there was no evidence of supernatural phenomenon, issuing a warning to the faithful to neither believe in Padre Pio's stigmata or visit him at San Giovanni Rotondo. The Calvary of Padre Pio continued, due to Gemelli's hasty, furious, and uninvited report. The persecution, calumny, and miscomprehension intensified, especially after *L'Osservatore Romano*, the official Vatican newspaper, published the decree of Padre Pio's condemnation on July 5, 1923.[7]

However, the persecution and the Vatican sanctions against Padre Pio did not stop crowds of Catholic faithful from Italy and all over the world, especially from the places where southern Italians have emigrated, from continuing to flock to San Giovanni Rotondo for Mass and confession or merely to get a glimpse of Padre Pio. More persecution was on the way for Padre Pio. The local religious authorities turned to Pope Pius XI, this time with a specific request: to suspend Padre Pio from administering the sacraments so the crowds of people would be stopped and contained. The accusation was that Padre Pio was unworthy to celebrate Mass; however, the pontiff was not convinced. On, July 16, 1933, Pope Pius XI reversed Padre Pio's ban, saying, "I have not been badly disposed toward Padre Pio, but I have been badly informed."[8]

Padre Pio the mystic had endured hard trials, heroically and patiently. Obedience and perseverance were his armor. Padre Pio was canonized by the people, by the *sensus fideli*, well before his canonization by the Church's magisterium. Pope John Paul II, who had personally known Padre Pio the mystic and stigmatist priest from his early days as a priest, on the occasion of his beatification, took a bold step in recognizing the distressing trials Padre Pio went through and his heroic endurance, saying,

> No less painful, and perhaps even more distressing from a human point of view, were the trials which he had to endure as a result, it might be said, of his incomparable charisms. It happens at times in the history of holiness that, by God's special permission, the one chosen is misunderstood. In that case, obedience becomes for him a crucible of purification, a path of gradual assimilation to Christ, a strengthening of true holiness.[9]

Mother Teresa faced trials because of her mysticism and the dark night of the soul, but probably not to the extent of the trials of Padre Pio. Initially, Mother faced some credibility challenges regarding her private revelations, hearing the Voice, which ordered her to leave the Loreto Sisters and start a new religious congregation to serve the poorest of the poor. Second, as explained in previous chapters, Mother went through an extraordinarily long dark night of the soul and spiritual suffering—a long-suffered invisible pain—and this obviously caused problems and misunderstanding within her religious community and between Mother and her Loreto superiors. Mother's dark night of the soul was as intense and long in suffering as Padre Pio's visible stigmata—they were both exactly fifty years long. From the letters published after Mother's death, which caused much controversy and misunderstanding, especially among the secular media, Mother admitted she did not share her spiritual dryness and aridity even with close friends and collaborators. Only her spiritual directors knew about it. From Mother's letters we also know that after several years of suffering in the silence of her heart and in complete obedience to her superiors, in March 1953, Mother disclosed her interior suffering to Archbishop Périer. In obedience to God, Church authorities, and her spiritual directors, Mother accepted darkness, actually came to love darkness as a gift and as a spiritual part of her work.[10] This is how mystics like Mother Teresa and Padre Pio before her coped and made peace with darkness, or turned their darkness and suffering into light to enlighten others.

Padre Pio's stigmata became a world phenomenon that attracted international attention. Padre Pio and his exceptional, extraordinary mysticism made controversial headlines during his lifetime. Additionally, when Padre Pio was beatified and canonized by Pope John Paul II, some of the same arguments against the stigmata and mysticism in general were renewed. In contrast, Mother's spiritual suffering never made headlines when she was alive. Mother died without knowing that her letters would be published. Actually, she wanted all her personal letters and correspondence of any sort to be destroyed and had specifically instructed Archbishop Picachy to destroy the letters that she had written to him. The reason was simple: she did not want media spotlight, controversy, and calumny about her spiritual darkness. Her mysticism was hidden, as mysticism indeed is mute and introverted (reflecting the meaning of the Greek root of *mysticism*), which is an indication of her humility and reverence for the work of God in her and through her.

When Mother's letters were published, shock waves came from her admirers and enemies alike. The woman who was until then the holy living saint had become the hunted saint, which, in fact, has often been the case with mystics, including Padre Pio. They were also both accused of impropriety. In 2005, almost four decades after his death, Padre Pio was accused of having sex with penitents.[11] The accusations were unfounded, and Padre Pio was exonerated. Mother Teresa was suspected by some of the members of her religious order of an inappropriate relationship with her spiritual director Fr. Van Exem. Under suspicion, Mother Teresa was immediately transferred by her provincial from Kolkata to Asansol, so that the supposed amorous relation would end due to physical distance:

> Some sisters of her community had noticed Mother Teresa's frequent and long conversations in confession with Father Van Exem in the months following her retreat in Darjeeling. From this simple fact, suspicion arose concerning the nature of their relationship. Obviously, the sisters had no clue about the reason for these prolonged meetings. Nonetheless, they deemed them inappropriate and brought them to the notice of her religious superiors. On the basis of these 'uncharitable suggestions and remarks,' the decision was made to transfer Mother Teresa to the Asansol community.[12]

Like Padre Pio, Mother followed in obedience and serenity the decisions of her superiors, although it was painful to leave behind St. Mary's school and her students. It was the same mysticism that she was persecuted for that provided solace to Mother Teresa. She considered her suffering, calumny, transfer, moving, and change as all being planned by the Voice. Obedience and considering everything as coming from God were characteristic of the diminutive

mystic throughout her life. Eventually, Archbishop Périer intervened, and wrote to Mother Gertrude, Mother Teresa's superior, on
January 13, 1948, explaining her trials and her steadfastness:

> In spite of her trials she has experienced from time to
> time in religious life, she is very loyal to the Institute of
> the Blessed Virgin Mary and I have never heard her com-
> plaining of superiors, or sisters, even when I knew she had
> been misunderstood.[13]

Extraordinary and Ordinary Mysticism

Sts. Padre Pio and Mother Teresa were mystics. St. Pio had
the extraordinary gifts of reading minds, bilocating, levitating, and
bearing the visibly bleeding stigmata for almost fifty years. Padre Pio
knew in advance the moment when he was going to die and had
prearranged for a spiritual daughter, the Marquise Giovanna Rizzani
Boschi, to be present at his deathbed, not physically but spiritually,
and follow every minute of his death. Unlike Padre Pio, Mother
Teresa did not know the moment of her death, neither had she made
any arrangements for people to be either physically or spiritually by
her side. Dissimilarly, her interior suffering and darkness accompanied her until her death and probably in sainthood, as she herself
wished it to become "a saint of darkness," which is highly unusual
for a saint to desire.[14] So Mother's mysticism was a simple, down-to-
earth mysticism, a more reachable and relatable mysticism. In a way,
even in her mysticism, Mother followed the little way, experiencing
the reality of God in her simplicity. Mother brought her gifts, her
talents, and a tailored form of mysticism that was totally hers to the
history of Christian mysticism. Mother's was an ordinary mysticism,
although both the visible and invisible suffering that the mystics suffered were extraordinary gifts, not for everyone to experience.

St. Padre Pio went through the dark night of the soul and experienced the same darkness, suffering, and loss of God that St. Mother

Teresa experienced. Padre Pio described his dark night of the soul as dark clouds gathering in the heavens, and he could not find even a feeble ray of light that could penetrate his troubled soul. The mystic felt in complete darkness, with an aching soul on the verge of death. His soul was tormented, yearning for God, and hell poured itself in his soul, Padre Pio wrote to Fr. Benedetto on May 4, 1914. By 1918, Padre Pio was completely overwhelmed by darkness. Literally, light had completely disappeared: "Completely cut off from the light of day, without a glimmer which might dispel my everlasting night, I crawl along in the dust of my nothingness, but I am powerless to move forward in the mire of my mysteries of all kinds."[15]

St. Mother Teresa underwent the same dark night of the soul—the invisible suffering—for fifty years. This is how Mother explained what she experienced:

> This terrible sense of loss—this untold darkness—this loneliness this continual longing for God—which gives me that pain deep down in my heart—Darkness is such that I really do not see—neither with my mind nor with my reason—the place of God in my soul is blank—There is no God in me—when the pain of longing is so great—I just long & long for God—and then it is that I feel—He does not want me—He is not there—…God does not want me—Sometimes—I just hear my own heart cry out—"My God" and nothing else comes—The torture and pain I can't explain.[16]

Nonetheless, Mother Teresa's mysticism was not as extraordinary as that of Padre Pio; her mysticism was a mysticism to which ordinary folks can relate and embrace. After all, the road to contemplative spirituality and *theosis* is open to all—and Mother, with her down-to-earth mysticism, made that possible for those who want to live a contemplative-active life. The *Catechism of the Catholic Church* makes the same argument:

Spiritual progress tends toward ever more intimate union with Christ. This union is called "mystical" because it participates in the mystery of Christ through the sacraments—"the holy mysteries"—and, in him, in the mystery of the Holy Trinity. God calls us all to this intimate union with him, even if the special graces or extraordinary signs of this mystical life are granted only to some for the sake of manifesting the gratuitous gift given to all. (#2014)[17]

So, St. Mother Teresa modeled a form of mysticism that served the poor and the destitute but also laypeople, her collaborators, and coworkers, who were searching for a contemplative spirituality to practice in their lives.

Objective and Subjective Mysticism

Hans Urs von Balthasar (1905–88), the eminent Swiss theologian and a Catholic priest, distinguishes between *objective* and *subjective* mysticism, while emphasizing a commonality between the two: all mysticism must be trinitarian, christological, and ecclesiological. For von Balthasar a special charism in the service of the word constitutes *objective* mysticism, which is experienced in a fashion proper and special to the mystic—*subjective* mysticism. Adrienne von Speyer (1902–67), a medical doctor, theologian, mystic, and stigmatic, who was baptized into the Catholic Church and was under the spiritual direction of von Balthasar, provided a further definition of *objective mysticism*: "what the mystic sees, hears, experiences can never be anything but one aspect of objective revelation, upon which a clearer, more intense light is shed in order to assist the understanding of people in the present time."[18] Instead, according to von Speyer, through *subjective* mysticism, "one has to surrender oneself completely, without introspection, so that what has been shown by God will be received undiluted."[19]

If von Balthasar's and von Speyer's definitions of *objective* and *subjective* mysticism are kept in mind, the mysticism experienced by St. Padre Pio and St. Mother Teresa were objective and subjective at the same time: they were *objective*, lived mysticism, lived exegesis of the mysteries of the Lord, and *subjective* mysticism, understood as a special grace from God to both saints.[20]

Eucharistic Mysticism

Besides being trinitarian-christological (through Christ the mystic gains access and partakes in the Trinity) and ecclesiological (a mystic is a microcosm of the Church, according to de Lubac),[21] Sts. Padre Pio and Mother Teresa's mysticism was also deeply eucharistic—the greatest of Christian mysteries where the faithful experience an epiphany, a meeting point in the Eucharist where Jesus comes to meet his people. The Eucharist is one of the greatest Christian mysteries and has attracted special devotion, especially on the part of mystics and the saints of the Catholic Church, beginning in the early centuries of Christianity to the present: from St. Basil the Great, St. Jerome, St. Gregory the Great, St. Ignatius, to medieval mystics St. Bernard of Clairvaux, St. Hildegard von Bingen, St. Bridget of Sweden, St. Catherine of Siena, St. Rita of Cascia, St. Teresa of Avila, to the modern-day saints St. John Bosco, St. Gemma Galgani, St. Faustina, to St. Padre Pio, St. Mother Teresa, and St. John Paul II.

The Eucharist was the centerpiece in the lives of Padre Pio and Mother Teresa. Both mystics nurtured a deep faith in the Lord, and consequently a deep devotion and reverence for the Eucharist. Since an early age, Padre Pio had a special devotion to the Eucharist. He would spend a considerable amount of time in his parish church in eucharistic adoration. The same goes for Mother Teresa: early in her childhood in Skopje, as she revealed to Fr. Neuner (her spiritual director), she had a special love for the Eucharist.[22]

People who have witnessed Padre Pio celebrating the Eucharist have testified about his deep devotion to the sacrament. Crucified

Jesus and Padre Pio carrying the sufferings of the stigmata were intimately united during the celebration of the Eucharist. Padre Pio lived intensely and closely the drama of Calvary.[23] When he was asked how could he stand for the entire duration of Mass carrying his wounds of the stigmata, Padre Pio responded, "During Mass I am not standing; I am hanging"—which is significant in understanding how mystically connected to Jesus on the cross Padre Pio was during the celebration of the Eucharist.[24]

In 2002, when Padre Pio was canonized and the world's attention was brought to the Capuchin stigmatic priest, the then Archbishop of Buenos Aires, Cardinal Bergoglio, future Pope Francis, was particularly attracted to Padre Pio's mission, vision, and especially the prayer groups founded by the saint. Bergoglio wanted Padre Pio's mission and vision to be brought to the Argentine capital, which was under his pastoral care. For this reason, Bergoglio sent a delegation to the source: he invited Fr. Marciano Morra, who for twenty-five years had served as general secretary of Padre Pio prayer groups, to pay him a visit in Buenos Aires.[25] Bergoglio was particularly interested to know the spirituality of Padre Pio and his devotion to the Eucharist. Fr. Morra explained to Cardinal Bergoglio that the centerpiece in Padre Pio's spirituality was the Holy Mass, the Eucharist, which Padre Pio celebrated early in the morning between 4:30 and 5:00—his life and his day practically centered around the Eucharist. For Padre Pio, skipping the Sunday Eucharist was a very serious sin. Padre Pio could absolve individuals in confession from other sins, but if he realized that there was no repentance on the part of the individual for having missed Mass, then he was very angry and would even send away the penitent without absolution.[26] Padre Pio might have had a direct and long-lasting influence on Bergoglio, as a decade later when he became pope, Francis would reflect on Padre Pio's lesson on the Sunday Mass understood as a source of renewal, saying,

How can we carry out the Gospel without drawing the energy needed to do it, one Sunday after another, from the limitless source of the Eucharist? We do not go to Mass in order to give something to God, but to receive what we truly need from him. We are reminded of this by the Church's prayer, which is addressed to God in this way: "although you have no need of our praise, yet our thanksgiving is itself your gift, since our praises add nothing to your greatness but profit us for salvation" (*Roman Missal*, Common Preface IV).[27]

Like Padre Pio, Mother Teresa had a great devotion to the Eucharist, which started early in her life, specifically when she was five and half and received her first holy communion in Skopje. Love for foreign missions was infused in her spirit since the day she received Christ in the Holy Eucharist. More than a decade later, she wrote to the Superior General of Loreto Sisters, explaining the special grace she had received on the day of her first communion, adding that it was the eucharistic Jesus who had consistently energized and sustained her to take a step into the unknown and go to foreign and far-away missions. What did the eucharistic Jesus want Sister Teresa to do?

The Voice to whom Mother refers in her correspondence was indeed the eucharistic Jesus, who had some special requests for Mother Teresa, changing her life forever. It was after receiving holy communion, when still on her knees, that Mother Teresa heard the locutions. She heard the same voice, the same locutions coming from the Holy Host, dictating what he wanted of her and what her future religious order would look like:

> I want Indian nuns, Victims of my love, who would be Mary & Martha. Who would be so very united to me as to radiate my love on souls. I want free nuns covered with my poverty of the cross—I want obedient nuns covered with my obedience of the Cross. I want full of love nuns

covered with the Charity of the Cross. Wilt thou refuse to do this for me?[28]

The eucharistic Jesus led Gonxhe Bojaxhiu from the Balkan periphery to the Indian periphery. It was a work of love, for the love of him, that "you have come to India for Me," to be his Spouse, the Voice said.[29] It was the eucharistic Jesus who prescribed her vocation and her life-long dedication to the poorest of the poor and to saving souls. Mother could have never done it without the continuous contact with and sustenance of the eucharistic Jesus. Additionally, it was he who designed and blessed the saris the Missionaries of Charity would wear in the field hospitals they serve worldwide: "Your present habit is holy because it is my symbol—your sari will become holy because it will be my symbol."[30]

How could Mother Teresa say no to the eucharistic Jesus who wanted to use her for his glory and to bring souls to him? As her devoted spouse, the eucharistic and mystical Jesus promised that he would be with her always, as she would bear torments and sufferings for his sake.

In 1947, in her correspondence with Archbishop Périer, when Mother was proposing and designing the first draft of the constitutions of her religious order, she wrote about the sisters receiving daily holy communion. She was worried about whether there were any impediments to this, and if there were, she was asking the archbishop for a solution. The way Mother concludes her letter to the archbishop is significant. Mother was convinced: if the Lord is received daily, nothing bad would happen either to the Sisters or to herself. She was convinced that the eucharistic Jesus would look after them.[31] When Mother organized the activities for the poor and the destitute, she made sure the Eucharist was present—she ensured the physical centrality of the Eucharist in the tabernacle for adoration. Ongoing eucharistic adoration meant constant communication and renewal for Mother and the Missionaries of Charity, as Pope Benedict XVI described the centrality of the Eucharist in Mother Teresa's mission:

185

But Mother Teresa who gave us this example and the community that follows in her steps, supposed always as the first condition of one foundation, the presence of a tabernacle. Without the presence of the love of God who gives himself, it would not have been possible to realize that apostolate. It would not have been possible to live in that abandonment to self. Only by inserting their self-abandonment in God, in this adventure of God, this humility of God, they could and can perform today this great act of love, this openness to all. In this sense, I would say that living the Eucharist in its original sense, in its true depth, is a school of life.[32]

Mother's relationship with Christ in the Eucharist was mystical and intense. In the same year (1947), her spiritual director Fr. Van Exem wrote to Archbishop Périer, explaining how Mother Teresa had asked him if she could do more penance, which included a strict regimen of night prayer. Mother had explained in detail her nightly longings to receive Holy Eucharist. This demonstrates her profound devotion to the Eucharist and the belief in Jesus's real presence in the bread and wine, but also Mother's longing to be in communion with Christ and the neighbor:

> The attraction for the Blessed Sacrament at times was so great. I longed for Holy Com. [Communion]. Night after night the sleep would disappear—and only to spend those hours in longing for His coming. This began in Asansol in Feb.—and now every night for one hour or two, I have noticed it is from 11 to 1, the same longing breaks into the sleep.[33]

At the dawn, first thing in the morning, Mother received holy communion in great devotion and humility. It was her daily routine. She always received the sacrament on the tongue, never in her hand:

the same tradition goes with the Missionaries of Charity sisters and brothers. Mother was very well aware that the faithful who wished to receive holy communion in the hand were allowed to do so by the Church "in areas where the bishops' conference with the *reco-gnitio* of the Apostolic See had given permission, the sacred host is to be administered to him or her,"[34] but nonetheless, she modeled her revered, time-tested way of receiving Communion—always on the tongue, as she was used to during her whole life serving in the periphery of the Church.

On September 23, 1950, Mother Teresa wrote to Archbishop Périer to express her gratitude that her order the Missionaries of Charity had received the official approval of the Church. But Mother was as joyful and grateful for another special reason—the possibility of having and celebrating Jesus in missionaries' chapel. The official approval meant that she would have the Eucharist present and celebrated in her convent by a validly ordained clergyman according to Article 1, Canon 900 of the *Code of Canon Law*.[35] Additionally, honoring the Eucharist, celebrating the tenth anniversary of the call within the call, Mother decided to have a "Eucharistic Year" for the Missionaries of Charity. The intention was sacramental and eucharistic as she wrote on December 15, 1955: "We will try to spread through the slums the love and the true devotion to the Blessed Sacrament in thanksgiving for our Society."[36]

Mother's theology of the Eucharist was simple: she went from receiving the Eucharist to serving the poorest of the poor; for Mother Teresa, those in most need were an extension of the Eucharist. For her, Jesus had a twofold presence: in the Eucharist and the poorest of the poor. Part V of the Missionaries of Charity *Constitutions*, written by Mother Teresa herself, explains the mystery and essence of eucharistic theology as united to and an extension of Jesus, which was Mother's understanding of the Eucharist. For her there was no difference between the two: Jesus in the Eucharist and Jesus in the slums, Jesus who was present "in the broken bodies of the poor."[37] Jesus in the Eucharist is the centerpiece in the spirituality of Mother

Teresa, and consequently in the spirituality of the Missionaries of Charity she founded. She explained in the *Constitutions*,

> From the contemplation of Jesus in the Eucharist we go to contemplation of him in the distressing disguise of the poorest of the poor and so proclaim the word of God to them in the streets and in the houses of the poor.[38]

The Eucharist and the daily reception of holy communion in devotion and reverence had the mystical power of spiritual renewal for Mother Teresa. Every day, through the mystery of the daily Mass, Mother and her sisters renewed the vows of poverty, chastity, obedience, and service to the poorest of the poor, and their desire to do more service, multiplied and intensified through the mystery of the Eucharist. Because of this lucid and pastoral understanding of the theology of the Eucharist, Mother insisted that her religious sisters participate in Mass and receive holy communion daily. Even if she is sick, a sister must be put in a room proximate to where Holy Mass is celebrated, so she can hear Mass from her bed and be able to receive the sacrament daily. In sum, the goal of the Missionaries of Charity life of service is union with Christ, and the means to achieve this desired *theosis* is Eucharist. Mother died convinced that if her order stayed firm and remained faithful to the centerpiece of the order's theology—the Eucharist—the Congregation will not run into any danger.[39]

IN PERSONA CHRISTI: THE THEOLOGY OF PRIESTHOOD OF PADRE PIO AND MOTHER TERESA

Why is Padre Pio's message still relevant, with people still flocking to San Giovanni Rotondo to pray for his intercession? And why is Mother Teresa's theology of the priesthood so intertwined with the vocations of all Christians? We now turn to explore the centrality of the priesthood to the spirituality and mission of both these saints.

Although the reasons to ask for his intercession might be as varied as the people visiting Padre Pio, he was a simple friar, a classic Capuchin, a Franciscan following in the footsteps of St. Francis of Assisi. Padre Pio was also a careful listener and confessor, spiritually close especially to the sick and the peripherals who flocked to his Masses and confessional asking for advice and intercession. Padre Pio through his priestly ordination acted *in persona Christi* as both a traditional-ordinary and nontraditional-extraordinary priest. Padre Pio was traditional-ordinary because he was a simple, peripheral priest from poor southern Italy, who was called to the vocation of priesthood to save souls and forgive the sinners; but he was also a priest with extraordinary charisms, who was fully dedicated to the love of God and love of neighbor, the reestablishment of the moral law in society, and universal mediation via his priesthood.[40] What captures Padre Pio's theology of the priestly vocation and acting *in persona Christi* are the words he pronounced and signed when he took the solemn vows at ordination:

> For You, may I be, in the world, the Way, the Truth, the Life, and for You, a holy priest, a perfect Victim. Padre Pio.[41]

When Padre Pio was ordained, he did not think of big projects and big accomplishments, diplomas and studies in theology, or dreams of missions in foreign and faraway lands, although when he was a student, he had asked his superiors to allow him to be a missionary. Instead, his priesthood and his priestly vocation began with a silent and painfully suffered participation in the passion of Christ via his mystical stigmata. Like Mother Teresa, Padre Pio felt a radical need to be united to Christ—*theosis*—living the gospel radically and literally. He considered his stigmata a way to grow in intimacy with Jesus and feel Jesus's suffering more profoundly—this is who

189

Padre Pio the priest was, and his understanding of suffering grew through his appreciation of his stigmata as bringing greater unity with Christ.

Pope John Paul II specifically commented on his gift as a confessor during his June 16, 2002, homily for the canonization of Padre Pio:

> Padre Pio was a generous dispenser of divine mercy, making himself available to all by welcoming them, by spiritual direction and, especially, by the administration of the sacrament of Penance. I also had the privilege, during my young years, of benefitting from his availability for penitents. The ministry of the confessional, which is one of the distinctive traits of his apostolate, attracted great crowds of the faithful to the monastery of San Giovanni Rotondo. Even when that unusual confessor treated pilgrims with apparent severity, the latter, becoming conscious of the gravity of sins and sincerely repentant, almost always came back for the peaceful embrace of sacramental forgiveness.[42]

Padre Pio was a confessor for fifty years, having no time to celebrate holidays, no breaks away from his convent, no pauses—his focus was on people who asked for a priest and who came from all over the world to be reconciled. Padre Pio the priest cared for the spiritual well-being of the individual who was asking for spiritual help and direction. His total focus was on the individual and his or her spiritual restoration and conscience, encouraging a convinced and deeply felt repentance. The embrace he offered to the penitent at the end of confession was a trace of his priestly vocation and acting *in persona Christi*—imitating a forgiving, loving, and fatherly prototype.

Similar to Mother Teresa, in his priestly vocation, Padre Pio was a little pencil in the hand of God; he did not want titles, prestige, attention, or media spotlight; he considered all these to be of no value for a priest who acts *in persona Christi*. Christ was the center and the reference point of his priesthood. For Padre Pio, the ordained priest ought to be holy and celibate; for him, personal-priestly holiness is necessary to make the priestly mission and the Christian message credible and effective among the people. This is how one can understand his butcher-priest dichotomy. In April 1913 Padre Pio wrote to his spiritual director,

> I saw Jesus who showed me a great crowd of priests and dignitaries of the Church. Jesus turned His horrified gaze away from those priests, as if tired of watching. Then, looking into my eyes, I observed with horror two tears running down His cheeks. He then walked away from that crowd of priests with a great expression of disgust on His face shouting, "BUTCHERS!" Then, turning to me, He said, "My son, do not believe that my agony lasted only three hours. No. On account of the souls who benefited more from Me, I will be in agony until the end of the world. During My agony, my son, one should not sleep. My soul does not go around looking for a drop of human pity [i.e., sympathy], but alas, they leave Me alone under the weight of indifference. My ministers' ingratitude and sleep make My agony even more difficult. What troubles Me the most is that these people add disbelief to their indifference."[43]

This is a harsh criticism on the part of Padre Pio, which was probably directed toward those priests who had fallen and were not acting *in persona Christi*.

Padre Pio's vows at ordination speak volumes about his understanding of priesthood as one called to be holy and a victim, to be holy priest, a perfect Victim, as he put it.[44] The priest was a victim, according to Padre Pio, because of the annihilation of self, or of the selfish I; instead, the priest lives for Thou by following radically and impersonating Thou *in persona*. In fact, it was the desire for sacrifice and annihilation of the selfish self that made Padre Pio enter the Capuchin convent. But, how was Padre Pio a victim? Being a victim for Thou meant total self-giving, total dedication by rendering his gifts available to people and showing them the way via confession and spiritual direction. "He has no need, as did the high priests, to offer sacrifice day after day, first for his own sins and then for those of the people; he did that once for all when he offered himself" (Heb 7:27), as Jesus who tasted death for every man, by sacrificing himself, voluntarily agreeing to be the Victim, so should the priests. This was Padre Pio's understanding of *in persona Christi*, which includes his victimhood. Understanding priesthood as the frontline victim for Christ and his people, Padre Pio became the first "priest victim," who obeyed the 1914 invitation of Pope Pius XI, a pontiff Padre Pio held in great regard, to offer himself as a victim for sinners, and to seek to prevent the impending disaster of World War I, about to be unleashed on Europe:[45]

> As many Catholics as there are throughout the world, and in the first place men from the clergy; whose duty, more-over, it will be, at the command of bishops, to carry out public supplications in every single parish, that the merci-ful God, exhausted as it were by the prayers of the pious, may take away the destructive flames of war—the sooner the better—and that, beneficent, He may grant to those who preside over civil affairs to think thoughts of peace and not of affliction.[46]

Mother spoke often of the two great gifts Jesus left behind to help Christians follow him. The first is his selfless giving, the gift of himself, which is his real presence in the Eucharist—the eucha-ristic Jesus in whom Mother strongly believed during all her life and mission. The second gift Jesus left behind according to Mother

Teresa is the gift of priesthood, serving *in persona Christi*, in mystical union with Jesus in obedience and chastity. For Mother, the priest was an *alter Christus*, another Christ, standing in the place of Christ. Mother understood priestly celibacy as a gift of emptiness—an emptiness that the priest receives, and eventually is filled with Jesus's love. There is no filling without the *kenosis*, emptying of self. Thus, for her, priests should guard a virgin heart and a virgin body in total service of and dedication to the people entrusted to their care. Once a holy priest told Mother Teresa, "Mother, Jesus is everything for me. I have neither time nor room in my life for other affections."[47] This is exactly what Mother Teresa wanted to see in priests understood as *in persona Christi*. This is the key in understanding the theology of priesthood of Mother Teresa and why she was not shy to express her views on celibacy, looking at priesthood as an imitation of Christ, who was celibate. Padre Pio and Mother Teresa have the same theology of priesthood. Keeping this theology of priesthood in mind, Mother wrote,

> Without priests, we have no Jesus.
> Without priests, we have no absolution.
> Without priests, we cannot receive Holy Communion.[48]

The eucharistic Jesus was the eucharistic priest for Mother Teresa. In a letter Mother wrote to Fr. Michael van der Peet, she had some prophetic words about priesthood and the Eucharist:

> You, I am sure, must feel often like that when at your word in your hands—the bread becomes the Body of Christ, the wine becomes the Blood of Christ.—How great must be your love for Christ.—No greater love—than the love of the priest for Christ His Lord & God.[49]

However, Mother had never aspired to a priestly ordination for herself or entertained any thought of women's ordination to the priesthood or diaconate, which were current topics widely discussed during her lifetime. Because of her opposition to women's ordination, Mother has been criticized by her staunchest critic, Christopher Hitchens, for lack of understanding and opposing women's empowerment.[50] She had a clear scriptural theology of priesthood and its source. She did not consider women's ordination to the priesthood or diaconate to be a human right or a women's emancipation or equality matter. Instead, Mother understood priestly vocation as coming from the economy of the mystery of Christ and the Church.[51] Fr. Sebastian Vazhakala, in his book dedicated to the years he spent with Mother Teresa, explains that Mother did not support women's ordination, arguing that if there was a woman worthy to be ordained, this should have been Mary, but Mary did not want to be a priest and Jesus did not want to ordain her.[52] The same argument she repeated in an interview granted to the editor of the Kolkata Catholic weekly the *Herald*, the Salesian Fr. C. M. Paul, on August 16, 1990:

> No one was a better priest than Mary. And yet she remained only the handmaid of the Lord. See, no one could say, not even you as a priest, this is my body, as she could, because the body of Jesus was in her. Beautiful no![53]

Mother felt her calling and vocation profoundly; it must have never occurred to her that what she was doing and her vocation were of a lesser value than of priest. As her mother Drana Bojaxhiu was, Mother Teresa was a very strong woman—Balkan tough and confident in the complementarity of men and women in religious life and in human life in general. Throughout her life and mission, Mother remained the handmaid of the Lord, following the example of Mary. She never saw women religious as of a lesser value than men religious. Neither did she see her vocation as submissive or subservient to men. Instead, Mother considered submission as a blessing and male-female-lay vocations as complementary. Only through her Christ-like virtue of submission and obedience could she go down to the level of the poorest of the poor she was serving; this way, she could identify with Christ of the slums. Thus, Mother considered submission for someone she loved, that is, Jesus in the poor, a blessing. For Mother, both women and men, lay and religious, were differently and specially called. The calling for her was identical; the difference was in how one lived and witnessed his or her special calling. For example, when governments requested that she open a Missionaries of Charity religious house, Mother insisted that governments ought to accept even a priest who would celebrate the Eucharist for the missionaries. The sisters could not go into the country without this guarantee.[54] For Mother, it all depends on how much love and dedication one puts into the calling and here lay the difference. While there is one calling with different expressions, her motto is always the same: to do small things with a great love, live your calling wherever you are with great dedication.

Cardinal Oswald Gracias, Archbishop of Bombay in India, remembers that during the Year of the Eucharist declared by Pope John Paul II (October 2004–October 2005) outside the chapels of the Missionaries of Charity all over the world, there was a little board with the inscription: "Priest of God, celebrate this Mass as if it is your first Mass, your last Mass, and your only Mass."[55] Mother had required the same dedication to the Eucharist to the Missionaries of Charity during her lifetime. She held priests to a high standard but would never aspire to seek ordination or act *in persona Christi*. Priests should do what they are called to do.

> [The Missionaries of Charity who worked in pairs] will encourage the sick, even if not dying, to ask for Holy Communion—for which they will also carry the required things and have the place and the sick ready for Our Lord's coming. They will notify the priest in time as to how many people wish to receive Our Lord.[56]

Mother was not blind to lukewarm priests, or to those who did not live up to their vows or their calling, or to those priests who were "not holy enough,"[57] to use St. Thérèse of Lisieux's terminology. However, like Thérèse, Mother wanted to help priests with her fervent prayers. How beautiful is the vocation *to preserve that salt* destined for souls! This is the vocation of Carmel, St. Thérèse of Lisieux wrote about the mission of the contemplative Carmelites describing the payers for priest, because the only purpose of our prayers and our sacrifices is to be an *apostle to the apostles*, to pray for them while they evangelize souls by words and above all by example.[58]

Consequently, Mother did not hesitate to provide some motherly advice to a priest in difficulty, offering her wisdom and practical steps to overcome his difficulties. This is Mother Teresa's September 22, 1985, letter to the priest:

> You know Mother's love for you. All these years you have been longing for this—and now when it is yours, do not lose it. This trial is a gift of Jesus to you to draw you closer to Himself so that you can share His Passion with Him. Remember, He has espoused you in tenderness and love, and to make this union more living [Jesus] made you His priest—His Eucharist. You have as much vocation to be an MC as I—to be an MC Priest of the Poorest of the Poor. Do not play with fire—fire burns and destroys. Pray often during the day: Jesus, in my heart I believe in Your tender love for me, I love You, and I want to be only all for You through Mary as an MC. Let us pray.

Every day at communion, Mother Teresa communicated two feelings to Jesus: One was of gratefulness, because he had helped her persevere to that day. The other was a special request: "teach me to pray."[59] In the second there is a special intention Mother had in mind: learning to pray for holy priests. Mother Teresa took her cue from St. Thérèse of Lisieux, who after her pilgrimage to Rome, realized how much prayer holy priests, who did not hide their weakness and fragility, needed. Mother Teresa was committed to praying for priests' holiness, and she was interested in and wanted the contemplative branch of her order to pray for the holiness of priests and the holiness of family life.[60] She entrusted Mary to guide and keep the priests in her heart. Mother wrote the following prayer for priests:

> Mary, Mother of Jesus,
> throw your mantle of purity over our priests.
> Protect them, guide them, and keep them in your heart.
> Be a Mother to them, especially in times of discouragement
>   and loneliness.
> Love them and keep them belonging completely to Jesus.
> Like Jesus, they, too, are your sons, so keep their hearts pure
>   and virginal.
> Keep their minds filled with Jesus, and put Jesus always on
>   their lips,
> so that he is the one they offer to sinners and to all they meet.
> Mary, Mother of Jesus, be their Mother, loving them and
>   bringing them joy.
> Take special care of sick and dying priests, and the ones most
>   tempted.
> Remember how they spent their youth and old age, their
>   entire lives serving and giving all to Jesus.[61]

CONTEMPLATIVE-ACTIVE MYSTICISM: THE MEDICINE OF MERCY

Padre Pio and Mother Teresa, two of the greatest mystic saints of our age, knew suffering—both physical and spiritual—firsthand. It was because they were sufferers, and through their mysticism cosufferers with Christ of the crucifix, that Sts. Padre Pio and Mother Teresa thought of and acted on to alleviate suffering in others. Since his youth, Padre Pio suffered ill health, so much so that people doubted if he was going to survive long enough to finish his religious training, let alone be able to live the austere rule of the Franciscans. The same had been true of Mother Teresa when she was young and growing up in Skopje. She suffered from coughs and malaria. She was frail and her health was fragile, which concerned her family and especially her mother. Both Padre Pio and Mother Teresa survived their medical trials. Their experiences with sickness and the physical suffering related to sickness made the saints champions of the sick and the suffering but also pioneers in finding innovative ways to alleviate the multitudes of suffering physically, spiritually, psychologically, and socially. This became their lifelong mission as their works of practicing evangelical medicine evidence.

Their active mysticism was not divorced and disassociated from contemplation. Rather, their mysticism was integrative or combined: they were contemplatives in action. Besides his life of prayer and contemplation, Padre Pio was known for his social commitment, which was supernaturally motivated and evangelically justified.[62] The active mystic Padre Pio always thought of solutions, when he noticed young people in their twenties waiting in line to receive alms from the convent. He then turned to his superior, Fr. Carmelo, saying, "Teach them an art or a trade. Go to Rome to our friends and do something. We absolutely must act!"[63] This was Padre Pio's way of prayer in action. The same goes for Mother Teresa. In her speech at Regina Mundi Institute in Rome, on December 20, 1979, Mother explained her understanding of active mysticism as this applies in the apostolate of the Missionaries of Charity: "We are contemplatives in the heart of the world. We are 24 hours a day with Jesus."[64] Mother Teresa and her religious sisters learned to be contemplatives in the slums they were serving and did not separate contemplation from action, prayer from praxis.

During the first centuries of Christian history, St. Basil the Great (330–79) wrote on the physician's role not only for the cure of the body but also for that of the soul, or what he called the "two right hands" of the art of medicine, which applies to both body and soul. St. Basil wrote *To Eustathius the Physician* in letter 189, exhorting that the physician practice "not confining the application of your skill to men's bodies, but by attending also to the cure of the diseases of their souls."[65] Medicine was understood as putting mercy into practice.

Padre Pio and Mother Teresa had a positive theology of illness: illness comes from God, and nothing that comes from God can be evil. Consequently, illness and the suffering related to it was seen as a means of unity with or returning to God. Both Padre Pio and Mother Teresa knew how to suffer mystically and physically. They knew firsthand the benefits of suffering and the fruits of suffering, by participation in the sufferings of Christ. Their homes for the relief of suffering were based on this understanding. Consequently, the ways to alleviate suffering were service following a theology of charity (caritas theology) and ministry of charity (caritas ministry).

In their homes of care for the poor and sick, they offered an integral and integrated health and hospice service model that combined the cure of the body with that of the soul, a method based on an integral anthropology, where science and wisdom, charity and service meet.[66] *Cura corporis* and *cura animae*—physical and spiritual wellness—was the motto of their homes for cure and accompaniment of dying patients. The innovation Padre Pio applied in his medical complex was humane medicine or a holistic approach to the patient, which focused on the whole person, body, mind, and soul, treating the patient as a person, not a number in a hospital or hospice room, nor as a disease to be cured. This approach was quite innovative, given the time in which the casa of Padre Pio was built. As art is a way of explaining theology, so is holistic patient care, or treating the patient as a person, not as an object to be cured. For Padre Pio, the human patient was not made up of parts that malfunctioned and needed either repair or replacement. Medicine, for him, was far more than restoring bodily wellness. The human person has a destiny and is directed to an end, which Padre Pio and Mother

Teresa understood as union with God—and for this, their suffering mattered.

Padre Pio's Home for the Relief of Suffering

St. Pio's art of modern medicine, combining curing the body with curing the soul, is applied in his foundation Home for the Relief of Suffering, an impressive modern complex near the church of San Giovanni Rotondo in the periphery of southern Italy. The name of Padre Pio's state-of-the-art hospital is significant. The home is the best setting in which to receive care and support—and, in the case of the home of Padre Pio, abundant Christian love. The second key expression is *relief of suffering*. This does not mean elimination of suffering, as eliminating suffering was not the focus of Padre Pio. He was convinced that human suffering could not be abolished or reduced by medical technology or by euthanizing the patient. That is why Padre Pio insisted that the structure, although it includes state-of-the-art medical equipment, still be called a home, which will give people hospitality and hope to live and cope with pain and suffering caused by illness. In Padre Pio's home, the sick person is called to a sanctified suffering, and the team of health-care providers have a special calling in assisting the suffering with the spirit of the Good Samaritan, using prayer and science. For Padre Pio relief of suffering meant carrying the cross, making its yoke lighter in Christ. For Padre Pio, as for Mother Teresa, Jesus was in the patients and in the poorest of the poor among the patients. Padre Pio liked saying of suffering,

> It is the only thing that the angels envy us…because it is the strongest and most sincere way of saying to God: "I really love you."[67]

For Padre Pio, love was suffering for the beloved and for the neighbor. When he was asked if the best thing to offer to God was love or suffering, Padre Pio without the slightest hesitation replied that it is suffering. So much did he believe in its redemptive power that above the door of his own cell is inscribed, "The cross is always ready and waiting for you everywhere."[68] It is in pain and suffering that the love of God is fortified, for Padre Pio. His theology of the cross was resignation to the cross of multiple sufferings and knowing how to carry it. That, in a nutshell, is the core purpose of his home for the relief of suffering—giving a theological meaning to suffering and learning how to carry it. Moreover, Padre Pio never entertained the idea of eliminating suffering altogether. Humans cannot go against the will of God, because it is God who arranges what Hans Urs von Balthasar called the theological states of the believer, plunging him at one time into the deep waters of the cross where he is not allowed to experience any consolation, and then into the grace given by resurrection of a hope, which brings with it the certainty that it does not deceive. No one can either manipulate or change the theological states, because they are christological and left to God's disposition.[69] Here, von Balthasar was referring to the spiritual suffering, which is not any different from the physical suffering. Padre Pio and Mother Teresa had experienced both sufferings firsthand. Padre Pio's home for the relief of suffering made patients aware of its Christian meaning. As Padre Pio himself instructed, "It is not suffering but knowing how to suffer that counts. Everybody suffers, but a handful know how to suffer."[70]

On January 9, 1940, Padre Pio announced his decision to create a home for the cure of the sick. He had a little money to offer to the project and an innovative idea of how to approach the complexity of human suffering. It was the beginning of the war, and the place chosen for the project was peripheral; the edifice was literally going to be built on a hard rock. Many doubted if a home of this kind could have ever been constructed or been possible in the peripheral province of Foggia. In fact, as Padre Pio would mention later in his life, it was indeed a grand earthly undertaking that is still bearing fruit and assisting the peripherals of southern Italy. Padre Pio's home is one of the most important hospitals and comprehensive care units in Italy where the practice of medicine and medical treatment is not isolated from or devoid of theology,[71] and the healing was not focused exclusively on the body. The medical doctors who joined Padre Pio's Home worked in teams with the patients and with one another, practicing the art of medicine and focusing equally on body and soul. Dr. Guglielmo Sanguinetti, the first medical doctor to join in Padre Pio's project, had once been what Italians call *mangiapreti* (anticleric; priest-hater), who was converted to faith and became a spiritual son of Padre Pio, reconnecting with his Catholic faith.

Padre Pio's Home for the Relief of Suffering was dedicated on May 5, 1956, officially opening its doors to the sick and the poor and all those who needed medical and spiritual assistance free of charge. Given the misery and unemployment plaguing southern Italy at the time, to some critics the house of Padre Pio might have seemed too lavish and out of place, a criticism Padre Pio was quick to address, arguing that "if I had it my way, I would have made even the beds out of gold, because where the patient is, the living Christ is."[72]

Initially the house could accommodate 250 patients, offering medical assistance in surgery and general medicine, obstetrics and gynecology, pediatrics, radiology, laboratories for clinical examinations, and orthopedics. On February 20, 1971, three years after the death of Padre Pio, Pope Paul VI would reflect on the enormous success of Padre Pio's approach to caring and his foundation. Prayer was the key to the success of Padre Pio's apostolate: "Look what fame he had....But why?...Because he said Mass humbly, heard confessions from dawn to dusk and was...the one who bore the wounds of our Lord. He was a man of prayer and suffering."[73]

The combination of the two, care for the body and soul via intercessory prayer, made the House for the Relief of Suffering a unique and sought-after institution. On the day of the dedication, Padre Pio had some prophetic words on the new house: "A seed has been planted on earth that He will warm with his rays of love. A new militia made up of renouncing and love is about to rise to the glory of God, for the comfort of souls and sick bodies."[74]

For the first anniversary of the work on May 5, 1957, Padre Pio continued to stress the focus of his foundation and the continuation of the work, which was bearing its fruit of taking care of the body/ soul duality. In his home, Padre Pio considered the body to be one with love, because according to Padre Pio love was the main ingredient to the relief of suffering:

> If this work were only for the relief of the bodies, it would only constitute a model clinic....But it is stimulated and urged to be an operative call to the love of God, through the call of charity. The suffering must live in it [in the hospital] the love of God through the wise acceptance of his suffering, and a serene meditation of his destiny to Him. In it [the hospital] the love to God should be strengthened in the souls of the sick, through love of Christ Crucified, which will emanate from those who assist the infirmity of his body and his spirit. Here, patients, physicians and priests will be wells of love, which the more abundant it will be in one, the more it will be communicated to others.[75]

The hospital on the top of the mountain became a temple of prayer, contemplation, and research, as was desired by St. Pio, soothing and alleviating human suffering. On May 8, 1957, on the occasion of the seventh National Congress of the Italian Catholic Physicians, which was held in the Home for the Relief of Suffering in San Giovanni Rotondo, Padre Pio recited for the first time "The Physician's Prayer" written by Pope Pius XII for the occasion. The prayer combined the Hippocratic oath and Christian ethics. During the last five years of his pontificate, Pius XII, who was facing serious health issues, reflected on medical ethics and death. He died a year after the Congress at the Home for the Relief of Suffering, on October 9, 1958. The Holy

Father's prayer captures Padre Pio's theology of illness and suffering and his way of dealing with or alleviating suffering.

Padre Pio's home on the mountain continues to be a temple of prayer, contemplation, and research as desired by the founder. Respecting the desire of Padre Pio, since 1978 the Home for the Relief of Suffering is dependent on and under the stewardship of the Holy See, via a special delegate.[76] The Vatican Secretary of State is ultimately responsible for the Foundation, which provides leadership for the house and its many affiliated entities.[77]

Mother Teresa's Home for the Dying—Nirmal Hriday

Saints work in harmony, probably without knowing it. This is the case of Sts. Padre Pio and Mother Teresa and their mutual understanding of mercy, although they never met in person. Mother Teresa and Padre Pio recognized Christ in every person, in the sick and destitute and those who were dying in solitude. Recognizing and serving Christ was Mother's theology: "whatever you did for one of these least brothers of mine, you did for me" (Matt 25:40). That is why Mother stressed that the Missionaries of Charity are not social workers in the service of the poorest of the poor; instead, they are contemplatives in action, because they recognize in every poor person the mysterious but real presence of Christ, the Lord.[78]

One of the first works of the apostolate of Mother Teresa where the same principles of Padre Pio's casa were applied was Nirmal Hriday—Mother Teresa's Home for the Dying, which she founded in 1952, two years after the foundation of the Missionaries of Charity. It was here that Mother started her mission of touching the periphery of the peripherals.[79] Upon Mother's request, the city of Kolkata gave her one of the shelters for pilgrims at the Kali temple that was not used by the Hindu pilgrims. Mother named the house Nirmal Hriday, which in Bengali means "pure heart," in honor of Mary's Immaculate Heart.[80] The beginning was not easy. According to a letter Mother sent to Archbishop Périer in August of 1953, she and her missionaries working in Nirmal Hriday were fearing for their lives. Mother knew that hard times were on the horizon, but she was more than determined to stand the test of charity.[81] The Hindu faithful feared that Mother and her Catholic nuns were desecrating the temple of Kali, so much so that an "official was determined to dismantle this insane project."[82] Other Indian officials responded, "Then bring your mother or sister to cure the dying and lepers, to replace Mother Teresa, and then we will let her [Mother Teresa] go."[83]

Mother and Nirmal Hriday passed the test of charity and gained the trust of the Hindus. The house provided home and hospitality, some rudimentary medical assistance, and an abundance of spiritual assistance, taking care of the body and the soul, to people who were suffering from tuberculosis, cancer, malaria, leprosy, cholera, AIDS, hepatitis, and many other diseases, most of them in need of a hospitable place to die. Neighbors living near Nirmal Hriday would report that they "were scared at first, and then after seeing them [the patients] treated, we [the local residents] thought, 'These are gods in human bodies,' 'If they can do it, so can I.'"[84] However, unlike Padre Pio's facility, Mother's Nirmal Hriday is not a hospital where the most advanced medical treatment, technology, medical cures, and research are conducted. Nirmal Hriday provides hospice care for the dying and offers some basic medical treatment to the dying patients, but not the same as provided at Padre Pio's home. *Hospitium* is a place of hospitality, providing a home to those who did not have one—the infirm or the peripherals; Mother's Nirmal Hriday is in the tradition of hospice care, understood as a place of rest for weary travelers[85] in the last stages of their journey. In the case of Mother Teresa's home, many of the patients are "returning home," so Nirmal Hriday is the final stop on their journey. However, what Mother Teresa's hospice care and Padre Pio's home have in common is their holistic approach to suffering and the dying—*cura corporis* and *cura animae* at a time when most twentieth-century hospitals are elaborately equipped for the diagnosis and rehabilitation of patients with acute illnesses, but this has usually been accompanied with a decrease in the holistic care that is the hospice hallmark.[86] Usually, hospice care starts where the hospital treatment has finished, and involves support from a number of people including clergy and social workers, to ease suffering and address grief associated with dying. In the case of Mother Teresa's Nirmal Hriday's patients, most of them have been either rejected or discarded from local hospitals or simply abandoned in the streets to die alone.

In 1991, Robin Fox, editor of *The Lancet* from 1990 to 1995, visited Nirmal Hriday. Fox described the medical care received in Mother's Nirmal Hriday as haphazard, while stressing that "the most important features of the regimen are cleanliness, the tending of wounds and sores, and loving kindness."[87] Fox was critical of Mother's hospice care for not administering analgesics, which were administered freely to terminally ill patients in palliative care units in the West, arguing that Mother Teresa's approach separates her from the hospice movement. However, in India at the time, as specialists testify, "most cancer patients...did not have access to any analgesia, because of lack of suitable drugs, of knowledge about the use of the drugs by the doctors as well as in some instances no understanding about pain management, and compounded by a lack of resources."[88] This makes a stronger case supporting Mother's approach in hospice and end-of-life-care, which in fact was bringing back *hospitium*, giving hospitality to all those who were unwanted and unloved who happened to be terminally ill following: "For I was...ill and you cared for me....'Amen, I say to you, whatever you did for one of these least brothers of mine, you did for me'" (Matt 25:35–40).

Indeed, Nirmal Hriday is not a hospital but a hospice, aiding sufferers in their last stages of suffering. It is not a place of death, but of hospitable breath, a spiritual place that brings joy and human love and support to patients. The most difficult lesson taught by Mother Teresa is how to love; her intention was never to resolve the big social issues but to focus on one human person at a time.[89] Vijay Prashad, a critic of Mother Teresa, admits that Mother Teresa's missionaries "certainly brought relief for many people, not in medical terms, but with love and affection. Mother Teresa's sisters attempted to soothe the ails of the ill and dying with the balm of love, since many had only rudimentary training in the arts of allopathic medicine (or any medical training for that matter)."[90]

Mother's approach at Nirmal Hriday was hands-on, searching for the destitute and the dying on the streets of Kolkata, those who had been denied medical treatment by the hospitals, and bringing them home, where they could find rudimentary medical assistance and a place where they could die with dignity and be buried or cremated with dignity, following the rituals of their particular religious tradition.[91] As volunteers who have worked in Nirmal Hriday testify, conversion to Christianity was not Mother's and is not the sisters' focus. Hiromi Josepha Kudo, who volunteered at Nirmal Hriday, explained, "When I worked in Nirmal Hriday as a volunteer, I recall having seen Sisters read the Quran to a dying Muslim and calling a Hindu priest from the temple to say the final prayers for dying Hindus. Her mission was not to convert non-Christians, but simply to serve the poorest of the poor in accordance with her Second Vocation."[92]

Mother's was a personalized service, establishing a personal connection with those who were unwanted and unloved by society—taking care of their ailing bodies but also of their souls. Mother liked austerity and simplicity in treatment. For her, machines and too much technology build barriers with people who were suffering. Hers was not a death house, where patients were bedridden, narcotized, depressed, or obtunded.[93] Instead, sisters and volunteers brought and still bring home and smiles to their deathbeds. The patients who come to Nirmal Hriday are society's discards and the most peripheral among the peripherals, as they are carrying the cross of their illness, poverty, and total abandonment. If John Paul II's analogy, "in every poor patient there is twice Jesus who suffers and who languishes,"[94] is used for Mother Teresa's patients of Nirmal Hriday, one can see and serve Christ thrice in their countenances: because they are sick, poor, and abandoned by all including their families. For Mother Teresa Nirmal Hriday was a "treasure house" of her congregation. The neglected, the rejected, the underserved closely reflect the suffering Christ—"Christ in distressing disguise"—and gave her the opportunity to "put her love into living action" and be a contemplative in action.[95]

Mother Teresa's patients were denied cures by government-run hospitals of Kolkata and literally discarded on the streets amid the city's waste. Because of the gravity of their medical conditions and total neglect, there was limited possibility for these individuals to survive. However, due to Mother Teresa's special care and rudimentary medical treatment, or medicine of mercy, several patients recovered. Those who died at Nirmal Hriday died like human beings, loved and cared for, because love is the first ingredient to the relief of suffering.[96] One of Mother's dying patients said, "I have lived like an animal in the street, but I will die like an angel, loved and cared for."[97]

Mother's model of hospice care, which follows in the footsteps of the Christian-monastic tradition of hospice care established in monasteries such as those of St. Basil the Great and St. Benedict, challenges the death-denying attitude of the modern health-care system, while championing a positive attitude toward the poor and dying in Kolkata and everywhere in the world where the Missionaries of Charity labor.

Mother regularly worked at Nirmal Hriday on Sundays. Her routine would be to pray and put on her apron, take the broom, and start cleaning and doing humble work. Whenever a dying person was brought in, Mother would be there to attend. Mother would touch each one tenderly and say a few words to them.[98] On February 3, 1986, Pope John Paul II visited Nirmal Hriday, greeting Mother Teresa's patients. The pontiff was so touched by what he saw, sharing the following reflection:

> Nirmal Hriday is a place of suffering, a house familiar
> with anguish and pain, a home for the destitute and

dying. But, at the same time, Nirmal Hriday is a place of hope, a house built on courage and faith, a home where love reigns, a home filled with love. In Nirmal Hriday, the mystery of human suffering meets the mystery of faith and love.[99]

Like Padre Pio's prayer groups made up of lay followers of Padre Pio, Mother Teresa's charism and her spirituality has been followed by many laypeople who volunteered at Mother's houses throughout the world. Out of these dedicated individuals, the Association of Co-workers of Mother Teresa was founded. On March 29, 1969, Paul VI blessed the constitution of the association. Among the lay collaborators of Mother Teresa are also physicians and health-care providers who volunteer in her houses for the poorest of the poor all over the world. As for the other lay followers, the intention of Mother Teresa for the physicians and health-care providers association was not the formation of a juridical organization, nor a simple aggregation of people who work with the Missionaries of Charity. Instead, and like Padre Pio's, Mother's approach was spiritual and later resulted in a spiritual family called the International Movement of the Collaborators of Mother Teresa. Mother asked her lay followers to undertake a sanctifying journey, which meant praying unceasingly, following her own and her religious sisters' example of contemplatives in action. In July 1981, Mother Teresa wrote the "Physician's Prayer," which captures her understanding of the medical profession and the Christian physician, who is called to live his or her professional life not only with science and conscience, but to act as a mediator of love and charity. The medical doctor was called to become a conscientious collaborator with Christ.[100] Mother Teresa and Padre Pio share the same understanding of the duality of body and soul, but also of evangelical medicine that centers on prayer. For Padre Pio and Mother Teresa the Christian physician ought to imitate the divine physician, serving an ailing Jesus in the sick:

Mary Mother of Jesus
give me your heart
so beautiful, so pure,
so immaculate,
so full of love and humility,
that I may be able to receive Jesus
in the Bread of Life, love Him
as you loved Him
and serve Him in the distressing disguise of the Poor.
In union with all the Masses
Being offered throughout the Catholic world
I offer Thee my heart
Make it meek and humble like yours.
God Bless you.

Mother Teresa m.c.
July 19, 1981[101]

It was at Nirmal Hriday that Mother practiced nursing and mercy combined. Mother had received an intensive training course with hands-on experience before starting her slum apostolate, and the religious sisters who joined the Missionaries of Charity were later trained in nursing and in the medical field. In a letter Mother wrote to her sisters on July 3, 1978, she said,

> In our Nirmal Hriday and Shishu Bhavan, I want you to have morning and evening prayer. Begin the leprosy and medical work with a prayer and put in a little more gentleness, a little more compassion with the sick. It will help you to remember that you are touching the Body of Christ. He is hungry for that touch. Will you not give it?[102]

Mother Teresa became an icon of God's tender mercy, radiating light and hope in the people she touched and served. She saw the suffering Jesus in the faces of the poor and the peripherals.

Two Mystics in Action

Sts. Padre Pio and Mother Teresa were mystics capable of reconnecting humanity to God's love. Through their contemplative-active missions they generously "dispensed" divine mercy and love through their contemplation and action, prayer, and active service in the Home for the Relief of Suffering and Nirmal Hriday, respectively. When the Salesian priest and mystic Fr. Cornelio Bertagnolli was asked to compare Padre Pio's and Mother Teresa's missions, he answered that both saints acted so much in harmony and symphony that one can say that one was Jesus and the other Mary. Padre Pio was Christ the priest and victim; Mother Teresa was the love and humility of the woman from Nazareth, of the wedding in Cana, of Calvary, of the Pentecost. There is an analogy even in their respective missions: the friar with the stigmata favored the poor who were sick, while Mother Teresa the poorest of the poor.[103] St. Padre Pio and Mother Teresa were not only harmonious but also complementary—where the rough benevolence of St. Padre Pio ended, there started the tenderness and smile of St. Mother Teresa.[104]

CHAPTER 7

THERE TO LEAD

THE FRUITFUL COLLABORATION OF ST. JOHN PAUL II AND ST. MOTHER TERESA

To bear our load—this world by God designed—
  That power we need:
Our Slavic Pope, brother to all mankind,
  Is there to lead!

Juliusz Słowacki, "Our Slavic Pope"[1]

THE PERIPHERIES OF WOJTYŁA: THE FALL OF COMMUNISM

Any attentive eye has probably not missed the special friendship between St. Mother Teresa and St. John Paul II. Pope John Paul II kissing the top of the head of the diminutive woman and she holding his hand in hers speaks volumes for their genuine bond of friendship and mutual admiration. Their friendship was as deep as it was intuitive. For the Polish pontiff, as George Weigel puts it, Mother Teresa was a personal message for the twentieth century and a living confirmation that the law of the gift graven in human nature could be lived in a way that led to the most profound happiness.[2] Without any exaggeration, Sts. John Paul II and Mother Teresa were the man and

212

the woman of the century, who together made and changed history. They were pilgrims of peace, individuals who were deeply in love with God and their neighbors, supporters of the poor, and promoters of human freedom and human dignity. Additionally, what John Paul II witnessed in Mother Teresa was what he called the mystery of a woman and the great works of God in and through the woman.

On October 16, 1978, the Catholic world was held in suspense, silence, and bewilderment when on the balcony of an overcrowded St. Peter's Square, the announcement of the election of the new pontiff was made. To the surprise of all, neither a traditional Italian nor a Western European name was pronounced. History was made, and more history was in the making with this announcement. This was the first Polish pope in the history of the papacy and the first non-Italian pontiff since the Dutchman Pope Adrian VI (1522–23) was elected to the See of St. Peter. "Undoubtedly his election surprised the world and I think it was a positive surprise,"[3] was how Cardinal Stanisław Dziwisz, Karol Wojtyła's longtime friend and collaborator even before he became Pope John Paul II, assessed the election of a Slavic pope. The Kremlin was highly concerned about the election of a Polish pontiff and the political circumstances related to the election.[4] Yuri Andropov, head of the KGB in Moscow, exploded at the KGB chief in Warsaw, saying, "How could you possibly allow the election of a citizen of a socialist country as pope?"[5] However, Rome had spoken, the election was final: the conclave, which had lasted for three days and eight ballots, had decided on the Polish Cardinal Karol Wojtyła—Pope John Paul II.

The first words the newly elected pontiff pronounced from St. Peter's balcony have remained unforgettable. The pontiff made the argument that he comes from a faraway land, from the East, a European country beyond the Iron Curtain, but one that represents the same faith and the same Christianity:

Dearest Brothers and Sisters: We are all still saddened by the death of our beloved Pope John Paul I. Behold, the

Most Eminent Cardinals have called/elected a new bishop of Rome. They called him from a faraway country…faraway, but always so close by through the communion in faith and Christian tradition. I was afraid to receive this nomination, but I accepted in the spirit of obedience to our Lord Jesus Christ and trust entirely in His Mother, the Most Holy Madonna.[6]

Italian, from now on, was considered "his" language, but the newly elected pontiff never forgot peripheral languages, which were as valid and valued as Italian in proclaiming the gospel. He used the same correction of pronouns as St. Francis of Assisi, Italy's copatron saint, who became "our" patron saint, not "your [Italian]" saint.[7] In fact, Wojtyła entrusted the Petrine ministry to St. Francis of Assisi. So, if another periphery can be added to the Slavic periphery and to what John Paul II was bringing to the papacy, it was the linguistic periphery. He was conscious that Polish would sound strange to people who until then were accustomed to Romance languages, German, or English. Nonetheless the pontiff was confident he would make the peripheral languages and cultures heard and appreciated. He would also make the artificial and politically imposed divide between East and West Europe known and corrected. He never ceased to see Poland as a profoundly European nation, with the same foundations of faith and traditions as other European nations. Europe for John Paul II was a united continent, and one of the main points of unity was the Judeo-Christian tradition.[8]

He knew that the diversity of people, languages, and cultures that made up the European consciousness, and the common roots and heritage of Europeans was an enormous treasure and strength for them. He thought of it as his mission, as a Polish pontiff, to reintroduce into the conscience of Europe and the communion of the Church the understanding of the words and of the languages that still sounded strange.[9] More broadly, Wojtyła, the humanist, understood connections between languages and cultures, and he viewed human experiences as connected and in dialogue despite unnaturally imposed borders by unjust political systems. The same with languages and their etymology, which, in spite of the well-known differences, even in way of writing, sound close and familiar one to another.[10] The election of a Slavic and Polish pope was, as theologian and papal biographer George Weigel emphasizes, an expression of God's purpose in his history, that his primary task was to "strengthen the brethren"; and that doing that would involve a persistent defense of basic human rights, especially the right of religious freedom.[11] Additionally, John Paul II believed that "in the designs of Providence there are no mere coincidences," as he said during his apostolic visit to Fatima on May 13, 1982.[12]

Leaving his beloved Poland and his people behind, John Paul II never hid nor downplayed his Polish national identity or personal history. Since the first moments of his election as the Bishop of Rome, he offered his integral self to the new mission of leading the universal Church. His bonds with peripheral Poland and his diocese of Krakow caused some of his critics to question his pontificate, suggesting that he would view and lead the Catholic Church through almost exclusively Polish lenses.[13] However, his vision and mission was neither Polish, Western, nor Eastern. Instead, John Paul II was the universal pastor, leading the Catholic Church to modernity. His view of the Church was universal, equally East and West. The concurrence of his papacy with the rise in recognition of Mother Teresa's mission was indeed fortuitous, introducing a fruitful collaboration.

But John Paul II's papacy would make other contributions: bringing the periphery to the center's attention—and, more specifically, bringing violations of human dignity and human rights of the peripherals to the center's attention. John Paul II's papacy would be focused on human rights, and the pope was the *defensor homini*, acting on behalf of the peripheral man, and more generally on behalf of humanity.[14] "The rights of man, indelibly inscribed in the inviolable rights of the people," ought to be respected, the newly elected pontiff said to the Poles on June 2, 1979, during his first visit to

Poland after his papal election.[15] But this did not make John Paul II a political pontiff. His papacy, as the papacy of Pope Francis, was deeply pastoral, and only through him being a vigorous pastor could he have an impact on the politics of the nations.[16]

The geopolitical periphery and the Church in the East came alive through his persona, a Slavic-Polish pope, and his pastorate, a vigorous defense of human rights and religious freedoms. The priorities of the new papacy were set: only a few months after being elected pope on October 16, 1978, John Paul II wrote his first encyclical letter, *Redemptor Hominis*, to all believers. Evangelization, vigorous defense of human rights, and religious freedom were among the priorities. For Wojtyła "the curtailment of the religious freedom of individuals and communities is not only a painful experience, but it is above all an attack on man's very dignity, independently of the religion professed or of the concept of the world which these individuals and communities have."[17] So human rights, for Wojtyła, flow from human dignity and are connected to the very nature of the human person—and Jesus Christ is the ultimate source of every right. According to *Redemptor Hominis*, the key to understanding human rights is christological: through the incarnation, Jesus Christ has restored the dignity of human beings by being in every human person. So, human rights and the human person are intimately connected: one cannot respect human rights before respecting the human person and his or her source. Consequently, Catholic teaching relies on recognizing the dignity of the human person, which compels preservation of human rights, as he explains in *Redemptor Hominis*. Thus, seeing and serving Christ, a christocentric understanding of human dignity and human rights as a derivate of human dignity, was what united John Paul II and Mother Teresa. The two shared a living witness to the unique value of every human person, even if the individual is at the very bottom of the social ladder.[18] Thus, failing to see and understand the transcendent nature of human dignity was a cause of concern for the pope, as it put human rights in jeopardy.[19]

Even his opposition to totalitarian regimes was in fact a fight to support human rights and human freedoms, which entailed, according to John Paul II, the right to freedom of thought, conscience, and religion, and the right to manifest one's religion either individually or in community, in public or in private.[20] Consequently, respect for human dignity requires respect for religious freedom; the very nature of the human person requires religious freedom.[21] The pontiff who lived under the communist regime of Poland knew it forced atheism on believers, and that communist governments give only atheism the right of citizenship in both public and social life. At the same time, people of faith were not tolerated "or are even—and this has already happened—entirely deprived of the rights of citizenship."[22] *Redemptor Hominis* and its contents had a particular appeal to the believers who were suffering behind the Iron Curtain. John Paul II knew from experience the high incompatibility between Catholic faith and communism, fueled by the communist hatred of people of faith and especially Christians (Catholics and Eastern Orthodox). John Paul II knew the opposition of the Church to any form of totalitarian regime by the state, and he was all too familiar with the atrocities committed in the name of communism. He also was a trained philosopher with deep knowledge of Marxist philosophy, and he was deeply aware of the fallacies of Marxism and its application. Pope Pius XI had warned about the danger of communism in his 1931 encyclical *Quadragesimo Anno* and cautioned all those who take the danger of communism and communist-imposed ideology lightly.[23]

Communism had sown fear in the hearts and minds of people who obeyed for the fear of government reprisals and persecution. The economic systems under the communist regimes was going from bad to worse, and the part of Europe behind the Iron Curtain was forced to starve for the sake of Marxist-Leninist principles and ideals. Communism strips humanity of the freedom to believe and forces them into the forced faith of atheism, as Bishop Fulton J. Sheen said:

217

And communism comes into a world that is sick with relativism, and offers an absolute, and men find a loyalty and a dedication and a consecration which gives them great faith in a political system, without imposing any individual morality.[24]

Wojtyła was not going to remain silent and avoid exposing atheistic communism, a forced militant atheism based on the dialectical and historical materialism of Karl Marx. He had seen the evils of the application of the teachings of Marx, Engels, Lenin, and Stalin firsthand. With the election of John Paul II, the Church of silence—the persecuted Church of the peripheries—was getting a voice, and her sufferings under the communist regimes was being revealed by a peripheral insider and a Slav, who had himself suffered the persecution and knew the weakness of the communist system, which included political-ideological, social, spiritual, and economic failures. Additionally, Wojtyła, besides being a professor of philosophy and an intellectual, had the bonus of the praxis and pastoral experience of working under repressive regimes. Consequently, his approach to the Vatican's *Ostpolitik* and diplomacy would build on the work of his predecessor Pope Paul VI and Cardinal Agostino Casaroli, the Vatican's top diplomat, who served under four popes. John Paul II's *Ostpolitik* was part of his general platform of the new evangelization: open wide the doors to Christ. The secularized West could not do alone without the East; and do not be afraid, as his saving power opens the boundaries of states and economic and political systems—this message was directed to the suffering Church behind the Iron Curtain. This involved not the preservation of the status quo but a change to address the human rights that were denied to the people living under the Soviet empire.[25]

Before the election of Wojtyła, the West knew little of what was going on beyond the Iron Curtain. The East and its Church were almost forgotten. The Church in the East had become the underground Church. When, on November 5, 1978, on a visit to

Assisi, someone from the crowd called on the newly elected pontiff, "Do not forget the Church of silence!" John Paul II responded, "There is no Church of silence anymore, because it speaks with my voice!"[26] Giving voice to the persecuted, voiceless Church of the isolated periphery was the mission to which the newly elected pontiff was called. How did he become one of the main world leaders who would bring down walls and borders, causing the fall of communism in Eastern Central Europe and the Soviet Union?

Wojtyła was also the millennial pope, under whose papacy the Church celebrated the two thousand years of Christian history. The primate of Poland, Cardinal Stefan Wyszynski, had told him when he was elected pope that the duty of the new pope would be to introduce the Church into the third millennium. John Paul II considered the jubilee as the climax of his pontificate, and as an occasion for renewal of the human spirit based on a rededication to the truth about humankind.[27] When Gorbachev introduced his wife to Pope John Paul II, he said, "I have the honor to present the greatest moral authority on Earth, and he's a Slav like us."[28] That phrase reminds us of one used about Mother Teresa and Kolkata: "Can anything good come from Nazareth?...Come and see" (John 1:46).

IN GOOD COMPANY—WHEN POLISH-TOUGH MEETS ALBANIAN-TOUGH

The communist system crumbled and fell in 1989. Berlin, Budapest, Prague, Warsaw, Sofia, and Bucharest were freed from the jaws of the oppressive system rather peacefully. John Paul II did not expect it "to fall so soon...and the last thing he expected was that freedom would come so swiftly and with so little bloodshed."[29] However, Albania, the country of Mother Teresa, where her family still lived, was the last bastion of communism. Communism only fell there in December 1990, when the anticommunist opposition won the elections, which led to the resignation of President Ramiz

Alia, second after dictator Enver Hoxha and last leader of People's Socialist Republic of Albania.

On April 25, 1993, Pope John Paul II paid a historic visit to Albania. The Polish-Slavic pope was the first ever Roman pontiff to visit Albania, a country with a Muslim majority where the Catholics make up roughly 10 percent of the population.[30] At his side, accompanying him on his visit, was Mother Teresa of Kolkata, who had returned to her country and her people after almost fifty years away. Mother Teresa was allowed to enter Albania only in 1989, and her visit was considered private by the communist authorities. Mother had suffered the communist repression and persecution of her close family and the Albanian people from a distance. If Mother Teresa's 1989 visit to Albania signaled the first signs of Albania's openness and the fall of the last bastion of communism in Eastern Central Europe, John Paul II's 1993 visit to Albania was a celebration of newly gained human and religious freedom in the country that paid a high human price to the communist dictatorship in human deaths and persecutions. The close friendship between Sts. John Paul II and Mother Teresa was marked also by the shared pain of suffering under repressive regimes, which both saints felt deeply and personally. Common suffering had made their bond even stronger.

Mother Teresa and John Paul II shared the same principles of apostolate; they opened wide the doors of the Church to the people and they brought to faith a sense of family and belonging. Their friendship was so deep and gentle that Msgr. Francesco Follo, Permanent Observer of the Holy See to UNESCO, who had worked closely with Missionaries of Charity in Italy and France, wrote in his book on John Paul II that their bond was so profound that Mother Teresa was "the feminine dimension of this great pontiff."[31] She was a mirror of John Paul II, as Mother's mission and vision concurred with the priorities of John Paul II's pontificate, which included the respect for life as the most basic right of the human person, human dignity and religious freedom, the rights of the peripherals and the voiceless, and the promotion of women's dignity.[32] Moreover, John

Paul II the philosopher and theologian provided the theological and philosophical foundation for understanding human dignity and human rights, and Mother Teresa applied what the great pontiff was teaching. They were complementary in theology as they were in life. But let us look back at the development of the special relationship between these two dynamic, humble, and world-changing figures.

Mother Teresa and then Cardinal Karol Wojtyła, Cardinal Archbishop of Krakow, had met for the first time in February 1973 while attending the 40th World Eucharistic Congress in Melbourne, which focused on the theme of Jesus's new commandment: "Love one another as I have loved you." It was Wojtyła's first exposure to the free world, and the future pope was impressed with the ecumenical spirit of the congress. The celebration of the Australian aboriginal Mass, which was part of the program of liturgical events, made an impression on Wojtyła. In his personal diary from the visit, the future pope mentioned meeting with Mother Teresa.[33] In fact, Mother Teresa's Sisters had a house in Melbourne. The Missionaries of Charity had opened their first house in Australia in 1970, helping people suffering from forms of poverty other than those rampant in India. In Australia, their work focused on those suffering from alcoholism and addiction and on meeting the spiritual needs of the lonely elderly. Three years later, in 1976, Karol Wojtyła and Mother Teresa met again in Philadelphia, at another Eucharistic Congress focusing on Jesus, the Bread of Life. Though the future pontiff and Mother Teresa were not yet well known in the Catholic world, their speeches resonated, and one could detect their common theologies. While Mother Teresa's address to the congress focused on physical hunger and love of small things—doing things her little way— Cardinal Wojtyła's focused on a different form of hunger: human hunger for freedom. However, at the core of their convergence were human dignity and human rights. The Polish cardinal was appealing in the name of those people who were living behind the Iron Curtain and were denied the most basic human freedoms, which included religious freedom. Hunger for bread, hunger for freedom, and the fight against human suffering and communist persecution were forging a lifelong friendship and common cause between the future saints.

The Melbourne and Philadelphia meetings with Mother Teresa and her missionary work in India must have had a profound and long-time effect on Wojtyła. According to Cardinal Dziwisz, the previous acquaintances were strengthened and cemented after Wojtyła's election. Cardinal Stanislaw Dziwisz, the long-time collaborator, friend, and personal secretary of John Paul II, recalls,

> Whenever she came to Rome, Mother Teresa would let me know and would come visit the Holy Father. She would always tell him about the expansion of the Missionaries of Charity and the new houses that she was able to open in countries such as Russia that were still otherwise totally closed to the Catholic Church.[34]

The bond of trust between John Paul II and Mother Teresa continued to grow substantially. In December 1979, when Mother Teresa was awarded the Nobel Peace Prize, John Paul II asked her to be his mirror, and a roving ambassador for life: "Go and say that everywhere [defense of life of the unborn]. And speak in my name in the places where I cannot go."[35] The request from the pontiff made Mother, who was humble and not much prone to public speaking, hesitant to accept the pontiff's offer; however, how could she say no to a pontiff and a close friend, as Wojtyła was for her? Mother was a fast learner, and sharing the values she cherished and profoundly believed in became her public mission, and she became a public and media-hunted face:

> Very quickly, though, she showed her true grit, if you'll pardon the expression, and became a real apostle of life. She went all over the world, proclaiming the dignity of the human person and the defense of life, from conception to

natural death. And the Holy Father was grateful for the way she threw herself into this mission and for the courage with which she carried it out.[36]

As the fame and media visibility of Mother Teresa and her apostolate were growing substantially, the requests for speeches, conferences, and media appearances grew exponentially. Mother Teresa decided to ask Pope John Paul II's permission to turn down the requests. She was not a public person and did not want to be in the media spotlight. Additionally, Mother was not interested in publicity and public speaking. Mother was also concerned that the time she spent in travel and public appearances meant time away from her religious congregation and her poor. However, John Paul II's advice was not something Mother wanted to hear: "Have proper care for your sisters, but a loving care for the good of the Church!"[37] Pope John Paul II had envisioned a new mission for the diminutive but Balkan-tough religious sister, who was indeed "a person message."[38] For John Paul II, Mother Teresa was his trustworthy ambassador, who with her gentleness, humility, and her broad smile could go to places that he could not and preceded him in places he had difficulties entering.[39] Mother Teresa overcame her unwillingness to participate in meetings and public speaking in obedience to the Holy Father. She would later say to Fr. Lush Gjergji from Kosovo, "The word of the Holy Father for me is law; it is the will of God."[40]

On May 13, 1981, when Pope John Paul II was shot in St. Peter's Square by Mehmet Ali Agca, Mother Teresa was in Florence to speak to the rally organized by the Italian March for Life, which was going to conclude there after similar gatherings were organized in the cities of Palermo, Naples, and Rome. All was meticulously prepared for Mother's appearance on the stage at 9:00 p.m. However, the great gathering of people supporting the life of the unborn was transformed into a manifestation of silence and prayer. People who were gathered in the plaza to hear Mother Teresa joined to pray for the life of the pope who was fighting for his life, for a leader, who, together with Mother Teresa, was one of the most ardent advocates of the right to life, the most fundamental among human rights, the denial of which shakes the very foundations of human rights.[41]

Through Mother's special inspiration, the gathering was transformed into a huge prayer for the health of Pope John Paul II. But Mother, with her intuition and feminine genius, was able to make connections between the deep pain she and the crowd were feeling for the life of the Holy Father, and the defense of life of the unborn child, which was the initial focus of the gathering. In front of a crowd, which was craving news from the Vatican, Mother started reciting the Lord's Prayer, followed by Hail Mary and Gloria. One could not fail to notice her very heavy heart and concern for John Paul II's life.[42] After the improvised prayer vigil, Mother Teresa launched an appeal in defense of life, which touched the consciences of people, saying that "today we have prayed for the Holy Father, but let's make a promise in this beautiful city: we cannot allow that children are killed in their mothers' wombs....If you fear the child who is about to be born, give her to me, I and God will take care of her....Let's offer this Mass for the Holy Father and all the mothers who fear the child who is yet born and pray to Mary who can help love all the children, those who were born and those who are not yet born, as she loved Jesus."[43]

Mother Teresa was neither a politician—she stayed out of politics—nor a trained philosopher or a theologian, although Msgr. Paulinus Costa, the then Archbishop of Dhaka, Bangladesh, called her "more theologian than we theologians."[44] However, Mother knew theology firsthand; her missionary and pastoral experience had taught her that the first and the most basic human right is the right to life. She was well versed in the economy and prioritized rights by praxis and action and protecting the rights of those who did not have a voice—the peripherals and the unborn babies. This focus for John Paul II and Mother Teresa became a defense of human rights. For Mother, Jesus identified with the poor, the marginal, the leper, the unborn, the small, and the voiceless—the rights of whom she was on the front line in defending. So, Mother's vigorous defense of life from conception to natural death was a human dignity and human rights issue that was deeply christological and christocentric: men, women, the unborn child are created for great things, to love and be loved, and Jesus Christ is both foundation and source of all rights. This, in a nutshell, was Mother's theological understanding of human rights. So, there is equality between creation and in creation. The dignity of the human life is equal for all and remains equal in its entirety, at every stage of human life—from conception to natural death, a philosophical-theological understanding Mother Teresa shared with Pope John Paul II.

"Why aren't you dead?" Mehmet Ali Agca asked Pope John Paul II when he visited him in the Roman prison of Rebibbia, adding, "I know I was aiming right. I know that the bullet was a killer. So why aren't you dead?"[45] he reiterated. John Paul II never forgot this question coming from his assassin and found it hard to answer. How different history would have been without the Polish pope, if he had died. Believers would answer that it was Providence and Our Lady who wanted John Paul II alive to continue his mission. United States President Ronald Reagan, who had survived a similar attempted assassination and near-death experience less than two months before the attack on John Paul II on March 30, 1981, believed that they had been spared by God for a purpose,[46] a conviction reinforced by Mother Teresa during a private White House meeting on June 4, 1981. Mother Teresa said to the president that

> she and her fellow Sisters of Charity had stayed up for two straight nights praying for him after his shooting. This comment humbled Reagan, but then Mother Teresa went further: "You have suffered the passion of the cross and have received grace. There is a purpose to this." And what was the purpose of his suffering? "This has happened to you at this time because your country and the world need you."[47]

After the attempted assassination, John Paul II resumed full speed his activity in leading the Church, jumping back into international travel. In 1982 he visited Argentina, Africa (Nigeria, Benin, Gabon, and Equatorial Guinea), Portugal, Spain, Great Britain, Brazil, and Geneva, followed by 1983 visits to Central America, the Caribbean islands, and his native Poland. In 1984, the Holy See restored diplomatic relations with the United States, which had been severed since 1867. President Reagan nominated William A. Wilson as ambassador to the Holy See. This was followed by a trip to Asia and the Pacific where, in Alaska on May 2, 1984, John Paul II met U.S. President Ronald Regan for the second time after their 1982 Rome meeting.

The friendship and mutual appreciation between John Paul II and Mother Teresa continued to get stronger based on similar interests and service to the periphery. In 1986, during his ten-day first visit to India, John Paul II prayed at Nirmal Hriday Ashram— Mother Teresa's Home for the Dying. The pope, led by Mother Teresa, stopped to visit each of the eighty-six patients, spoon-feeding the sick, the dying, and the lepers. On the pavement in front of the house, the pope hugged Mother Teresa tightly, as if to thank all the Missionaries of Charity for their extraordinary witness of love. And the nun seemed even smaller, like a little bird, in the pope's arms.[48] The most important mission of Mother Teresa's Home for the Dying was the defense of human dignity of every human person who was not able to defend themselves, but instead was thrown away and discarded by society. Returning dignity to those who were denied dignity, giving a voice to those who had no voice, bringing the periphery to the center forged the friendship and the sainthood of Pope John Paul II and Mother Teresa. This is what John Paul II said about the dignity of the human person after his February 3, 1986, visit to Nirmal Hriday:

Nirmal Hriday proclaims the profound dignity of every human person. The loving care which is shown here bears

226

witness to the truth that the worth of a human being is not measured by usefulness or talents, by health or sickness, by age or creed or race. Our human dignity comes from God our Creator in whose image we are all made. No amount of privation or suffering can ever remove this dignity, for we are always precious in the eyes of God.

The historic visit of St. John Paul II to India and his meeting with Mother Teresa are memorialized in two life-size statues of Pope John Paul II and Mother Teresa on the St. Thomas Apostle to India National Shrine. John Paul II was impressed by the mission of the diminutive woman and her self-giving for the poorest of the poor, always with a smile on her face. So moved by poverty and human suffering was the pontiff from what he witnessed in India, that two years after his visit to India, on May 21, 1988, during the special Marian Year, the Gift of Mary, a home for poor, was inaugurated and entrusted to the Missionaries of Charity at the Vatican. The Gift of Mary Home developed out of a conversation between John Paul II and Mother Teresa. Both future saints shared a special devotion to Mary. Nonetheless, for the Vatican, the project was something totally new, unthought of and unfathomed before: to have a house for the poorest of the poor of Rome inside the Vatican's imposing surrounding walls. As Joaquin Navarro-Valls, who for twenty years served as director of the Vatican Press Office, explained in his 2016 interview with the Vatican Radio,

> It [the project] came out during a conversation between the two of them in the Vatican....When the Pope reflected on it a little, he said: "Let's do it!—It can be done!" Of course, it was a surprise! It was unheard of [before] that these people who lived in the streets, who slept in the streets, who had no family, who were sick, could be received inside the Vatican—because that space is inside the Vatican. And so, it [the house] was inaugurated in 1988: exactly two years

after the Pope's trip to India. I think that John Paul II was inspired, in some way, by what he himself witnessed in India. So, even if there are so many differences between the city of Kolkata and Rome, we can say that these cities are similar in the fact that both cities have many suffering people, who are sick, who have no family, people who are abandoned by all. The Pope did not doubt for a moment and was fully aware that this decision would present a great novelty in the Vatican.[49]

Mother Teresa's Gift of Mary Home is still in place and serving the poorest of the poor in the city of Rome. Pope Benedict XVI during his January 4, 2008, visit to Mother Teresa's home explained that it was Mother Teresa's desire to call the new home Gift of Mary, "hoping, that it might always be possible to experience in it the love of the Blessed Virgin. For anyone who knocks at the door, it is in fact a gift of Mary to feel welcomed by the loving arms of the Sisters and volunteers."[50]

The friendship between John Paul II and Mother Teresa grew over the years of John Paul II's pontificate. They both became highly visible public and media figures and so did their friendship. Joaquin Navarro-Valls recalls how impressed he was with the extraordinary harmony between the two, a harmony that, according to Navarro-Valls, was cemented by love of Jesus and love of neighbor. Navarro-Valls added that their love was like that of a brother and a sister.[51] The friendship of John Paul II and Mother Teresa testifies to the great respect that John Paul II showed toward women, or what he called the feminine genius. Coincidentally, during the same year as the establishment of Mother Teresa's Gift of Mary Home, Pope John Paul II issued the apostolic letter *Mulieris Dignitatem*, focusing on the dignity and the vocation of women on the occasion of the Marian Year. It was issued on August 15, 1988, on the Solemnity of the Assumption of the Blessed Virgin Mary. The pontiff thanked every woman and considered them equal to men in their shared journey:

Therefore the Church gives thanks for each and every woman: for mothers, for sisters, for wives; for women consecrated to God in virginity; for women dedicated to the many human beings who await the gratuitous love of another person; for women who watch over the human persons in the family, which is the fundamental sign of the human community; for women who work professionally, and who at times are burdened by a great social responsibility; for "perfect" women and for "weak" women—for all women as they have come forth from the heart of God in all the beauty and richness of their femininity; as they have been embraced by his eternal love; as, together with men, they are pilgrims on this earth, which is the temporal "homeland" of all people and is transformed sometimes into a "valley of tears"; as they assume, together with men, a common responsibility for the destiny of humanity according to daily necessities and according to that definitive destiny which the human family has in God himself, in the bosom of the ineffable Trinity.[52]

The same pontiff would again focus on women and their dignity in his 1995 *Letter to Women*, written as a sign of solidarity and gratitude on the occasion of the Fourth World Conference on Women, in Beijing, where he stresses the urgent need for women to achieve real equality with men in every area.[53] The friendship between John Paul II and Mother Teresa should be viewed within this framework—the great appreciation that John Paul II had for women and their equal contribution to the Church and society following the example of Mary, the feminine image of the Church. In Mother Teresa and her missionary work, John Paul II saw the genius of a woman put to work and bearing fruit by putting herself at the service of others. Mother's was a service of love.[54]

But there was more that united the brother and sister—Mother Teresa's family, her mother, Drana Bojaxhiu, and Age Bojaxhiu, were living in Albania, suffering human rights violations under one of the most repressive communist persecutions in the Soviet-bloc countries. For two decades Mother Teresa was longing to visit her country and say goodbye to her dying mother. Mother had not seen her mother and sister since she left to join the Loreto Sisters in Ireland, but this was not possible until 1989. If the election of John Paul II was considered by believers providential especially for the fall of communism, the 1989 visit of Mother Teresa to the last bastion of communism in Eastern Europe was similarly providential, and this combined with the papacy of a Polish pope was doubly providential. The visit of Mother Teresa two years before the fall of communism and the freedom regained by the martyred people of Albania prepared the way for Pope John Paul II's 1993 visit as the first pontiff ever to visit the country—she was his extraordinary ambassador, probably the first Catholic religious woman to visit the country before the fall of communism. Obviously, there was symmetry between John Paul II and Mother Teresa in their intimate experiences with the communist regimes of Poland and Albania, respectively, and these experiences strengthened their friendship and their determination to give a voice for the human rights of the peripherals who were suffering persecution in the communist gulags. What was Mother Teresa's plight with respect to the communist government of Enver Hoxha, the Albanian dictator—and to his dictatorship?

MOTHER TERESA: AN INSTRUMENT OF PROVIDENCE?

If the bond between Pope John Paul II and President Ronald Reagan was providential, as both of them have stated, Mother Teresa was also an added bonus of feminine genius in the providential plan for the Cold War to come to such a rapid and peaceful end and for her martyred Albanian people who were living beyond the Iron Curtain. As John Paul II's ambassador, the diminutive Mother

Teresa could go where the powerful men of nations could not go. She was a mediator, bridge builder, and peace builder through her littleness, and knew how to put what John Paul II called the genius of women in action.

Pope John Paul II knew about the communist persecution in Albania and the martyrdom of the Albanian Church. On October 5, 1980, John Paul II was on a pastoral visit to the southern Italian Adriatic port city of Otranto, which lies just fifty miles from the Albanian coast. The occasion was the celebration of the five hundredth anniversary of the Martyrs of Otranto. On August 14, 1480, all eight hundred older men of the city were, one by one, beheaded by the Ottomans who had taken over the city of Otranto, while younger men and women were enslaved and eight thousand of them were shipped off to the neighboring Albania. According to chronicles, Gedik Ahmet Pasha had the eight hundred men beheaded when they refused to convert to Islam, leaving their remains unburied on what is known as the Hill of the Martyrs.[55] The martyrdom happened on the eve of the Feast of the Assumption. The eight hundred Martyrs of Otranto were canonized by Pope Francis on May 12, 2013.[56]

Pope John Paul II expressed his spiritual support for the people of the neighboring Albania (without mentioning them specifically) who were being martyred because of their faith and their rights were being denied. John Paul II called it a special duty of all Christians to sustain those brothers and sisters on the other side of the Adriatic Sea whose fundamental rights were violated. "Do not forget the martyrs of our time. Do not behave as if they do not exist....We must pray that the Lord will support these brothers of ours with his grace in these difficult trials," John Paul II said, referring to modern martyrdom.[57]

This concern for the Albanian periphery signaled a difference between John Paul II's and Paul VI's pontificates, especially in their *Ostpolitik*. Paul VI seemed to be more pessimistic and less hopeful about the fall of the communism and his *Ostpolitik*, or *modus non moriendi* (a "way of not dying"), proved highly unsuccessful in the communist-East-bloc countries that were part of the Warsaw Pact. Until 1968, Albania was member of the pact, but left it when Warsaw Pact troops invaded Czechoslovakia. Vatican *Ostpolitik* tactics included a cessation of all public Vatican criticism of communist regimes, and endless negotiations with communist governments, which did not bring any results.[50] During Paul VI's pontificate, in 1967, the communist government of Albania proclaimed state-militant atheism, which made Albania the first atheistic country in the world, banning any form of religion. Religion was considered reactionary, backward, and an opium to the people. Religious women and men who had served in the country before the establishment of the communist regime were either executed, imprisoned in labor or "reeducation" camps, or expelled from Albania as undesired individuals. Religion in general, and any personal religious leaning and activity, was severely persecuted.

Due to the religious purge, 2,200 mosques, churches, chapels, monasteries, and other religious buildings were vandalized and closed. Of that number, 327 were Roman Catholic. On November 22, 1967, the government published Decree No. 4337 ordering the annulment of the religious charters and of all laws pertaining to state-church relationships. All religious rites were prohibited, and grave penalties were imposed on violators. The remaining priests were sent to forced-labor camps for reeducation.[59] The Albanian Party and government boasted that it had become the first atheistic country in the world. The abolition of religion in Albania did not make headlines. Albania was more peripheral than other Eastern-bloc countries that continued to be part of the Warsaw Pact. The situation changed with the pontificate of John Paul II, rightly called the human rights pope, who took a more vocal and direct anticommunist stance on the violation of human rights.

Clearly, the Polish pontiff was aware of the communist persecution taking place in the neighboring-peripheral Albania. On February 26, 1984, Pope John Paul II was on a pastoral visit to the city of Bari, in southern Italy, which was historically connected to Albania via the Adriatic Sea and the port of Durazzo (Durrës), a connecting bridge to the East. This time the pontiff spoke directly to the suffering people of Albania, who were hermetically closed off from the rest of the world under the communist dictatorship of the proletariat:

> From this city [Bari] which, due to its geographical and cultural location, is a bridge looking beyond the Mediterranean Sea, my thoughts also go to our brothers and sisters of Albania, who cannot externally express/celebrate their religious faith, which is a fundamental human right. While I commend them to your prayers, I wish to assure them that they are particularly present in my heart and that I entrust them to the protection of the Madonna.[60]

The pontiff's tone against the religious persecution in Albania went hand in hand with the strength in friendship with Mother Teresa. Two years after Bari, the pontiff met with a group of Albanians who lived in Rome at the parish of St. Gregory VII at Gelsomio in Rome, on April 27, 1986. The Albanian community of Rome was established well before the takeover of the communist regime. This was the first meeting of its kind, the first time for a Roman pontiff to meet the Albanian community of Rome. The pontiff confessed that every day especially at the eucharistic sacrifice, he tried to live the martyrdom of the Albanian believers behind the Iron Curtain. John Paul II prayed not only for Catholics and Christians, who in Albania are a minority, but for all believers including Muslims and Bektashi, as well as atheists. Two layers of the Church existed in the communist countries, the external and the internal, which Pope John Paul II knew from experience in his native communist Poland. He knew firsthand the vitality of the underground Church and the role of the underground Church to keep faith alive. He knew that faith could not be erased from the hearts and souls of the people:

> But we know well that the Church cannot disappear
> from hearts [of the believers] because it is instituted by
> the Holy Spirit, by the word of Christ, by the same Christ
> who lives in his faithful. I deeply believe, together with
> you, that Christ lives, as he lives within us here in Rome,
> in your Albanian Roman community, he also lives in the
> martyred brothers of your homeland. When he lives, the
> Church lives. One can't kill Christ! Yes, they killed him;
> they crucified him; he died on the cross. But he is risen.
> You can't kill Christ![61]

Consequently, the Church and Christ lived, invisibly, in the hearts of the people of Albania. John Paul II never ceased to be hopeful about the temporary nature of the wall that divided East and West, that hermetically divided peripheral Albania from the rest of the world. It was the theological virtue of hope that helped believers during the almost fifty years of martyrdom to reach interior peace. For him, as evidenced throughout his long pontificate, humanity has rights—fundamental and inviolable rights, and governments are called and required to respect those fundamental rights. The argument of Wojtyła is philosophically and anthropologically sound: if human rights are not respected then it means that the world has lost its humanity and has turned into an antihuman world. Here is the lucidity of Wojtyła's philosophy and profound concern for the violation of human rights, coming from a humanist pope.

How did the pontiff see his role in upholding the human rights of an oppressed and peripheral nation with a Muslim majority and a Catholic Christian minority? He was not afraid to expose the evil of the denial of human rights in Albania to the entire world. To use Pope Francis's center-periphery paradigm, John Paul II was bringing the periphery of the human rights violations in a tiny country—a stronghold of communism—to the center's or world's attention. He promised Albanians that he would continue to do so "in front of the world because the world ought to understand this suffering, ought to understand this injustice."[62] Mother Teresa with her "little" ways helped Wojtyła, and her presence and action proved providential for the Albanian people and their freedom—she was John Paul II's mirror in a personal and personalized way. Thus, it was in the Albanian periphery that Polish-tough and Balkan-tough met. What had happened to Mother Teresa's family in Albania during communism?

Mother Teresa had known the suffering and injustice of human rights violation of her people. Around 1965, Mother Teresa wrote to the then Albanian embassy in Rome, given that she as a religious could not enter an atheistic country, instead asking that her mother be granted a visa to travel to Italy for medical treatment, accompanied by her sister, Age. She explained that she had not seen her mother and her sister for over thirty years, and this was probably the last chance for Mother to see and serve her mother. The answer from the Rome embassy was a cold no. This was followed by a second attempt in 1968, the possibility of a visa via France. Maurice Couve de Murville, the French foreign minister who personally knew Mother Teresa, presented Mother's request for a visa entry to Albania to Javer Malo, Albanian ambassador in Paris. Malo informed the dictator Enver Hoxha in Albania that Mother Teresa's visa issue had been brought to the attention of various Albanian embassies in the West over the past couple of years. The answer from Albania was an obstinate no. Additionally, other foreign diplomats and state dignitaries knew of Mother's great desire to visit her country and meet her family. According to her brother, Lazër, who had fled Albania for political reasons and lived in Palermo, Italy, Mother had asked for help from President John F. Kennedy, the first lady Jacqueline Kennedy, French president Charles de Gaulle, and the king of Sweden, Gustaf VI Adolf, with no result.

The argument Tirana was making for not granting travel visas for her mother and sister for medical reasons was that Drana Bojaxhiu's condition would not permit her to travel, and that the public health-care system and public hospitals in Albania could provide the needed medical expertise and care for Drana. The response was also an attack on Mother Teresa and her brother, Lazër Bojaxhiu, who had abandoned their family in Albania. A comment was also made that before Mother Teresa and Lazër Bojaxhiu chose to leave the country, they should have thought about the consequences of leaving their mother and sister. The logic behind the government decision not to grant exit visas to Drana and Age Bojaxhiu is as follows: if both women were granted permission to travel abroad, they would probably not return to Albania. The Bojaxhiu family had two members, Mother Teresa and Lazër, living outside Albania, and in the eyes of the communist government the Bojaxhiu family was not loyal enough to the government, not to be trusted, and in communist terminology the Bojaxhius had a "bad biography." Further, Mother Teresa, being a Catholic nun, was an enemy of the people who could "contaminate" people with her religiosity and religious blindness.

Mother Teresa made another attempt at requesting a visa, but the answer was again no. The dictator Enver Hoxha and the Albanian authorities were unmoved by Mother Teresa's pleas to visit her mother and sister and by the pressure from foreign diplomats. Obviously, Mother Teresa suffered from the government's decision, but she accepted the fact that her dream of seeing her elderly mother alive was not going to happen. On July 12, 1972, her mother died at the age of eighty-three. This is what Mother wrote in her native Albanian to her first cousin File Çuni, who was living in Melbourne, Australia, at the time:

> Nana Loke ka shkue n'shpi te Zoti dashtun—se tash e kam...nje telegram Agi ka shrue: "12 korrik ora 05 Nana vdiq. Agi." Tash na kemi Loken mu lut per ne. Une e di se si ti e ke dashet Loken, je motra jone e vogla—dhe tash ajo ka sigurisht me na ndihmue ma teper. T'lutem archb. T'lutem lute argjipeshkvin Knox dhe motrat e jona mu lutë për loken....Si jeni ju? Une jam mire me shnet vetem qe tash kam shum pune. (Mommy returned to the house of the Father. I have just received a telegram from Agi [her sister] who

wrote: "Mother died at 5:00 [a.m.] on July 12. Agi"
Now we have Mommy to pray for us. I know how
much you have loved Mummy; you are our little
sister—and now she will help us even more....Please
ask Archb Knox [James Robert Cardinal Knox, cardinal
archbishop of Melbourne] and my sisters [Missionaries
of Charity of Melbourne] to pray for Mummy. How are
you? I am doing well health wise but now I have a lot
of work.

Signed Mother Teresa mc[63]

In 1974 her sister died, at the age of sixty-nine. Their deaths and the inability to see them might have devastated Mother Teresa, but she kept it all to herself. The pain of the loss might have been hard for Mother, but she carried the suffering—she did not make any public announcements or media appearances to express her discontent or revolt against the Albanian communist government. Neither did she criticize the dictator Enver Hoxha. Mother Teresa believed that it was neither her calling nor her vocation to criticize governments or enter any political-ideological controversy that would cause more persecution to the people who were living in Albania and were close to the Bojaxhius. Mother's vocation was elsewhere: she was more interested in fighting against materialism and indifference. However, she never lost the hope of visiting her country and requesting a visa to visit and pay homage to the graves of her mother and sister and visit their home in the Albanian capital, Tirana.

However, the Albanian Secret Police was monitoring Mother Teresa, especially after she received the Nobel Peace Prize and because of the media attention she was receiving for her missionary work in India. Additionally, mother was not hiding her origins. "By blood, I am Albanian,"[64] she told the media when she was awarded the Nobel Prize in 1979. But this was problematic for the Albanian communist state and its ban of religion. According to Prof. Nevila Nika, former director of the Albanian State Archive, the communists feared Mother Teresa's fame and her becoming an international icon, thinking that human rights violations and religious persecution in Albania behind the Iron Curtain would be brought to the world's attention. Albanians who were living under the regime were kept completely ignorant of the fame of their conational: "While Mother Teresa was being honored around the world, Albanians did not know what was happening. None of the [Albanian] citizens knew of her or what she had done to win such an award. But the communist leadership knew it well and they could not underestimate it any longer."[65]

In June 1982, the Albanian minister of internal affairs sent a classified report to Ramiz Alia, who at that time was serving as the head of the Presidium of the People's Assembly, reporting about the danger of Mother Teresa's activities and labeling her as "a conspirator against the regime" serving "the Vatican's hostile activities towards Albania."[66] The fear that the Albanian communist regime had about Mother Teresa becoming an international personality was the same fear the KGB and the UB (Polish Secret Police) had about the election of John Paul II. The 1982 report also mentioned a gathering of seventy Albanian Catholic clergy in Rome in March 1982 from Albania (who had managed to escape the dictatorship) and from Kosovo, organized by Mother Teresa. Again, in November 1982, Albanian intelligence accused Mother Teresa of organizing anti-Albanian propaganda, saying, "The Vatican and Pope Wojtyła are personally and widely using the nun Tereza Bojaxhiu for propaganda activities against our country."[67]

Albanian communist isolation turned into paranoia, and the state engaged in labeling and blaming individuals as enemies of the people or accusing them of anticommunist agitation and propaganda. These mere accusations were used freely and extensively to imprison people—and worse, to suffocate human rights and free thinking. "I arrest you for agitation and propaganda against the state!" Back goes the prisoner for ten more years of communist reeducation.[68] The paranoia about a planned foreign invasion and anticommunist agenda to overthrow the regime is still part of Albania's landscape—one cannot get rid of the more than three hundred thousand concrete bunkers spread

throughout the country. The bunkers were the brainchild of dictator Hoxha, who was convinced in paranoia that everyone, including
Greece, the then Yugoslavia, Italy, NATO, even the former allies, was
after Albania to invade it.[69] The fear of Mother Teresa's anti-Albanian
activities is part and parcel of this communist paranoia about everything foreign and everyone living in the West.

Following the dictator's death—Enver Hoxha died on April
11, 1985, at the age of seventy-six—and the appointment of his
close collaborator and designated successor, Ramiz Alia, the Albanian government began to follow a milder policy toward religion.
Alia, under international pressure, began to reconsider granting the
denied visa to one of the most famous Albanians living abroad. The
thinking was that by allowing a highly celebrated Catholic humanitarian to visit the country, Alia would signal a new direction for his
country after almost half a century of severe dictatorship.

According to Bashkim Pitarka, who was Albania's chief delegate to the United Nations, Alia was contemplating a possible
appearance before the United Nations General Assembly with the
goal of reestablishing diplomatic ties with the United States, which
were officially broken in 1946. Nevila Nika argues that Alia was possibly motivated by the devastating economic situation of Albania,
and Alia thought that perhaps Mother's visit would bring international attention to Albania and "she [Mother Teresa] could provide
humanitarian aid" for the impoverished country.[70] Moreover, the
secretary general of the United Nations, Javier Pérez de Cuéllar, had
brought up the thorny issue of human rights violations and freedom
of movement, especially the case of the celebrated Mother Teresa.
According to Pitarka, de Cuéllar strongly encouraged Alia to end the
decades-long mistake of visa denial for Mother Teresa and allow the
celebrated religious to visit her country.

Mindful of the situation in Albania, where the communist system was still in place, and the long-time hostility toward granting
entrance to Mother Teresa, Alia thought of presenting a possible visit
of Mother Teresa to Albania by granting an entry visa strictly for

"private" reasons, meaning nonofficial or nongovernment-related reasons. "I will never forget the day, in early August 1989, when Mother Teresa came to the Albanian Embassy in Rome to receive her first visa—a visa that would enable her to travel back to her homeland after almost sixty years away from it. I was a minister-counsellor for cultural affairs in the embassy at the time. It was during a period when the weakened communist government of Albania was allowing breezes of pluralism to blow through the bureaucracy," Gjovalin Shkurtaj, who at the time was serving as minister-council for cultural affairs in the Albanian Embassy in Rome, explained in an interview on September 2, 2016, on the occasion of Mother's canonization.[71]

It took almost twenty-five years for Mother to be granted permission to visit her country. Shkurtaj recalls that when the approval from the government of Tirana reached the Albanian embassy of Rome, the embassy contacted the Missionaries of Charity in Rome to let Mother know that she was granted a visa to visit Albania. To the surprise of all, Mother Teresa herself went to the Albanian embassy to pick up the visa:

> On that early afternoon, on a very hot day in August, an old car pulled into the driveway of our embassy in Rome's via Asmara, driven by one of the missionary sisters. Mother Teresa slowly got out. In front of us was a tiny lady, stooped over, wearing dark sandals on her feet, dressed in her simple, white and blue sari. The only adornment she wore was a Roman Catholic rosary around her neck. Inside the embassy hall, we had prepared a huge banquet in her honor. Neither she, nor the two Sisters accompanying her, ever touched it. She didn't stay long, meeting briefly with our ambassador, and in parting saluted all of us in rusty Albanian—*Zoti qoftë me ju* (May God be with you).[72]

In early August of 1989, Mother visited Albania, which was still a communist country, and her visit was conducted under strict

Albanian Secret Police surveillance.[73] Mother's dream of visiting her country finally came true, as she wrote to the Albanian President Ramiz Alia on August 16, 1989, when she was still visiting in Tirana:

> After many years of prayer and desire to visit my own country after visiting so many throughout the world, at last the Good God gave this beautiful gift to come and see my people. My own family lived here for many years and they also died here so I was able to visit their graves.[74]

Mother Teresa paid homage to the graves of Drana and Age Bojaxhiu in the cemetery of Sharra near Tirana and visited the home where they had lived and died in the Albanian capital. Her visit was barely covered by the state-controlled media. What had happened to Mother's family who were living beyond the Iron Curtain and suffering persecution because of their Catholic faith? What was the fate of Drana and Age Bojaxhiu, who were suffering persecution because of Mother Teresa's status as a religious, and because of Lazër Bojaxhiu, who was living outside Albania?

After Mother Teresa left to join the religious sisters of Loreto, her mother and sister had moved away from Skopje, first settling in Scutari, and later moving to the Albanian capital, Tirana. Prof. Inis Kraja, daughter of the famous Albanian opera singer Marie Kraja, a close lifelong friend of the Bojaxhiu family, in an interview explained that Age Bojaxhiu was an exceptionally intelligent woman. When she moved to Albania, leaving everything behind in Skopje, Marie Kraja and Age worked for Tirana Radio. The families from Kosovo and North Macedonia who had moved to Albania tended to stay together, and that was the case with the Bojaxhius and Krajas.[75] Age, due to her linguistic abilities—she was fluent in German, Serbo-Croatian, Turkish, Italian, and her native Albanian—and education, was the breadwinner, taking care of her mother.[76] Age was employed by the Tirana Radio Serbo-Croatian program since Tirana Radio's foundation on November 28, 1938, during the reign of King Zog of the Albanians. Age was a translator, commentator, and speaker in the program until 1955/56, when the communist dictatorship was ruling the country with a heavy hand; because the communists deemed her family's connections and activities suspicious, she was disenfranchised. Age had worked briefly for the Yugoslav embassy of Tirana, but with the break in the Albanian-Yugoslav relations she lost her job at the embassy.[77]

After her suspension from Tirana Radio and until her death in 1974, Age made use of her other talents, such as tailoring in private, though this was not something the communists allowed, as private property, ownership, and private business were strictly prohibited. The economic situation of the two women drastically deteriorated, and they both died very poor, looking for alms from neighbors to pay for rent and goods. Prof. Kraja remembers that Drana and Age received news from Mother Teresa rather indirectly, usually via Lazër Bojaxhiu, who lived in Italy. Letters from abroad were strictly monitored by the communist authorities, let alone correspondence with a religious sister. Mother Teresa knew this and after the communist takeover, to save her family in Albania from persecution, she limited correspondence.

When asked about Drana, Prof. Kraja explained that she remembered her as she was growing up:

> She was a silent, few-words-woman...thoughtful. Always hospitable with a smile on her face...she had Mother Teresa's physiognomy. Clean and meticulous. When I first saw Mother Teresa live, Lokja (Mommy), as we called her, came to mind. She was a diminutive woman, dressed in black.[78] (Wearing black was a tradition among Albanian women whose husbands had died.)

According to Prof. Kraja, Drana's dream was to see Mother Teresa. She always called her Gonxhe (Gjyli in Turkish). When asked about religion and how Drana and Age lived their faith during the dictatorship, Prof. Kraja explained that both women kept religion very personal and shared it with her mother, Marie Kraja—obviously it was impossible to celebrate one's faith in Albania during the communist dictatorship and especially after 1967, when Albania became the world's only atheistic country:

> They were believers deep in their hearts. Christmas and Easter were celebrated in the intimacy of home, we never forgot to celebrate them.[79]

It is that inner Church or the Church of the catacombs that persisted in the heart of the people that no dictator, however strong, was able to eradicate—the Church that could not disappear from the heart of the people, as John Paul II said to Albanian pilgrims in April 1986.[80]

Part of Mother's visit to Albania was a formal lunch meeting with Mrs. Nexhmije Hoxha, the dictator's wife, lifelong comrade, and strong confidant, and her daughter Pranvera Hoxha in the dictator's villa. Besides paying homage and visiting the graves of her mother and sister, Mother Teresa put a bouquet of flowers and prayed at the grave of dictator Enver Hoxha at the Nation's Martyrs Cemetery, which became controversial, especially among Mother's most ardent critics like Christopher Hitchens. In a 1995 *New York Times* article, Walter Goodman criticized Mother for paying tribute to the grave of Hoxha, stating that "Mother Teresa gives more unto Caesar than is strictly required by Scripture."[81]

However, Albanian media revealed that Mother Teresa never knew that the grave she visited at the Nation's Martyrs Cemetery was that of the dictator. The visit at the dictator's grave was part of the protocol of visiting a communist country, the first tribute ought to go to the cult of the leader. But there is another important detail in this puzzle: Nexhmije Hoxha, the dictator's wife, recalls the lunch with Mother Teresa in the dictator's villa. According to Mrs. Hoxha, when Mother Teresa saw a big portrait of Enver Hoxha in the living room, she asked, "Who is this man?" Mrs. Hoxha explained that the person who accompanied Mother Teresa to Hoxha's grave (Mr. Jorgo Melica) reminded her that "he is the man on whose grave you put the flowers."[82] It is true that Mother Teresa never publicly criticized Hoxha, or any other government or institution in Albania. She never wanted to enter the politics of the country, and she feared for the well-being of her close family and relatives who were living in Albania. A public appearance of Mother denouncing communism, and the dictatorship, might have caused people to be either locked in communist reeducation camps or killed by public execution. She knew what dictatorships and dictators were capable of, while her critics criticizing her from the free West did not know what living under communist dictatorship meant.

Mother Teresa went into the places where Pope John Paul II could not go, and the hermetically closed, communist Albania was one of those places.[83] She was the soft power, who with her littleness brought Albania up to speed and opened hearts and doors to freedom. According to Albanian political observers, the visit of Mother Teresa to her country signaled a new opening. It was the first sign of positive changes on the way, foretelling the fall of communism. November 4, 1990, was a memorable day in the hearts and minds of the people of Scutari and of all Albanians, a day that testified to what John Paul II had told the Albanian community in Rome in 1986— one can't kill Christ! One cannot kill the Church![84] Indeed, faith and hope were alive and never abandoned the suffering people of Albania. Almost five thousand people, Catholics and Muslims, participated in Mass on November 4, 1990, the first public Mass since 1967. The main celebrant was the Albanian Fr. Simon Jubani, who had been in the communist prisons and labor camps for twenty-six years and was released in 1989. The Catholic cemetery was the only holy ground left in Albania at that time, as all churches were either destroyed, transformed, or repurposed. Albania was showing signs of resurrection. Providentially, it was in the same Rrmaj cemetery of Scutari that Blessed Fr. Giovanni Fausti, SJ, professor of philosophy and rector of the Jesuit Pontifical Albanian Seminary of Scutari, was executed and buried in a collective grave on March 4, 1946, by the communists. The historic Scutari cemetery, where Fr. Fausti and thirty-seven other martyrs found their end, was anticipating the resurrection of faith and the fall of communism.[85]

For Albanians, whether Christian, Muslim, Bektashi, or atheist, Mother's visit was providential for gaining human and religious freedoms, which were restored only a year after her visit, with the free postcommunist elections.[86] Going where the pontiff could not go? Indeed, Mother generously could, and with her soft demeanor made Alia change his ways. The revolution of conscience that John Paul II was successfully winning in his native Poland, Mother was winning in Albania. On December 1, 1990, Ramiz Alia issued a decree honoring Mother Teresa, on the occasion of her eightieth birthday, with First Class Merit Order of "Naim Frashëri," which was the country's highest honor named after the Albanian poet and prominent patriot Naim Frashëri, with the following citation:

> To Mother Teresa, Anjeze Gonzhe Bojaxhiu:
> A world-renowned personality who, inspired by endless love for people, especially the poor, the sick, and the hungry, who has dedicated all her life to them. Mother Teresa's selfless activity, the rare spirit of sacrifice and the high sense of humanism, has won her the respect of all humankind. Albanians are proud of their great and honorable daughter.[87]

After receiving Albania's highest honor, Mother Teresa renewed her request to the Albanian communist leader, exploring the possibility of bringing the Missionaries of Charity to Albania. Mother wrote insistently and with some urgency for the sisters to come to Albania. Her intention was not to score points by establishing religious houses in another country—no, she had enough religious houses already throughout the world, as Mother's is one of the fastest growing Catholic religious orders.[88] Aroup Chatterjee, one of

Mother's critics, maintains that Mother Teresa's travels to communist countries and Muslim-run nations were more self-serving than altruistic.[89] This criticism does not apply to Albania and it would be hard to make an argument, without a lucid understanding of the Catholic theology of suffering and serving, about other countries where Mother served. If Mother's missionary work is emptied of theology, it is an empty mission.

The insistence of Mother on bringing the sisters to Albania as soon as possible was so that they could start immediately rebuilding and support the healing process. She noticed poverty, bitterness, and wounds—both physical and spiritual—that needed immediate attention. She was feeling those wounds firsthand—her mother and sister had suffered under the dictatorship, and she had suffered from afar the regime's consequences. There was no time to wait to begin reconstructing. This was the charism of her order: to pick up the suffering and revive them. "In many places of the world, when things go really, totally wrong, when things are very, very difficult, the Missionaries of Charity are still present. They don't leave," said American-born Archbishop Charles Brown, current apostolic nuncio to Albania.[90] This is was what Mother wanted for her sisters—to be there and not leave.

Additionally, her approach to theology was practical and hands-on, bringing solace to broken people. Jesus's hunger that she had satiated around the world now was in her home: she was called to her native Albania, to give back what she had received freely from her mother, as her mother continually helped the poor. Part of her practical theology was her forgiveness of the communists who persecuted her family and her, by not allowing her to return home.[91] Her mother, according to a testimonial of her brother, Lazër, who was also banned from reentering Albania, had died desperately holding Gonxhe's picture on her chest. "The woman who had cared for the world's dying was denied the honor of providing some care and spiritual solace to her own dying mother," said Lazër in an interview with the Italian *Gente* in December 1979.[92]

It was a teaching moment for Mother, because she knew first-hand that Albanians would find it very hard to forgive. Have the love to forgive and the humility to forget was her advice when anyone was faced with any offense.[93] She knew the words of Jesus on the cross and acted on them: "Father, forgive them, they know not what they do" (Luke 23:34). Did Mother forgive the communist dictator for her personal suffering? This is what Nexhmije Hoxha, the wife of the Albanian dictator Enver Hoxha, had noticed during Mother's 1989 visit to communist Albania. In a September 6, 2010, interview, when asked by a journalist, "Was Mother Teresa angry with the regime who had banned her from entering the country?" Mrs. Hoxha responded by explaining what she had observed during the time she spent with Mother Teresa at her home: "No, no, this needs to be known. Mother Teresa was not angry, she did not hold grudges."[94] Mother explained her theology of forgiveness, which she applied in the country where she was hurt the most, in her speech in Nagasaki on April 26, 1982:

> Suffering makes it important, first of all, that we pray, because we need courage to forgive. And to be able to forgive we need lots of love in our hearts. Forgive! And also we must know that we need to be forgiven. And for that we need a humble heart. So humility and love will help us to forgive each other; and instead of hurting each other we will begin to love each other and to see what is beautiful in each other. Every one of us has something beautiful. If we only take the trouble to see it, we will be able to love that person—even that person who hurts us most. If we have a free heart, we will be able to forgive that person.[95]

From, this letter, which Mother wrote to Ramiz Alia on December 4, 1990, one can tell that Mother had experience dealing with communist governments. She did not enter into polemics and criticism but kept her focus on contributing to the healing of a country without watering down her theology or hiding who she was: a religious sister. She signed the letter with the forbidden "God bless you." It seemed that Providence was having a say and a signing hand in Albanian affairs via this diminutive woman, who was more than determined to give a helping hand and contribute her share to benefit her broken people:

Tirana 4th December [19]90

Dear Mr. President,

After accepting the invitation to come to Albania for the purpose of arranging and finalizing the details necessary to bring 4 of my sisters to Albania, I cancelled all engagement with the hope that after meeting with you all will be settled: I would be able to bring the sisters. They are waiting in Rome and are ready to leave tomorrow (Wednesday). I just want to make it clear to you—that we are not an institution—therefore we will not have any public religious ceremonies—for the present we will need a simple small house where the sisters can live their consecrated life in private. I assume all financial support for my sisters. For the present we will begin by giving a helping hand to the hospitals. Therefore, I ask you again to give us a place where I can bring the sisters tomorrow and together begin the work of love for the glory of God and the good of our people.

My gratitude to you is my prayer for you and the people you serve.

God bless you,
M. Teresa mc[96]

A few days after Mother's letter to the president, on December 11, 1990, came the fall of Albanian communism. Albania's first attempt at free elections was in March 1991. Providentially, Mother Teresa's Missionaries of Charity house in Tirana opened in March 1991. Obviously, Mother Teresa did not cause communism to fall in Albania, but her presence and being among the first Catholic religious to enter her atheistic country was providential. To use John Paul II's remarks when he commented about his attempted assassination, in the designs of Providence, there are no coincidences and there is a "motherly hand" that can intervene.[97] He had also declared that "the destiny of all nations lies in the hands of a merciful Providence."[98]

Mother Teresa's presence and assistance during the fall of communism was motherly and providential for Albania. She had been the prophetess banned to enter her own land for more than twenty-five years under communist and Sigurimi's surveillance—"no prophet is accepted in his own native place" (Luke 4:24). However, Mother Teresa's 1989 grand entrance signaled the fall of the last bastion of communism in Eastern-bloc countries: she went before anyone else "to prepare his ways" (Luke 1:76) and the coming of the much longed-for freedom and hope for the martyred Albanian people.

John Paul II's visit to Albania on April 25, 1993 was historic, the first time ever that a Roman pontiff set foot in the country. If Mother Teresa with her littleness opened the way, John Paul II reconstituted the Catholic Church's hierarchy for the country, after the fall of communism. During his visit, Pope John Paul II ordained four Albanian bishops in the Cathedral of the Sacred Heart in Scutari, which was transformed during the years of the persecution to a sport stadium and had been consecrated back to a Catholic cathedral.[99]

The speech that Pope John Paul II delivered to the crowds gathered in Scanderbeg Square in the capital, Tirana, has remained memorable in the consciousness of the Albanian people. John Paul II recognized the wounds communism had left behind and the tragedy of communist oppression. He pointed to the main argument he had used in fighting against communism: the denial or deprivation of fundamental human rights and freedom of conscience, which in Albania was accompanied by unspeakable brutality toward priests and the faithful, who suffered persecution and death in communist concentration camps. He touched the wounds of the Albanian nation, which was in desperate need of healing. The heaven-on-earth the communist regimes in Eastern-bloc countries aspired to build had failed miserably, because, according to John Paul II, the system destroyed the human person and his or her inviolable rights. John Paul II used Albania and the persecution under the communist regime in the country as motivation for the European continent to never forget the atrocities committed in the name of an ideology.[100] In his speech, John Paul II recognized Mother Teresa, a daughter of this martyred land, and her universal mission to feed the world's hungry, saying,

> How can I fail to mention, a chosen/elect daughter of the Albanian people, Sister Teresa of Calcutta, mother of the world's poorest of the poor? With a warm faith, this small-great woman carries within herself the generous and indomitable impulse of the Albanian heart.[101]

Even during the times of Albania's complete isolation, when nobody knew what was going on in Albania and many had not even heard of it, Mother Teresa was bringing the country to the world's attention. It was this humble religious, this humble servant of the poorest of the poor, who carried around the world the name of the country, bringing Albania to the center's attention. John Paul II ended his *Regina Coeli* with the following acknowledgment of the humble Mother Teresa, who was in the audience:

> Dear friends, I cannot fail to greet a very humble person who is here with/among us. It is Mother Teresa of Calcutta. Everyone knows where he comes from, what his country is. His homeland is here. Even in the times of complete isolation of Albania, there was this humble religious, this valuable servant of the poorest of the poor who carried the name of your country [Albania] all over the world. In Mother Teresa, Albania has always been

esteemed. This is her mission and of all those who, like her, are true followers of Christ, apostles of Christ and apostles of charity. I thank you today in the name of the Universal Church, thank you, dear Albanians, for this daughter of your land, of your people. We all thank the Lord for this day.[102]

On Friday, September 5, 1997, when the little woman and the great missionary Mother Teresa died, her death shook and shocked the world. Tributes to a life in service poured in from every part of the world: Catholics, Muslims, Hindus, Buddhists, presidents, prime ministers, heads of state, cardinals, and the media showed the collective pain over Mother's death. "Mother Teresa, Hope of the Despairing, Dies at 87," wrote the *New York Times*; "A Day That Shook the World: Death of Mother Teresa," wrote the British *The Independent*; India, Mother's adopted country, in a departure from protocol, gave Mother a state funeral, normally reserved for senior officials, and declared Saturday, September 6, a day of national mourning. All flags across the country were flown at half-mast on the day of Mother's funeral. The angel of Kolkata had died. These and similar expressions of sorrow and mourning were expressed on Mother's death, as so many considered her a living saint or as one of "the saints next door," as Pope Francis calls them.[103] She was a saint before she was beatified and canonized by people. She was the every-day saint of the everyday people.

The death of Mother, a close friend, was particularly hard on Pope John Paul II, who, as soon as he heard about her death, started praying. According to Cardinal Dziwisz, John Paul II was very saddened by the news, saying that she had left everybody a little orphaned. For John Paul II she was a sister. According to Cardinal Dziwisz, "on the evening he received the news, he frankly expressed his hope that she would quickly be made a saint."[104] So much he admired Mother Teresa for her dedication to the poorest of the poor that he waived the five-year waiting period after the candidate's death, making it only two before the process of Mother Teresa's beatification and canonization could start. According to canon law, the reigning pontiff can waive the waiting period, and the move by John Paul II for the cause of Mother Teresa was a smart one; she was already considered a saint by popular acclaim. Cardinal Dziwisz provides some key details:

> He also put the proceedings on the fast track. He didn't force anything, though, because he was convinced that she was a saint. Plus, no one could ignore the fact that her witness had cut across ideological, cultural, and religious divisions and had won over the whole world. And I've no doubt that he was happy, in a spiritual sense, that he was able to raise to the glory of the altars a woman like Teresa, whom he had known personally.[105]

Two years before his death, on October 19, 2003, John Paul II beatified Mother Teresa in the presence of four hundred thousand people. According to the Italian daily *Corriere della Sera*, 80 percent of the pilgrims were Italian; foreign pilgrims came from Europe and the United States, and a few thousand came from India. Official delegations from India and Albania attended. Many Italian politicians and institutional authorities, including the mayor of Rome, Walter Veltroni, were there. However, the first section, the one closest to the altar in St. Peter's Square, was reserved for two thousand poor people from Rome, accompanied by hundreds of nuns and volunteers.[106] How could the poor not be part of the celebration? Speaking of providential coincidences, the beatification of Mother Teresa was preceded by the celebration of the twenty-fifth anniversary of John Paul II's pontificate on October 16, 2003. It was also providential that her beatification took place on World Mission Sunday. Mother was a missionary par excellence. This is how John Paul II announced Mother's beatification:

Mother Teresa of Calcutta, Foundress of the Missionaries of Charity whom today I have the joy of adding to
the Roll of the Blesseds, allowed this logic to guide her. I
am personally grateful to this courageous woman whom
I have always felt beside me. Mother Teresa, an icon of
the Good Samaritan, went everywhere to serve Christ in
the poorest of the poor. Not even conflict and war could
stand in her way.[107]

Mother was canonized by Pope Francis in September 2016 and she
became St. Mother Teresa of Kolkata. Her canonization followed
that of her friend St. John Paul II, who was canonized by Pope
Francis on September 30, 2013: friends in life and for life, raised
one after the other to the glory of the altars.

What united Sts. John Paul II and Mother Teresa? They came
from the peripheries of Poland and the Balkans; they both knew
and suffered under communism; they never lost the theological
virtues of faith and hope; they never conceded to the tyranny of
the possible and the present. They shared a profound and saintly
friendship—where one could not go the other could, where one left
off the other picked up. The two not only were friends in the faith
but emerged in their own ways as patron saints of the modern world.
They were Polish-tough and Albanian-tough who providentially met
and served.

PART III

CONTEMPORARY PERIPHERIES

CHAPTER 8

THE POPE OF THE PERIPHERY AND THE MOTHER OF THE PERIPHERY

POPE FRANCIS AND ST. MOTHER TERESA

God, Father of mercy and all goodness,
we thank you for giving us the life
and the charism of Saint Mother Teresa.

Pope Francis[1]

On May 7, 2019, Pope Francis visited the periphery of North Macedonia and the city of Skopje, birthplace of St. Mother Teresa. On that occasion, the Holy Father composed and prayed the following prayer of gratitude to St. Mother Teresa, which is also a prayer tribute to the periphery—and the good that the Balkan periphery can produce. The pontiff's gratitude goes a long way: from the city and the people of the North Macedonian periphery who educated the future saint; to the nuclear Bojaxhiu family; and to the Skopjen church where St. Mother Teresa received the sacraments and her future religious vocation to go deeper into the world's periphery and serve the world's poorest of the poor in India. This is how Pope Francis prayed for the intercession of St. Mother Teresa, first in silence before the statue of Mother Teresa in the Memorial House's courtyard and later in the Memorial House's Chapel, in the presence of Skopje's religious leaders who were gathered for Pope Francis's visit:

> Saint Mother Teresa, mother of the poor, we ask for your special intercession and help, here in this city where you were born, where you had your home. Here you received the gift of rebirth in the sacraments of Christian initiation. Here you heard the first words of faith in your family and in the community of the faithful. Here you began to see and meet people in need, the poor and the helpless. Here you learned from your parents to love those in greatest need and to help them. Here, in the silence of the church, you heard the call of Jesus to follow him as a religious in the missions.
>
> Here in this place, we ask you to intercede with Jesus, that we too may obtain the grace to be watchful and attentive to the cry of the poor, those deprived of their rights, the sick, the outcast and the least of our brothers and sisters. May he grant us the grace to see him in the eyes of all who look to us in their need. May he grant us a heart capable of loving God present in every man and woman, a heart capable of recognizing him in those who experience suffering and injustice. May he grant us the grace to become signs of love and hope in our own day, when so many are poor, abandoned, marginalized and migrants. May he grant that our love not only be on our lips, but that it be effective and genuine, so that we may bear credible witness to the Church whose duty it is to proclaim the Good News to the poor, freedom to prisoners, joy to the afflicted and the grace of salvation to all.[2]

The laboratory of the Skopje periphery was not a peripheral school for Mother Teresa to formally learn to start a lifelong religious vocation to serve the poorest of the poor. Instead, the school of Skopje was life-giving and life bringing for the future saint. It was in the periphery that Mother Teresa learned and lived by the transformative Christian virtues and values she then took with her to her next periphery in Kolkata. The Skopjen-Albanian periphery proved to be much more resourceful and transformative than anyone could have expected. Much good came from the Balkans, which trained the saint of the gutters. Francis's visit to a country with a Catholic minority—North Macedonia—can be understood within the framework of his theology of the peripheries: the Holy Father's special care for society's borders and peripheries, which he views as vital and vitally enriching to the center.

Because of the earthquake of 1963, there is nothing left of Mother Teresa's family's home, which was centrally located in Skopje, or of the church in which Mother Teresa was baptized and which her family frequented. Mother wrote of the centrality of the church and the church community in her family's life and in her upbringing. As she said, her family grew up in the church's courtyard. Mother cherished what she had learned in the laboratory of the periphery and brought what she had experienced in Skopje to India. The home-made sanctity of her mother, Drana, and the virtues and values of the people of Skopje that had shaped and educated her, stayed with Mother through her entire life and mission.

It was the periphery and the Mother of the periphery and the poor to whom the pope of the periphery paid tribute when he visited Mother Teresa's Memorial House in Skopje in May 2019, in the presence and with the participation of the Missionaries of Charity; the city's poor; and the religious leaders of Skopje: Stefan Veljanovski, the Orthodox Metropolitan of Skopje; Sulejman Rexhepi, the head of the North Macedonia Islamic Religious Community; Rev. Michail Cevoc, representative of the Evangelical-Methodist Church; and Berta Romano-Nikolic, representative of the Jewish community.[3] On the altar of the church of Mother Teresa's Memorial House were exposed a relic of St. Mother Teresa, some of her personal objects, and five burning candles representing the diverse religious communities of Skopje.[4]

FRANCIS'S FIRSTS

Latin America—Argentina

The announcement from the balcony of St. Peter's of the election of a new pontiff, who was largely unknown outside Roman circles, caught 1.2 billion Catholics by surprise.[5] Pope Francis was born and raised in Argentina, which is both a geographical and existential periphery in the Americas. As Archbishop of Buenos Aires, the largest city and capital of Argentina, and the second largest metropolitan area in South America, with a population of close to 13 million, he witnessed firsthand city peripheries where most of the social and religious life was lived and suffered. Francis is the first Latin American pope, and the first non-European pontiff in modern times, leading the world's 1.2 billion Catholics. In his first improvised address to the crowd in St. Peter's Square immediately after his election, the newly elected pontiff had this to say to the world: "You know that it was the duty of the conclave to give Rome a bishop. It seems that my brother cardinals have gone to the ends of the earth to get one…but here we are."[6]

Francis did not identify himself with the center where he now stood. Instead, his identity mark was the "ends of the world"—the margins, the world's edges. A distinct peripheral trajectory became quickly evident in his papacy: Francis departs from the peripheries to arrive at the center. This is what he did in Italy, the country where he as pontiff is a primate. The first place in Italy he visited was the tiny Sicilian island of Lampedusa in early July 2013, which is a major point of arrival for refugees trying to enter Europe and home of the boat people of the peripheries. The first big Italian city Francis would visit in Italy was Naples. The same peripheral-bound geography has followed in his European visits. He did not visit the capitals of Europe where Catholicism is an important historic reality; instead he chose to visit Albania and Bosnia and Herzegovina, with Muslim majorities. Bergolio's Christianity accomplishes a preferential choice—for the peripherals and the peripheries. This is scriptural geopolitics, the theme of Vatican II—the Church of the poor. Francis calls upon Christians to visit the peripheries of the world, beginning with the poor and the marginalized where they live in Lampedusa, Naples, Cuba, or Albania.

Francis is the first pontiff in the history of the papacy originating from the Americas. But there are other firsts for Francis: the pontiff's father immigrated to Argentina from northern Italy (Piedmont) in the 1920s. His mother was born in Buenos Aires to Italian immigrant parents. This makes Pope Francis the first modern pontiff born of immigrant parents. From 1876 to 1976, around 24 million immigrants left Italy, and among this immigrant population, 3 million settled in Argentina. According to statistics, among 44 million Argentinian inhabitants, 6 million—or 15 percent of the population—are of Italian descent.[7] Coming from a family of immigrants, knowing firsthand the struggles of immigrants, explains Pope Francis's intimate closeness to the plight of the immigrants living in the socioeconomic peripheries: their struggle to find employment, stability, and acceptance in the host country. On September 22, 2013, during his visit to Cagliari, the main city of the Italian island of Sardinia, in his meeting with workers, Francis spoke openly about the sufferings of his immigrant family in Buenos Aires:

> My father went to Argentina as a young man full of illusions "of making it in America." And he suffered in the dreadful recession of the 1930s. They lost everything! There was no work! And in my childhood, I heard talk of this period at home....I never saw it, I had not yet been

born, but I heard about this suffering at home, I heard talk of it. I know it well![8]

It is true that Pope Francis was not born in Italy, but by blood Jorge Mario Bergoglio is 100 percent Italian. Actually, as he himself put it, "I am the most Italian among my family members."[9] He spent a considerable amount of time with his grandparents since the early age of thirteen months old. In fact, his Italian grandmother Rose (Nonna Rosa, as he calls her) was his first teacher of faith and Catholic catechism and a transmitter of life's wisdom, as Pope Francis explained in the general audience on March 11, 2015, *Special Catechesis on the Family—Grandparents*:

> How beautiful, however, is the encouragement an elderly person manages to pass on to a young person who is seeking the meaning of faith and of life! It is truly the mission of grandparents, the vocation of the elderly. The words of grandparents have special value for the young. And the young know it. I still carry with me, always, in my breviary, the words my grandmother consigned to me in writing on the day of my priestly ordination. I read them often and they do me good.[10]

In addition to appreciating the value of the elderly as transmitters and preservers, the future pope had grown up to see other treasures in the elderly. He esteemed the valued role of the elderly as pontiffs or, literally, "bridge builders," and for the dialogue their role fosters between generations. That is why, for Francis, the elderly ought to be never marginalized, forgotten, or worst of all discarded—which have become plagues of modernity. So, the pope is quite keen to bring to the world's attention the periphery of the elderly.[11]

One important way in which grandmother Rose was a bridge builder for the young Jorge was in her role as a transmitter and teacher of Italian language and everything Italian. The future pope learned and spoke in perfect Piedmont dialect. For his immigrant father, Italy, Italian, and everything related to his native country was a very difficult subject, so he preferred to not speak the language. Italy and Italianism were taboos for his father, who was probably seeking full acceptance and integration into the Argentinean society, which, as other societies, required one to be wholly of the new society, which consequently causes one to lose their original national identity and assimilate. Bergoglio, due to his maternal grandparents, preserved the Italianism his father was trying to suppress. Bergoglio witnessed firsthand the suppression of identity, or the involuntary language loss and assimilation among immigrants, which are still current problems among immigrants in Europe, the United States, and elsewhere. Native language marginalization and assimilation are problems of the immigrant periphery that Francis has made central to his pontificate.

Moreover, Buenos Aires, Argentina's megacapital, where Jorge Mario Bergoglio was born, is the largest city in the country. Over the years, as is the case in other megalopolises, a considerable number of urban populations have moved there and live in the city's slums—or, as they are called in Argentina, *villas miserias*, where they live in poverty and suffer chronic unemployment. These *villas miserias* are cities within cities. They emerge at the margins of another city—unplanned shantytown communities that lack roads, potable water, and hygiene. *Villas miserias* is the definition of the modern geographical and existential periphery growing around the modern metropolitan cities. According to the most recent national census conducted in 2010, in the Greater Buenos Aires area, the urban agglomeration concentrating 32 percent of the country's population, more than a fifth of households live in inadequate housing conditions.[12] The future pontiff lived among the people of the urban existential peripheries and the priests serving the people of the *villas miserias*, which for the most part were either abusively occupied or abusively constructed buildings in precarious and hazardous conditions.[13]

The then cardinal Bergoglio was a supporter of the *curas villeros*—the priests of the slums, those Catholic priests who labored with the people living in the tenements or shantytowns. The *curas villeros* worked with the disadvantaged youth and immigrants and dealt with family violence and the plague of drugs and addiction, which were present even in the center city of Buenos Aires, but in a more camouflaged way.[14] The priority of Jorge Mario Bergoglio's church when he was Archbishop of Buenos Aires was the *villas miserias* and the *curas villeros*—the people of the periphery and the priests serving in the periphery. One of these priests was Fr. Pepe di Paola, a *cura villero* who was in constant contact with Archbishop Bergoglio during his apostolate in the Buenos Aires slums, as he explains in his January 10, 2014, interview.[15] The priests of the peripheries like Fr. Di Paola, who had made the heroic vocational choice to serve in the multiple layers of Buenos Aires's periphery, among the twenty-one dangerous slums of the Argentine capital to be exact, were then as they are now Bergolio's heroes. After his appointment as Archbishop of Buenos Aires, Bergoglio chose the peripheries, the *villas miserias*, as the center of his pastoral mission, bringing their problems to the attention of the archdiocese. The archbishop's priority was reaching out to the peripheries, to those who lived in the margins, recognizing their dignity as human persons, their right to a life free from poverty, hunger, injustice, and the criminal threat.[16] The future pontiff's priests were men of action, who had identified with the peripherals; they were those who lived with the peripherals and in the shantytowns. The *curas villeros* did not look at the problems of the marginals from afar. Instead, these missionary priests were there to share and participate in resolving their problems. The *villas* and the slums had a theology to teach, which is called the theology of the slums—which teaches a more human and humane face of poverty because this is indeed a lived and shared poverty. Thus, it is in the *villas miserias* that the Church and the people became one: the priests and all members of the Church are cosharers and cosufferers with the poor. Additionally, Bergoglio's periphery became a teaching periphery. Values like solidarity; sacrificing one's life for the other; preferring life over death; giving a Christian burial to the dead; looking after the sick, making room for the sick person at home; breaking bread with those who are hungry because where ten people can eat, twelve can also eat; patience and fortitude in the face of great adversity—these were all values cultivated in the periphery, are values the archbishop cherished.[17] Bergoglio would give a strong yes to the question, "Can anything good come from Nazareth?" (John 1:46). The future pope trusted in the good value system that came from the periphery.

Moreover, the culture of the multicultural *villas miserias* have preserved the evangelical values neglected by the more affluent and secularized city people—the *porteña*. The center city has a different value system compared to the Buenos Aires periphery. It organizes itself around power, wealth, and vanity, which is a common expression of ideologies from both right and left.[18] The culture of encounter is the culture of the *villera*, which *porteña* seems to have lost—the lived and learned culture of encounter and dialogue of the *villera* is the culture Pope Francis has in fact been bringing to the center of the Church since early in his pontificate. The Argentinian pontiff is reevaluating and revaluing the multiple layers of the periphery by bringing the values and virtues of the periphery to the Church's attention. However, Bergoglio's model of center-periphery is not internally conflicted or confrontational. He views center-periphery in harmony, as he explained in his *Letter to the Catechists* on August 21, 2007: "Our way out to the periphery will not be to move away from the center, but to remain in the vine and thus give true fruit in his love."[19] This is a christological-scriptural understanding of the periphery by making Christ the center and applying John 15:5: "I am the vine, you are the branches. Whoever remains in me and I in him will bear much fruit, because without me you can do nothing." Moreover, Bergoglio's center and periphery, or going to the periphery to meet Christ, is not an abandonment of the center. Instead, it is going out to the periphery and simultaneously remaining in the center; it is going out and staying to discern and to act. It is a reflect-reform trajectory while keeping Christ as the center piece—seeing Christ as a tenant of the *villas miserias*. This is Bergoglio's center-periphery coinfluential and integral balance.

RELIGIOUS ORDER—THE JESUITS

In the history of the papacy—266 pontiffs—only thirty-six pontiffs have belonged to religious orders. The Benedictines boast seventeen Roman pontiffs, starting with Gregory I, known as Gregory the Great (AD 590–604) in the seventh century, and most recently the Benedictine Camaldolese, Gregory XVI, Roman pontiff from 1831 to 1846; the Augustinians seven (Zachary, Eugene IV, Honorius II, Innocent II, Lucius II, Gregory VIII, and Adrian IV); the Dominicans four (Innocent V, Benedict XI, Pius V, and Benedict XIII); five Franciscans (Nicholas IV, Sixtus IV, Sixtus V, Julius II, and Clement XIV); and two Cistercians (Eugene III and Benedict XII). Pope Francis is the first pope coming from the Society of Jesus, an all-male religious order.[20]

St. Ignatius of Loyola did not want his brothers to be bishops or either directly or indirectly to seek positions, dignity, or prelacy within the Society of Jesus or widely in the Church's hierarchy. St. Ignatius was so much against ambitions for ecclesiastical positions that he wanted to demote all those brothers who were suspected to have sought after higher positions, saying, "One who can be proved to have sought such a prelacy becomes ineligible and disqualified for promotion to any prelacy."[21] The reason behind St. Ignatius's firm opposition was to save his brothers from the danger of careerism, ambition, and vainglory, which according to the Jesuits' founder was the mother of all evils among the members of a community or congregation. Additionally, the Jesuits are missionaries, which requires movement, mobility, and no attachment to one particular place. Assuming a bishopric or other prelacy/hierarchal positions would make the religious brothers committed to one place with less free-dom to exercise their vocation for either domestic or foreign missions. Moreover, and from a practical perspective, Jesuits taking ecclesiastical positions meant fewer Jesuit brothers to serve Jesuit apostolates.

However, despite Ignatius's aversion, historically, there have been Jesuit bishops, archbishops, and cardinals, and with Pope Francis a new milestone, a first was reached: a Jesuit being elected Roman pontiff. According to *Jesuit Constitution* 817, "they are compelled by an order from the one who can command them under pain of sin,"[22] and the *Code of Canon Law*, Canon 705 states, "A religious raised to the episcopate remains a member of his institute but is subject only to the Roman Pontiff by virtue of the vow of obedience and is not bound by obligations which he himself prudently judges cannot be reconciled with his condition."[23] Assuming hierarchal position might be justified, under specific circumstances and under obedience. Moreover, in the case of a Jesuit pontiff, when one is elected pope, he does not cease to be a Jesuit. Once a Jesuit, always a Jesuit—a member of the Society of Jesus. In other words, one's belonging to the religious order never expires, even if he becomes a pontiff. After all, "Man is created to praise, reverence, and serve God our Lord, and by this means to save his soul. And the other things on the face of the earth are created for man and that they may help him in prosecuting the end for which he is created," so there is "freedom" for man to serve the Lord—that is the end for which man is created.[24] Obedience or promptness is required to obey "in all, the true Spouse of Christ our Lord, which is our holy Mother the Church Hierarchical,"[25] so in the case of Jesuit Pope Francis, he had to obey the Church, which chose him to be her leader. St. Ignatius of Loyola's *Spiritual Exercises* approved of these reasons. Francis, according to his biographer, Austen Ivereigh, continues to put *SJ* after his name and is deeply imbued with the spirituality of the Society's founder, St. Ignatius of Loyola.[26]

In addition to being the first Jesuit pontiff, Pope Francis was also the first Jesuit Archbishop of Buenos Aires—this makes Francis score another first.

WHAT IS BEHIND THE NAME?

The Jesuit pontiff did not take the name of Francis Xavier, SJ, the sixteenth-century Jesuit missionary and the cofounder of the Society of Jesus, as many in St. Peter's Square speculated when the newly elected pontiff come out on the balcony. Francis's choice was to take the name of the founder of another religious order, the Franciscans—St. Francis of Assisi. Francis's name choice was significant, as with this choice he is marking another first among the 266 Roman pontiffs since St. Peter (AD 64 or 67): the first to be named Francis. Among the most popular pontiffs' names in the history of papacy are John (23), Gregory (16), Benedict (16), Clement (14), Innocent (13), Leo (13), and Pius (12).[27] It seems as if Francis the pontiff wants to tread his own path in the papacy, in discontinuity with the popular names taken by Roman pontiffs since the time of St. Peter, but continuing in the footsteps of St. Francis of Assisi, emulating Christ, focusing on the poor and the peripherals, dialogue, and the culture of encounter, the same values shared by the thirteenth-century saint of Assisi and patron saint of Italy. Three days after the election, in a special audience to representatives of the communications media, the newly elected pontiff gave his reasons for his name choice:

> I will tell you the story. During the election, I was seated next to the Archbishop Emeritus of São Paolo and Prefect Emeritus of the Congregation for the Clergy, Cardinal Claudio Hummes: a good friend, a good friend! When things were looking dangerous, he encouraged me. And when the votes reached two thirds, there was the usual applause, because the Pope had been elected. And he gave me a hug and a kiss and said: "Don't forget the poor!" And those words came to me: the poor, the poor. Then, right away, thinking of the poor, I thought of Francis of Assisi. Then I thought of all the wars, as the votes were

still being counted, till the end. Francis is also the man of peace. That is how the name came into my heart: Francis of Assisi. For me, he is the man of poverty, the man of peace, the man who loves and protects creation; these days we do not have a very good relationship with creation, do we? He is the man who gives us this spirit of peace, the poor man....How I would like a Church which is poor and for the poor![28]

Francis laid the stepping-stones of his papacy starting with his first homily as a Roman pontiff on March 19, 2013, which marked the start of his Petrine ministry. The newly elected pontiff spoke about the protection and care of all creation, and the beauty of the created world, following in the footsteps of the saint of his name-sake, St. Francis of Assisi, who showed the way:

> It means respecting each of God's creatures and respect-ing the environment in which we live. It means protecting people, showing loving concern for each and every person, especially children, the elderly, those in need, who are often the last we think about. It means caring for one another in our families: husbands and wives first protect one another, and then, as parents, they care for their children, and chil-dren themselves, in time, protect their parents. It means building sincere friendships in which we protect one another in trust, respect, and goodness. In the end, every-thing has been entrusted to our protection, and all of us are responsible for it. Be protectors of God's gifts![29]

Francis is a pope of many additional firsts. He is the first pope in six hundred years to take office after one who had resigned, Pope Benedict XVI—whose resignation shocked the Catholic world. More-over, Francis is the first pontiff of the modern age who has coped with a living prior pontiff or a pope emeritus. Additionally, unlike his immediate antecedent pontiffs St. John Paul II and Pope Benedict XVI, who both participated in the deliberations of the Second Vatican Council, Francis is the first postconciliar pontiff—not only did he not participate at the Second Vatican Council but he also studied theology and was ordained after the council's closure.[30] However, Francis's thought and theology is greatly influenced by his predecessors St. Paul VI, John Paul I, St. John Paul II, and Benedict XVI, which makes Francis both traditional and progressive—or as his fellow Jesuit, James Corkery, SJ, calls him, an innovative heir, a person who responds creatively to what he has received from the Church's tradition.[31]

POPE FRANCIS'S THEOLOGY OF PERIPHERY

In Christian theological terms, Francis's theology of periphery is to be understood in terms of Christ's teaching to his apostles, "Go into the whole world and proclaim the gospel to every creature" (Mark 16:15). This vocation can be fully accomplished only if one has lived and experienced the geographical and existential periphery. Jesus himself experienced this life fully, living in the periphery for thirty years and, during his ministry, never losing sight of society's existential periphery—the poor, the lost sheep, the abandoned, the discarded, the prostitutes, the troubled women. So, the peripheral identity and trajectory was distinct and distinctive in Jesus and his mission. Similarly, for Francis, the Church—following in the footsteps of the prototype Jesus—is called to come out of herself and go to the ends of the earth, to the peripheries of our times: geographical and existential peripheries, which need the light of the gospel.

Francis's reference to the periphery is a metaphor that goes much deeper than mere geography or material poverty. As he says,

> I am convinced of one thing: the great changes in history were realized when reality was seen not from the center but rather from the periphery. This is a hermeneutical

question: reality is understood only if it is looked at from the periphery, and not when our viewpoint is equidistant from everything. Truly to understand reality we need to move away from the central position of calmness and peacefulness and direct ourselves to the peripheral areas. Being at the periphery helps to see and to understand better, to analyze reality more correctly, to shun centralism and ideological approaches.[32]

Francis's vision of the periphery is decentralized and nonhegemonic, contesting a prevailing, power-centered vision of the world and the Church. Beyond the official history—Pope Francis suggests—an alternative trajectory of the same history is at work: we must explore this neglected and marginalized side to truly understand the unfolding story of humankind. Pope Francis anchored his theology in the direct experience of true life in the periphery by being the pastor of the peripheral people. "This is really very important to me," he said, "the need to become acquainted with reality by experience, to spend time walking on the periphery in order really to become acquainted with the reality and life-experiences of people. If this does not happen, we then run the risk of being abstract ideologists or fundamentalists, which is not healthy."[33]

Furthermore, the role of the Church as seen by Pope Francis is a vigorous movement from the "center" (a self-referential attitude), via a dynamic engagement with the world. Francis's theology and direction of the Church "go outside" through a dialectical process to produce a more open and committed attitude well beyond the invisible walls of the community of believers:

There is a tension between the center and the periphery. We must get out of ourselves and go toward the periphery. We must avoid the spiritual disease of the Church that can become self-referential: when this happens, the Church itself becomes sick. It's true that accidents can happen when you go out into the street, as can happen to any man or woman. But if the Church remains closed onto itself, self-referential, it grows old. Between a Church that goes into the street and gets into an accident and a Church that is sick with self-referentiality, I have no doubts in preferring the first.[34]

In Pope Francis's view, "accidents" are preferable to "sickness."

According to Francis's theology of periphery and geopolitics, the world is not a hierarchal pyramid and even less a sphere. Francis defends a more nuanced vision of a world that is interconnected and interdependent—a world without a dominant center, whose units are, to some extent, equally peripheral and whose problems equally important: "Here our model is not the sphere, which is no greater than its parts, where every point is equidistant from the center, and there are no differences between them. Instead, it is the polyhedron, which reflects the convergence of all its parts, each of which preserves its distinctiveness."[35]

WHAT UNITES THE POPE OF THE PERIPHERY TO THE MOTHER OF THE PERIPHERY

The Good Samaritan

In the Third Congress of the Catholic Communicators/Media held in Buenos Aires on October 10, 2002, the then archbishop Bergoglio stressed the role of the media in transmitting information truthfully and accurately, which meant communicating the reality in its entirety in a clear and harmonious way.[36] When the future pope talked about the media communicating the beauty of love, which shares joys and sorrows, Archbishop Bergoglio focused on the parable of the Good Samaritan, when he "approached the victim, poured oil and wine over his wounds and bandaged them. Then he lifted him up on his own animal, took him to an inn and cared for him" (Luke

10:34). The archbishop was connecting the parable of the Good Samaritan to two contemporary good Samaritans, making specific reference to the Mother of the Poor, Mother Teresa of Kolkata, and Blessed Artemide Zatti (1880–1951), a Salesian brother who, inspired by Don Bosco, ran a hospital and pharmacy for the sick and the poor for forty years in Viedma, Argentina, and who was beatified by John Paul II in 2002.[37] Mother Teresa and Fr. Zatti, the modern Samaritans, were Bergoglio's religious models of Christian mercy:

> [They] shine without tricks or special effects, but of that brilliance that only mercy brings forth when it is spent in caring for those most in need, anointing them with the perfumed oil of its tenderness.[38]

For Archbishop Bergoglio the best Samaritans, like the original Samaritan described in the Gospel, were those who originated from the periphery, and who live with and help the peripherals. The Samaritans of Scripture were indeed peripherals and looked down upon, as the Samaritan woman said to Jesus: "How can you, a Jew, ask me, a Samaritan woman, for a drink? (For Jews use nothing in common with Samaritans)" (John 4:9). Mother Teresa, a woman who came from the Balkan periphery, and Fr. Zatti, an Italian immigrant to Argentina, were the future pontiff's model religious. Putting others first, offering a generous and selfless love was Mother Teresa's and Fr. Zatti's way of life. This is how both put their faith into action, since faith without works is indeed a dead faith. These modern Samaritans' hearts were filled with mercy and compassion for the poorest of the poor and the needy, recognizing the magnificent beauty of God in the neighbor. They saw and witnessed God in the suffering neighbor.

Archbishop Bergoglio continued his speech at the Third Congress of the Catholic Communicators/Media, making another important reference to Mother Teresa, whom he had met very briefly in 1994 at the Bishops' Synod in Rome.

When we think of someone as Mother Teresa of Kolkata, our heart is filled with beauty that does not derive from her physical appearances or the stature of that woman, but instead from the sparkling light of charity towards the poor and the underprivileged that accompanies it [our heart].[39]

Archbishop Bergoglio was reflecting on where people can go in search of beauty and how to discover the genuine beauty that is far beyond superficial appearances or mundane fashion. For Bergoglio, there is beauty to be found in all men and women who fully live their vocation of religious, laity, parenthood, motherhood, widowhood, by giving all of themselves unconditionally to the other, their families. Bergoglio's beauty is an all offering-gratuitous beauty that one gives without expecting anything in return and those people like Mother Teresa, who have discovered and live this beauty, are those who lay the foundations for a culture of solidarity and social friendship.[40]

Solidarity with the Poor

For Pope Francis, Mother Teresa is the Good Samaritan woman, who gave without expecting, who showed mercy and compassion in abundance. But more connects Bergoglio and Mother Teresa—the pope of the slums and the mother of the poor. From December 2010 to 2013, right before his election as Roman pontiff, Cardinal Jorge Mario Bergoglio had worked with Rabbi Abraham Skorka and the Protestant minister Rev. Marcelo Figueroa to share their views on interfaith dialogue on Buenos Aires archdiocesan Channel 21. The program, which was moderated by Rev. Figueroa, was called *Bible: A Valid Dialogue* and explored current topics including solidarity, forgiveness, love, suffering, inclusion, and many others of interest to religious viewers, both Christian and Jews. Figueroa referred to Genesis 4, the story of Cain and Abel. In one of the TV episodes Cardinal Bergoglio and Rabbi Skorka were asked to reflect on the topic of solidarity—its many dimensions, meanings, and applications. Rev. Figueroa started the discussion by bringing forth Genesis 4 from the Old Testament—the story of Cain and Abel, posing the same scriptural question the Lord asked Cain, to the religious leaders Bergoglio and Skorka: "Where is your brother Abel? He answered, 'I do not know. Am I my brother's keeper?'" (Gen 4:9). It was an angry demand on the part of Cain, which in a way marked the origin of human indifference toward the neighbor—or worse, selfishness and self-centeredness. The question can also be framed as this: Am I my brother's custodian, the person responsible for taking care of him? Am I the protector of my brother? Should I watch over my brother so that nothing harmful happens to him? The essence of Cain's question is this: Who is the neighbor or the other for me? Cain's questions can be expanded to include who my brother is—is he my neighbor; friend; the individual belonging to another faith, religion, or a different religious community; the unborn child—and the list can go on and on. When a person searches for the other in self, when he or she finds a collective of individuals in the self and treats them as if they were the self, there is a unity with the other person: one becomes an integral part of the other. Consequently, one cannot ignore the other, because he or she is part of the other. Thus, recognizing the stranger, the other, in me, treating the other as I would like to be treated—this is the transcendent nature of solidarity as understood in Christian theology as transcendent love of God-with-us, who is in total solidarity with his people. It was Christ-God who modeled solidarity first, by taking upon himself the suffering and frailties of his people, walking side by side with us.

Returning to Cain's question "Am I my brother's keeper?'" (Gen 4:9), what exactly was Cardinal Bergoglio's answer? Bergoglio's answer was a firm yes. For Bergoglio, the strong yes meant solidarity in action, a walking solidarity similar to that of the Lord. This is a universal value, and with the coming of Christ has become a shared value, between the giver and the taker, the one who gives gratuitously and the one who receives. Thus, taking responsibility, protecting the brother, the afflicted neighbor, the immigrant in difficulty searching for a job or a home, for Cardinal Bergoglio meant that the person who was helping had overcome selfishness, had overcome the small self, or what Bergoglio called "my small world" centered on "I, me, with me, for me."[41]

Pope John Paul II argued along the same lines in his 1987 encyclical *Sollicitudo Rei Socialis* (On Social Concern) on the occasion of the twentieth anniversary of Paul VI's 1967 encyclical *Populorum Progressio* (On the Development of Peoples), writing,

> In the light of faith, solidarity seeks to go beyond itself, to take on the specifically Christian dimension of total gratuity, forgiveness and reconciliation.[42]

This gratuity in giving makes Christian solidarity a duty to be sustained, or what Paul VI called "the duty of promoting human solidarity."[43] Going out of self, or abandoning self, is what solidarity means for Bergoglio then and for Pope Francis now.

During the same TV program on Buenos Aires archdiocesan Channel 21, focusing on the same topic of solidarity, Cardinal Bergoglio and Rabbi Skorka explored Jesus's message during the final judgement, or the judgement of the nations:

> For I was hungry and you gave me food, I was thirsty and you gave me drink, a stranger and you welcomed me, naked and you clothed me, ill and you cared for me, in prison and you visited me. Then the righteous will answer him and say, "Lord, when did we see you hungry and feed you, or thirsty and give you drink? When did we see you a stranger and welcome you, or naked and clothe you? When did we see you ill or in prison, and visit you?" And the king will say to them in reply, "Amen, I say to you, whatever you did for one of these least brothers of mine, you did for me." (Matt 25:35–40)

Solidarity is a Christian virtue that goes hand in hand with Christian charity. You did it for me—this is Bergoglio's essence of Christian solidarity. Solidarity means identification with the peripherals and the disadvantaged, and through them serving none other but Christ. Moreover, the future pontiff considered solidarity and the love of neighbor to be a way toward human perfection, a way of bringing one closer to God. Everyone is created and is part of creation: all are brothers and sisters, children of the same Father, the cardinal explained.[44] Bergoglio concludes his argument on solidarity by urging the viewers to be solidary and take care of the neighbor, as solidarity is urgent and by no means can it be put off until tomorrow or forgotten altogether.

Bergoglio's theology of solidarity and Mother Teresa's theology of solidarity are identical—in fighting the selfish self and instead giving gratuitously to the neighbor or brother, who was created equal by God. The pope of the Argentine slums and the mother of the poor are both champions of the Christian virtue of solidarity, as both had experienced solidarity by working in the slums and with the poor. Mother Teresa, reflecting on finding Christ in the poor, the marginal, the peripheral, the sick, the abandoned, and the elderly had this to say about solidarity:

> We are at the service of the poor. But are we capable, are we willing to share the poverty of the poor? Do we identify with the poor whom we serve? Do we really feel in solidarity with them? Do we share with them just like Jesus shares with us? The poor anywhere in the world are Christ who suffers. In them, the Son of God lives and dies. Through them, God shows his face.[45]

Moreover, Mother Teresa, like Cardinal Bergoglio, considers solidarity with the poor and serving the poor a privilege:

> I am grateful to God to have given me this opportunity to be with you and to share with you the gift of God, the

privilege of being with the poor, the privilege of being twenty-four hours in touch with Christ. For Jesus has said, and He cannot deceive us, "You did it to Me. I was hungry and you gave Me to eat; and I was thirsty, and you gave Me to drink; and I was sick and in prison and you visited Me, and I was homeless and you gave Me a home. You took Me in." We are trying to do [this], you and I together, to bring that joy of touching Christ in the distressing disguise.[46]

When Cardinal Bergoglio was exploring these topics on Buenos Aires archdiocesan Channel 21 and at the 2002 Third Congress of the Catholic Communicators/Media, he would have never thought that a decade later he would be elected the 266th Roman pontiff and, in that role, would return to the parable of the Good Samaritan and solidarity with the poor, and the modern-peripheral Samaritan— Mother Teresa of Kolkata. The parable of the Good Samaritan, the compassionate and merciful love of the Father and solidarity with the peripherals, Archbishop Bergoglio's favorite theology, continued to be the focal themes of the now Pope Francis's Extraordinary Jubilee of Mercy that he himself called from December 8, 2015, to November 20, 2016. When the Holy Father opened the Holy Door of Mercy of St. Peter's Basilica, he had this to say for the gift of grace for the Jubilee of Mercy and solidarity with the poor:

> To pass through the Holy Door means to rediscover the infinite mercy of the Father who welcomes everyone and goes out personally to encounter each of them. It is he who seeks us! It is he who comes to encounter us! This will be a year in which we grow ever more convinced of God's mercy. How much wrong we do to God and his grace when we speak of sins being punished by his judgment before we speak of their being forgiven by his mercy (cf. Saint Augustine, *De Praedestinatione Sanctorum*, 12,

24)! But that is the truth. We have to put mercy before judgment, and in any event God's judgement will always be in the light of his mercy. In passing through the Holy Door, then, may we feel that we ourselves are part of this mystery of love, of tenderness. Let us set aside all fear and dread, for these do not befit men and women who are loved. Instead, let us experience the joy of encountering that grace which transforms all things.[47]

Three months before the conclusion of the Extraordinary Jubilee of Mercy, on September 4, 2016, Pope Francis raised the mother of the poor and the Good Samaritan woman of modern solidarity to the glory of the altars. Mother Teresa became St. Mother Teresa of Kolkata but also Francis's saint. Mother will forever be remembered as Francis's saint and the model for applying Francis's theology of the peripheries and solidarity.[48] Thus, St. Mother Teresa and Pope Francis will be forever bound together in their love of God's mercy and how both of them creatively dispensed God's mercy among the people. The peripheral-modern Samaritan woman whom Francis set on center stage had the following saintly virtues, as Pope Francis explained in the homily on the occasion of her canonization in front of an overflowing St. Peter's Square:

Mother Teresa, in all aspects of her life, was a generous dispenser of divine mercy, making herself available for everyone through her welcome and defense of human life, those unborn and those abandoned and discarded. She was committed to defending life, ceaselessly proclaiming that "the unborn are the weakest, the smallest, the most vulnerable." She bowed down before those who were spent, left to die on the side of the road, seeing in them their God-given dignity; she made her voice heard before the powers of this world, so that they might recognize their guilt for the crime—the crimes!—of poverty they created. For Mother Teresa, mercy was the "salt" which gave flavor to her work, it was the "light" which shone in the darkness of the many who no longer had tears to shed for their poverty and suffering.[49]

But the lives of St. Mother Teresa and Pope Francis have been woven together in even more directions. Francis love for the world's peripheries brought him to Albania in 2014, the country of origin of Mother Teresa and an overwhelmingly Muslim country. Francis paid tribute to the mother of the peripheries, evidencing a particular wealth of the periphery—the culture of encounter and solidarity, following in the footsteps of Mother Teresa. Pope Francis had this to say to the Albanian young people during the Angelus:

> Dear young people, you are the new generation, the new generation of Albania, the future of the country. With the power of the Gospel and the example of your ancestors and the martyrs, you know how to say "No" to the idolatry of money—"No" to the idolatry of money, "No" to the false freedom of individualism, "No" to addiction and to violence; you also know how to say "Yes" to a culture of encounter and of solidarity, "Yes" to the beauty that is inseparable from the good and the true; "Yes" to a life lived with great enthusiasm and at the same time faithful in little things. In this way, you will build a better Albania and a better world, in the footsteps of your ancestors.[50]

St. Francis of Assisi

Besides the two being Good Samaritans for the peripherals, channeling God's love and mercy to the poor, and modeling solidarity to the neighbor, St. Mother Teresa and Pope Francis's bond of unity goes deeper, to two Catholic saints, who were their namesakes: St. Thérèse of Lisieux and St. Francis of Assisi, respectively—saints whose vision and mission Mother Teresa and Pope Francis made their own. Franciscan spirituality is profound in Mother Teresa's and Pope Francis's missions and visions. Since his election in 2013, the son of the Italian immigrants to Argentina has had the same name as a beloved saint of Italy from Assisi—a name now associated with both notable medieval and modern men. Behind a name there is a mission and significance. Obviously, there is a mission and vision in Pope Francis's pontificate, and the bond of Pope Francis with St. Francis is clear.

In the 2002 *Letter to the Catechists* Cardinal Bergoglio reflected on Matthew 4:10, "The Lord, your God, shall you worship and him alone shall you serve." Cardinal Bergoglio was referring to a wounded society, which was anticipating the grand entrance of the Lord who was no other than the Way, the Truth, and the Life, and who is capable of effecting reconciliation.[51] Bergoglio explained that the worship due to God means prostrating in humility and recognizing the greatness of God. While explaining the proper way to worship God to his audience, Cardinal Bergoglio used the example of his favorite Italian saint, St. Francis of Assisi, and how the great saint from Assisi loved the entirety of God's creation. Little did Bergoglio know at that time that after a decade he would be called Francis and lead the universal Catholic Church toward an integral ecology, which means living in harmony with God, the neighbor, the earth, and oneself, the core of St. Francis of Assisi's view of creation:

> Worship means going towards unity, discovering that we are children of the same Father, members of the same family, as Saint Francis had discovered: singing his praises in harmony with all of Creation and all humans [part of creation]. It means re-establishing the bonds we have severed with the earth, with our brothers; it means recognizing him as Lord of all things, a good Father of the entire world.[52]

Care for creation means solidarity and care for the poor and the peripherals. The newly elected pope was making known his pontificate's priorities. On July 24, 2013, a few months after his election, on the occasion of the 14th World Youth Day, Pope Francis visited Rio De Janeiro. Part of Francis's apostolic journey was the visit to St. Francis of Assisi of the Providence of God Hospital—he called this hospital a shrine of human suffering. Francis had the occasion to talk about his favorite saint, who was the hospital's patron saint. The pontiff spoke against worldly riches and comforts as St. Francis of Assisi did regarding his own wealth and property. Only by leaving everything behind, returning to Lady Poverty, becoming poor among the poor, could St. Francis understand where true joy came from—embracing the leper, the peripheral. Pope Francis explained,

> True joy and riches do not come from the idols of this world—material things and the possession of them—but are to be found only in following Christ and serving others. Less well known, perhaps, is the moment when this understanding took concrete form in his own life. It was when Francis embraced a leper. This suffering brother was the "mediator of light...for Saint Francis of Assisi" (*Lumen Fidei*, 57), because in every suffering brother and sister that we embrace, we embrace the suffering Body of Christ. Today, in this place where people struggle with drug addiction, I wish to embrace each and every one of you, who are the flesh of Christ, and to ask God to renew your journey, and also mine, with purpose and steadfast hope.[53]

On October 4, 2014, on the occasion of the opening of the Synod on the Family, Pope Francis referred to his namesake as he explained how Franciscan spirituality would lead the Church's and society's renewal:

With the joy of the Gospel we will rediscover the way of a reconciled and merciful Church, poor and a friend of the poor; a Church "given strength that it might, in patience and in love, overcome its sorrows and its challenges, both within itself and from without" (*Lumen Gentium*, n. 8).[54]

Pope Francis considers St. Francis—the saint of the poor, dialogue, and encounter—his personal saint, as he himself has admitted on several occasions. On November 23, 2016, as reported by *Interfax*, Pope Francis congratulated Patriarch Kirill of Moscow and All Russia on his seventieth birthday and presented him with a very special gift: a relic of St. Francis of Assisi, whom Francis called his "heavenly protector."[55] The pope said in a message to the patriarch, "In expressing again my gratitude for presenting me with a piece of the holy relics of Saint Seraphim of Sarov, I am glad to present you with a relic of St. Francis of Assisi, my heavenly protector."[56] St. Seraphim of Sarov (1754–1833) was a great Russian ascetic who followed the prayer regimen prescribed in the Rule of St. Pachomius (292–348). "May these two marvelous God pleasers, already united in paradise, pray for us that we labor even more unitedly for the sake of attaining peace and total unity that Jesus Christ prayed for," Pope Francis wrote in his message to the Russian patriarch.[57]

Following in the footsteps of St. Francis of Assisi, his hand-picked saint and heavenly protector, Pope Francis starts his 2015 encyclical letter *Laudato Si'* (Praise Be to You, My Lord), from the *Canticle of the Brother Sun*, otherwise known as *The Canticle of the Creatures*. The *Canticle* was composed by St. Francis of Assisi, the first great poem in Italian vernacular, where St. Francis views creation as interwoven and interdependent, paying special homage to the sun, light, and fire.[58] Pope Francis in his *Laudato Si'* joins his voice to St. Francis's in being thankful for God's creation and the common good that God created for all, adding,

Saint Francis of Assisi reminds us that our common home is like a sister with whom we share our life and a beautiful mother who opens her arms to embrace us. "Praise be to you, my Lord, through our Sister, Mother Earth, who sustains and governs us, and who produces various fruit with colored flowers and herbs."[59]

Pope Francis, as St. Francis of Assisi, supports an integral ecology that is based on recognition of the interconnectedness among all creatures and the Creator. St. Francis considered the surrounding world very close—as close as a brother is to a sister and vice versa. Pope Francis evidenced that austerity and asceticism lived by St. Francis of Assisi are not to be understood as veneers or superficial asceticism. Instead St. Francis's lifestyle meant a refusal to turn reality into an object to be used, controlled, and manipulated. What St. Francis modeled was in fact respect for creation. And this applies not only to the planet Earth but to all God's creation because all is connected. This is why he writes,

> Francis helps us to see that an integral ecology calls for openness to categories which transcend the language of mathematics and biology and take us to the heart of what it is to be human. Just as happens when we fall in love with someone, whenever he would gaze at the sun, the moon or the smallest of animals, he burst into song, drawing all other creatures into his praise. He communed with all creation, even preaching to the flowers, inviting them "to praise the Lord, just as if they were endowed with reason." His response to the world around him was so much more than intellectual appreciation or economic calculus, for to him each and every creature was a sister united to him by bonds of affection. That is why he felt called to care for all that exists. His disciple Saint Bonaventure tells us that, "from a reflection on the primary source of all things,

284

filled with even more abundant piety, he would call creatures, no matter how small, by the name of 'brother' or
'sister.'" Such a conviction cannot be written off as naive
romanticism, for it affects the choices which determine
our behavior. If we approach nature and the environment
without this openness to awe and wonder, if we no longer
speak the language of fraternity and beauty in our relationship with the world, our attitude will be that of masters, consumers, ruthless exploiters, unable to set limits
on their immediate needs.[60]

St. Francis of Assisi lived in harmony with God, with the neighbor, and
with self—and this is how Pope Francis understands inclusiveness.
Francis's understanding of the culture of inclusion is the same as
that of St. Francis of Assisi. But the central piece in the inclusiveness
and integral ecology of both Francises is harmony with God—the
Creator. This is an important piece that unites the two Francises
with each other but also with Mother Teresa.

The thread that connects the two Francises and Mother Teresa
is "I thirst, I am thirsty"—Jesus's call from the cross. The fulfillment
of Scripture is in this call for help, as John showed in his Gospel. The
cry of the poor and the marginalized was synthesized and became
actual in the "I thirst" for the Francises and for Mother Teresa. It
does not necessarily signify only physical thirst for water—it signi-
fies a plethora of things. Jesus's "I thirst" from the cross is more than
thirst and hunger, it is a different kind that does not have an expira-
tion date—it is a thirst for love. St. Francis of Assisi, Mother Teresa,
and Pope Francis share this understanding of "I thirst" and have
their pastoral ways of applying or satiating its multiplicity. In his
speech for the 2016 World Day of Prayer for Peace in Assisi, Pope
Francis explained,

> "Love is not loved": this reality, according to some
> accounts, is what upset Saint Francis of Assisi. For love

of the suffering Lord, he was not ashamed to cry out and grieve loudly (cf. *Fonti Francescane*, no. 1413). This same reality must be in our hearts as we contemplate Christ Crucified, he who thirsts for love. Mother Teresa of Calcutta desired that in the chapel of every community of her sisters the words "I thirst" would be written next to the crucifix. Her response was to quench Jesus' thirst for love on the Cross through service to the poorest of the poor. The Lord's thirst is indeed quenched by our compassionate love; he is consoled when, in his name, we bend down to another's suffering. On the day of judgment they will be called "blessed" who gave drink to those who were thirsty, who offered true gestures of love to those in need: "As you did it to one of the least of these my brethren, you did it to me" (Matt 25:40).[61]

Jesus was thirsting for love, and through expressing his thirst Jesus called all to respond. Jesus's "I thirst" became the call to action and affection of Mother Teresa and her Missionaries of Charity. She dedicated her life to that call. It is Jesus's "I thirst" for love and souls that organically and integrally connects the two Francises and St. Mother Teresa.

St. Thérèse of Lisieux

But there is another bond between Pope Francis and Mother Teresa—the devotion to St. Thérèse of Lisieux, Mother Teresa's namesake. Inside the famous black and worn-out briefcase Pope Francis still carries with him on his trips, there is a constant—*The Story of a Soul: The Autobiography of St. Thérèse of Lisieux*, a book by a young saint, a doctor of the Church, who has constantly sustained Francis through her intercessory prayer. In his message for Lent 2015, Pope Francis makes a specific mention of St. Thérèse of

Lisieux, her sustenance in prayer, and the communion between the Church in heaven and the Militant Church on earth through prayer:

> The Church in heaven is not triumphant because she has turned her back on the sufferings of the world and rejoices in splendid isolation. Rather, the saints already joyfully contemplate the fact that, through Jesus' death and resurrection, they have triumphed once and for all over indifference, hardness of heart and hatred. Until this victory of love penetrates the whole world, the saints continue to accompany us on our pilgrim way. Saint Therese of Lisieux, a Doctor of the Church, expressed her conviction that the joy in heaven for the victory of crucified love remains incomplete as long as there is still a single man or woman on earth who suffers and cries out in pain: "I trust fully that I shall not remain idle in heaven; my desire is to continue to work for the Church and for souls" (Letter 254, July 14, 1897). We share in the merits and joy of the saints, even as they share in our struggles and our longing for peace and reconciliation. Their joy in the victory of the Risen Christ gives us strength as we strive to overcome our indifference and hardness of heart.[62]

In this message, Francis was inviting the Church to open up in two directions: toward heaven and toward earth. There is an inherent connection between the Church in heaven and the Church on earth. From the saints in heaven, including the Little Flower, the Church on earth learns that their triumph in heaven is in fact also a triumph for the people on earth: the saints in heaven render their intercession to the Church on earth to ease their journey toward heaven. What Pope Francis was teaching through his 2015 Lenten message are the works of mercy and the help for the neighbor, which are expected to increase during the period of Lent. The works of mercy do not finish here, on Earth. But the works of mercy of those in heaven are not free tickets to heaven, either. The saints and angels who reside in heaven are the best example: they continue to intercede for their neighbors as they did before, when they were among the earthly. So, works of mercy continue in heaven, and works of mercy on earth are a taste of heaven for the earthly, in anticipation of heaven. That is why St. Thérèse of Lisieux promised to continue to work in heaven for souls. Similarly, St. Mother Teresa promised that she will continue to intercede for her poor on earth, "to light the light of those in darkness on earth."[63]

In Thérèse's little way, the ordinary things of life, when done with extraordinary love, are transformed into something extraordinary— this was Mother Teresa's principle in life, too. Mother was always ready to contribute her little part, to alleviate suffering and carry the cross, as she said during her 1984 visit to the famine-stricken Ethiopia. Mother did not hesitate to do her little part to help the world's hungriest nation:

> Ethiopia is an open Calvary, not an open hell. You and I
> can do our little part and then life will be saved.[64]

For Mother Teresa what she gave graciously was always considered little and unimportant. However, what she always taught her sisters was the love one puts into the little things. This is what mattered to Mother Teresa, following in the footsteps of St. Thérèse of Lisieux:

> Just to do that humble work....We have determined to
> remain with the humble work and...it is not a waste of time
> just to feed and to wash and to scrub and to love and to take
> care and to do these little things. Because it is directly done
> to the hungry Christ, the naked Christ. He cannot deceive
> us; it is that touching Him twenty-four hours.[65]

On September 7, 2019, Pope Francis visited the cloistered contemplative nuns of Carmel of St. Joseph in Antananarivo, Madagascar.

Francis was keen to mention the little way of St. Thérèse of Lisieux, reflecting on the daily simple routine or "the little steps" the nuns undertake in their way to Christian perfection. He recognized that

> all of you cloistered nuns have come to be close to the Lord, to seek the way of perfection. But the way to perfection is found in these small steps on the way of obedience, small steps of charity and love. With steps that seem nothing.[66]

Francis, after giving his prepared text to the nuns, preferred to reflect on a true story about St. Thérèse of Lisieux and her endurance and humility dealing with Sister Pierre, an elderly sister in her religious community who was refusing St. Thérèse's help, saying she should not touch her or help her. It seems like old age had made this nun hard to deal with. But nonetheless, St. Thérèse overcame her hostility and always had a smile on her face, understanding the frailty of sister's old age. St. Thérèse, with her little way of caring, prepared the meal for the elderly nun. This is life in the family, solidarity and help, being your brother's keeper with little acts of kindness—charity in small and big things. Pope Francis concluded his remarks to the contemplative nuns at the Carmel of St. Joseph in Antananarivo with a confession about his spiritual bond with St. Thérèse of Lisieux and her little ways of kindness. St. Thérèse of Lisieux accompanies the Holy Father, now an old man, as he called himself:

> She [St. Thérèse of Lisieux] is a faithful friend. And for that reason, I did not want to talk to you about theories but about a saint. Of what a saint is capable of, of the path of holiness. Go forward and be brave![67]

On September 4, 2016, which coincided with the nineteenth anniversary of her death, Pope Francis, the pope of the slums, canonized the mother of the slums during the Extraordinary Jubilee of Mercy. St. Mother Teresa will forever be remembered as Pope Francis's saint, who was called from the Balkan-Indian periphery to satiate the thirst of Christ and invite the others to do the same. Pope Francis and St. Mother Teresa are people through whom mercy has satiated thirst, turning mercy into love. St. Mother Teresa will be remembered as the small-great Saint of Pope Francis, who never tires of asking for her intercession:

> Saint Mother Teresa, mother of the poor, we ask for your special intercession and help, here in this city where you were born, where you had your home. Here you received the gift of rebirth in the sacraments of Christian initiation. Here you heard the first words of faith in your family and in the community of the faithful. Here you began to see and meet people in need, the poor and the helpless. Here you learned from your parents to love those in greatest need and to help them. Here, in the silence of the church, you heard the call of Jesus to follow him as a religious in the missions.[68]

It is the nature of fallen humanity to separate humankind into central and peripheral. Until all disunity is ended—until we are in heaven—we will see injustice, famine, illness, and suffering. However, the spirituality, life, and intercession of St. Mother Teresa are equalizing forces, encouraging us all to spread the gospel message of mercy and love. If we are faithful to this call, we can, as the saints who inspired St. Mother Teresa herself, bring joyous glints of heaven to earth. By performing small actions of mercy with great love, we can make God's kingdom present, eliminating the disparity between center and periphery and holding up the beauty of Christ through all and in all.

NOTES

PROLOGUE

1. Andrea Riccardi, *Periferie. Crisi e Novità per la Chiesa* (Milan: Jaca Book, 2016), 104.

2. Alver Metalli, *Tierras de América*, September 2, 2016, "Santa Teresa de Calcuta. La religiosa que será canonizada el domingo por el Papa Francisco contada por el postulador Brian Kolodiejchuk, quien llevó adelante la causa hasta su culminación," http://www.tierrasdeamerica.com/2016/09/02/santa-teresa-de-calcuta1-la-religiosa-que-sera-canonizada-el-domingo-por-el-papa-francisco-contada-por-el-postulador-brian-kolodiejchuk-quien-llevo-adelante-la-causa-hasta-su-culminacion.

3. The Republic of Macedonia changed its name to the Republic of North Macedonia on February 12, 2019, ending decades of controversy with neighboring Greece.

4. John XXIII, Allocution of Pope John XXIII Announcing the Roman Synod, Ecumenical Council and Update of the Code of Canon Law, January 25, 1959, http://w2.vatican.va/content/john-xxiii/it/speeches/1959/documents/hf_j-xxiii_spe_19590125_annuncio.html.

5. John Paul II, Homily for the Inauguration of His Pontificate, October 22, 1978, https://w2.vatican.va/content/john-paul-ii/en/homilies/1978/documents/hf_jp-ii_hom_19781022_inizio-pontificato.html.

6. Benedict XVI, General Audience, Wednesday, November 21, 2012, http://w2.vatican.va/content/benedict-xvi/en/audiences/2012/documents/hf_ben-xvi_aud_20121121.html.

7. Elisabeth A. Johnson, "Galilee: A Critical Matrix for Marian Studies," *Theological Studies* 70 (2009): 331.

8. Richard A. Horsley, *Galilee, History, Politics, People* (Harrisburg, PA: Trinity Press International, 1995), 189.

9. Orlando E. Costas, "Christian Mission from the Periphery," *Faith and Mission* 1, no. 1 (Fall 1983): 1.

10. Richard A. Horsley, *Archaeology, History, and Society in Galilee* (Harrisburg, PA: Trinity Press International, 1996), 151.

11. Costas, "Christian Mission," 2.

12. Costas, "Christian Mission," 4.

13. Ernest van Eck, "The Baptism of Jesus in Mark: A Status Transformation Ritual," *Neotestamentica* 30, no. 1 (1996): 196.

14. Costas, "Christian Mission," 7.

15. Riccardi, *Periferie. Crisi e Novità*, 33.

16. Rodney Stark, *The Rise of Christianity* (San Francisco: HarperSanFrancisco, 1997), 47.

17. Marta Sordi, *The Christians and the Roman Empire* (Norman: University of Oklahoma Press, 1986), 6.

18. Charles Pietri, "La Conversion de Rome et la primauté du pape (IV–VIes.)," in *Il Primato del Vescovo di Roma nel Primo Millennio: Ricerche e Testimonianze*, ed. Michele Maccarrone, Atti del Symposium Storico-Teologico, Roma, 9–13 Ottobre 1989 (Vatican City: Libreria Editrice Vaticana, 1991), 219–43.

19. A. M. Sellar, *Bede's Ecclesiastical History of England* (London: George Bell and Sons, 1907), 91.

20. Paul Philibert, "When Not in Rome: Lessons from the Peripheries of the Church," *America*, March 13, 2014, https://www.americamagazine.org/issue/when-not-rome.

21. Philibert, "When Not in Rome."

22. Francesco Russo, *Monachesimo Greco e Cultura in Calabria*, Conferenza tenuta il 16–12–1976, Centro "Studi Sedes Sapientiae" (Reggio Calabria: Edizioni Parallelo 38, 1977), 19.

23. David Paul Hester, *Monasticism and Spirituality of the Italo-Greeks* (Thessalonike: Patriarchikon Hidryma Paterikōn Meletōn, 1992), 123.

24. Jared Wicks, "Yves Congar's Doctrinal Service of the People of God," *Gregorianum* 84, no. 3 (2003): 546.

25. Yves Congar, "Theology in the Council," *American Ecclesiastical Review* 155 (1966): 220.

26. Yves Congar, *True and False Reform in the Church* (Collegeville, MN: Liturgical Press, 2011), 239.

27. Congar, *True and False Reform*, 253.

CHAPTER 1

1. Jennifer Wallace, "A (Hi)story of Illyria," *Greece & Rome* 45, no. 2 (October 1998): 213.

2. "Mother Teresa of Calcutta (1910–1997)," Biography, http://www.vatican.va/news_services/liturgy/saints/ns_lit_doc_20031019_madre teresa_en.html.

3. Gonxhe was Mother Teresa's Albanian name before baptism and taking the religious vows. It means "rosebud-flower."

4. Kathryn Spink, *The Miracle of Love: Mother Teresa of Calcutta, Her Missionaries of Charity, and Her Co-workers* (San Francisco: Harper & Row, 1981), 17–18.

5. David Porter, *Mother Teresa: The Early Years* (Grand Rapids: Eerdmans, 1986), xi.

6. Robert Royal, "Albania: The First Atheist State," *Arlington Catholic Herald* (2000), https://www.catholiceducation.org/en/controversy/persecution/albania-the-first-atheist-state.html.

7. Angelo Comastri, *Madre Teresa, Una Goccia d'Acqua Pulita* (Milan: Paoline Editoriale, 2016), 19.

8. Sebastian Vazhakala, *Life with Mother Teresa: My Thirty-Year Friendship with the Mother of the Poor* (Cincinnati: St. Anthony Messenger Press, 2004), 10.

9. Comastri, *Madre Teresa*, 19.

10. Christopher Peterson and Martin E. P. Seligman, *Character Strengths and Virtues: A Handbook and Classification* (New York: Oxford University Press, 2004), 521.

11. Cristina Siccardi, *Madre Teresa. Tutto Iniziò nella Mia Terra* (Milan, San Paolo Edizioni, 2013), 23.

12. St. Thérèse of Lisieux, *Story of a Soul: The Autobiography of St. Thérèse of Lisieux*, trans. John Clarke (Washington, DC: ICS Publications, 1996), 194.

13. Maria Pandevska, "Periodizacija velikogo vostoč nogo krizisa, 1875–1881," in *Balkanot i Rusija: Ops 'toto i specific 'noto vo istoriskiot i kulturniot razvitok (prilozi od zaednic 'kiot proekt pomegju Institutot za nacionalna istorija I Institutot za slavistika pri RAN)*, ed. Todor Cepreganov and Elena Guskova (Skopje: Institut za nacionalna istorija, 2010), 23–34.

14. The Congress of Berlin in 1878 declared Serbia, Montenegro, and Romania independent kingdoms. It also sanctioned establishment of an autonomous Bulgarian principality, which in 1885 annexed Eastern

Rumelia and in 1908 declared its complete independence and received recognition as a kingdom. For more, see Andrew Rossos, *Macedonia and the Macedonians: A History* (Stanford, CA: Hoover Press, 2008), 60.

15. Robert Austin, "Greater Albania: The Albanian State and the Question of Kosovë, 1912–2001," in *Ideologies and National Identities: The Case of Twentieth-Century Southeastern Europe*, ed. John Lampe and Mark Mazower (Budapest: Central European University Press, 2004), 237.

16. Austin, "Greater Albania," 237.

17. "Mémoire über Albanien (Ende 1901 bis Anfang 1905)," 1; Kral to Calice, Monastir, 18 July 1902, HHStA, Ges. Arch. Konstantinopel, Fasz. 422 cited in Stavro Skendi, *The Albanian National Awakening* (Princeton, NJ: Princeton University Press, 1967), 144.

18. Thoma Murzaku, *Kur u Caktuan Kufijtë e Shqipërisë (1912–1914)* (Tirana: Akademia e Shkencave të Shqipërisë, 2017), 21–22.

19. Leon Trotsky, *The Balkan Wars, 1912–13: The War Correspondence of Leon Trotsky* (New York: Monad Press, 1980), 268.

20. Trotsky, *The Balkan Wars*, 268.

21. Rossos, *Macedonia and the Macedonians*, 130.

22. Robert Elsie, *Historical Dictionary of Kosova* (Lanham, MD: Scarecrow Press, 2004), xxii.

23. Skender Asani, *Shkupi Ndërmjet Dy Luftërave Botërore*, Pjesa 1 (Skopje: Logos-A, 2015), 16.

24. Isa Blumi and Yavuz M. Hakan Yavuz, *War and Nationalism: The Balkan Wars, 1912–1913, and Their Sociopolitical Implications* (Salt Lake City: University of Utah Press, 2013), 44.

25. Brian Kolodiejchuk, ed., *Mother Teresa: Come Be My Light* (New York: Image, 2007), 15.

26. Vilma Antoni Bejtullahu, interview with author, October 22, 2017. Vilma Antoni Bejtullahu (1940) was a cousin to Mother Teresa, daughter of Lorenc Antoni, whose grandmother Maria was sister to Mother Teresa's father, Nikollë Bojaxhiu. Lorenc Antoni, Mother Teresa's cousin, was the same age as Mother Teresa.

27. Dante Alighieri, *The Divine Comedy of Dante Alighieri. The Italian Text with a Translation in English Blank Verse and a Commentary by Courtney Langdon*, vol. 3, *Paradiso* (Cambridge, MA: Harvard University Press, 1921), 269.

28. Navin Chawla, *Mother Teresa* (Rockport, MA: Element, 1996), 2.

29. Thérèse of Lisieux, *Story of a Soul: The Autobiography of St. Thérèse of Lisieux* (New York: Cosimo Classics, 2007), 67.

30. Vazhakala, *Life with Mother Teresa*, 10.

31. Skender Asani, Albert Ramaj, and Natasha Didenko, *Familjet Katolike Shqiptare në Shkup, Dokumente, Fotografi dhe Dëshmi* (Catholic Albanian Families in Skopje) (Skopje: Instituti I Trashëgimië Shpirtërore E Kulturore Të Shqiptarëve & Acta Non Verba, 2018), 89. A photocopy of the original certificate of baptism of Mother Teresa, ibid. 297. The document was released on August 11, 1928, from the parish and is signed by Fr. Anton Buković, a Catholic priest from Croatia who was serving in the Sacred Heart Cathedral of Skopje.

32. Albanisches Institut, St. Gallen, http://albanisches-institut.ch.

33. William Shakespeare, *Romeo and Juliet*, act 2, scene 2.

34. Mother Teresa, *Constitutions of the Missionaries of Charity* (Calcutta: Missionaries of Charity, 1988), 14–15.

35. Kathryn Spink, *Mother Teresa: A Complete Authorized Biography* (San Francisco: HarperSanFrancisco, 1997), xii.

36. Ali Caka and Nebi Caka, "Prejardhja dhe Shprëndarja Rajonale e Mbiemrave të Shqiptarëve të Kosovës," in *Studime Shoqërore* (Pristina: Akademia e Shkencave dhe e Arteve e Kosovës, 2008), 344.

37. Caka and Caka, "Prejardhja dhe Shprëndarja Rajonale," 322.

38. Porter, *Mother Teresa: The Early Years*, 5.

39. Caka and Caka, "Prejardhja dhe Shprëndarja Rajonale," 322.

40. Lush Gjergji, *Madre Teresa. La Madre della Carita* (Bologna: Editrice Velar, 1990), 35.

41. Zija Shkodra, *Qyteti Shqiptar gjatë Rilindjes Kombëtare* (Tirana: Akademia e Shkencave, Instituti I Historisë, 1984), 249–50.

42. Vilma Antoni Bejtullahu, interview with author, October 22, 2017.

43. Lush Gjergji, "Pesë Vizitat e Shën Nënë Terezës në Kosovë," *Drita e Përmuajshme Fetare-Kulturore e Kishës Katolike*, http://www.drita.info/2017/01/05/pese-vizitat-e-shen-nene-terezes-ne-kosove-2/.

44. Comastri, *Madre Teresa*, 13.

45. Comastri, *Madre Teresa*, 13.

46. Comastri, *Madre Teresa*, 335.

47. Josepha Hiromi Kudo, *Mother Teresa: A Saint from Skopje* (Gujarat, India: Gujarat Sahitya Prakash, 2006), 45.

48. Vilma Antoni Bejtullahu, interview with author, October 22, 2017.

49. Asani, Ramaj, and Didenko, *Familjet Katolike Shqiptare në Shkup*, 339.

50. *Kanuni i Lekë Dukagjinit/The Code of Lekë Dukagjini.* Albanian Text Collected and Arranged by Shtjefën Gjeçovi. Translated, with an introduction by Leonard Fox (New York: Gjonlekaj Publishing, 1989), 26.

51. Asani, Ramaj, and Didenko, *Familjet Katolike Shqiptare në Shkup*, 360.

52. Asani, Ramaj, and Didenko, *Familjet Katolike Shqiptare në Shkup*, 336.

53. Chawla, *Mother Teresa*, 1; Spink, *Mother Teresa: A Complete Authorized Biography*, 4.

54. Eileen Egan, *Such a Vision of the Street: Mother Teresa—the Spirit and the Work* (New York: Doubleday, 1985), 7.

55. Brian Kolodiejchuk, ed., *Mother Teresa: Come Be My Light; The Private Writings of the Saint of Calcutta* (New York: Image, 2007), 29.

56. Mother Teresa, *In My Own Words* (Liguori, MO: Liguori Publications, 1997).

57. Lush Gjergji, *Mother Teresa: Her Life, Her Works* (Hyde Park, NY: New City Press, 1991), 14.

58. Gjergji, *Mother Teresa*, 14.

59. Mother Teresa, *Constitutions of the Missionaries of Charity*, 65–66.

60. Vazhakala, *Life with Mother Teresa*, 9.

61. Vilma Antoni Bejtullahu, interview with author, October 22, 2017.

62. Vazhakala, *Life with Mother Teresa*, 7.

63. Vilma Antoni Bejtullahu, interview with author, October 22, 2017.

64. Siccardi, *Madre Teresa*, 41.

65. John Paul II, Apostolic Exhortation *Familiaris Consortio*, no. 42, http://w2.vatican.va/content/john-paul-ii/en/apost_exhortations/documents/hf_jp-ii_exh_19811122_familiaris-consortio.html.

66. Spink, *Mother Teresa: A Complete Authorized Biography*, 3.

67. Gjergji, *Mother Teresa: Her Life, Her Works*, 12.

68. Most probably it was the Feast of St. Catherine of Alexandria, or St. Catherine of the Wheel, a saint celebrated both in the East and the West. Her feast day is celebrated in the Roman Catholic Church on November 25.

69. Vilma Antoni Bejtullahu, interview with author, October 22, 2017.

70. Gjergji, *Mother Teresa: Her Life, Her Works*, 12.

71. Gjergji, *Mother Teresa: Her Life, Her Works*, 15.
72. Brian Kolodiejchuk, ed., *Mother Teresa: A Call to Mercy; Hearts to Love, Hands to Serve* (New York: Image, 2016), 3–4.
73. *Kanuni i Lekë Dukagjinit/The Code of Lekë Dukagjini*, 132.
74. Kolodiejchuk, *Mother Teresa: Come Be My Light*, 31.
75. Vilma Antoni Bejtullahu, interview with author, October 22, 2017.
76. Gjergji, *Mother Teresa: Her Life, Her Works*, 13.
77. Saverio Gaeta, *Madre Teresa, Il Segreto della Santità* (Milan: San Paolo, 2016), 8.
78. Most recent research excludes poisoning and other speculation. "Nikollë died of natural causes," Asani, et al., *Familjet Katolike*, 336.
79. Gaeta, *Madre Teresa*, 8.
80. Kolodiejchuk ed., *Mother Teresa: A Call to Mercy*, 219.
81. Mother Teresa, *In My Own Words*.
82. Porter, *Mother Teresa: The Early Years*, 10.
83. Gjergji, *Mother Teresa: Her Life, Her Works*, 13.
84. Comastri, *Madre Teresa*, 15.
85. Kolodiejchuk, ed., *Mother Teresa: A Call to Mercy*, 204.
86. Mother Teresa, *In My Own Words*.
87. Thérèse of Lisieux, *Simply Surrender* (Notre Dame, IN: Ave Maria, 2008), 95.
88. Gjergji, *Mother Teresa: Her Life, Her Works*, 16.
89. Gjergji, *Mother Teresa: Her Life, Her Works*, 15.
90. Comastri, *Madre Teresa*, 23.

CHAPTER 2

1. Saverio Gaeta, *Madre Teresa, Il Segreto della Santità* (Milan: San Paolo, 2016), 11.
2. Frok Zefi, Župa Letnica, and Zajednica Kosovskih Hrvata, *Letnica*, http://zkhletnica.com/monografija/.
3. Sebastian Vazhakala, *Life with Mother Teresa: My Thirty-Year Friendship with the Mother of the Poor* (Cincinnati: St. Anthony Messenger Press, 2004), 73.
4. Mother Teresa, *Constitutions of the Missionaries of Charity* (Calcutta: Missionaries of Charity, 1988), 7.

5. Eileen Egan, *Such a Vision of the Street: Mother Teresa—the Spirit and the Work* (New York: Doubleday, 1985), 15.

6. *Kanuni i Lekë Dukagjinit/The Code of Lekë Dukagjini*, 46.

7. Vazhakala, *Life with Mother Teresa*, 9.

8. Lufti Alia, *Agnes Gonxhe Bojaxhiu: Nënë Tereza* (Tirana: Erik, 2015), 23.

9. Bill Hamilton, "Mother Teresa Speaks," *BBC Breakfast News*, https://www.youtube.com/watch?v=xrppvaHZjXs.

10. Brian Kolodiejchuk, ed., *Come Be My Light* (New York: Image, 2007), 351.

11. BBC News, February 11, 2019, "The Albanian Bunkers Built in the Midst of the Cold War," https://www.bbc.com/news/in-pictures -47157127.

12. "Letër e Nënë Terezës e Shkruar në Gjuhën Shqipe," *Drita e Përmuajshme Fetare-Kulturore e Kishës Katolike*, http://www.drita.info/2017/ 09/28/leter-e-nene-terezes-e-shkruar-ne-gjuhen-shqipe.

13. "Letër e Nënë Terezës e Shkruar në Gjuhën Shqipe."

14. Afrim Krasniqi, "Nderim apo Pushim për Nënë Terezën?" *Dita*, October 19, 2015, http://www.gazetadita.al/nderim-apo-pushim-per -nene-terezen/.

15. Angelo Comastri, *Madre Teresa Una Goccia D'Acqua Pulita* (Milan: Paoline Editoriale, 2016), 18.

16. Prof. Inis Kraja, interview with author, April 24, 2017.

17. Kolodiejchuk, *Come Be My Light*, 312.

18. Albino Luciani (John Paul I), *Illustrissimi: Lettere ai Grandi del Passato (I doni della Chiesa)*, Associazione Amici del Papa.

19. Mother Teresa, *In My Own Words* (Liguori, MO: Liguori Publications, 1996).

20. Mother Teresa, *Constitutions of the Missionaries of Charity*, 28–29.

21. Kolodiejchuk, *Come Be My Light*, 48.

22. Angelo Devananda Scolozzi, *Una Chiamata nella Chiamata. Testimonianza dei Miei Ventun Anni di Vita Accanto a Madre Teresa di Calcutta* (Vatican City: Libreria Editrice Vaticana, 2014), 129. These are never-before published diaries of Mother Teresa written between 1948 and 1949.

23. Cardinal Joseph Ratzinger, Homily, St. Peter's Basilica, April 18, 2005, http://www.vatican.va/gpII/documents/homily-pro-eligendo -pontifice_20050418_en.html.

24. Christopher Hitchens, "Mommie Dearest: The Pope Beatifies Mother Teresa, a Fanatic, a Fundamentalist, and a Fraud," *Slate*, October 20, 2003, https://slate.com/news-and-politics/2003/10/the-fanatic-fraudulent-mother-teresa.html.

25. Kolodiejchuk, *Come Be My Light*, 232.

26. Scolozzi, *Una Chiamata nella Chiamata*, 79.

27. Kolodiejchuk, *Come Be My Light*, 293.

28. Benedict XVI, Encyclical Letter *Caritas in Veritate*, June 29, 2009, http://w2.vatican.va/content/benedict-xvi/en/encyclicals/documents/hf_ben-xvi_enc_20090629_caritas-in-veritate.html.

29. *Caritas in Veritate*, no. 7.

30. Mother Teresa, *In My Own Words*.

31. Kolodiejchuk, *Come Be My Light*, 286.

32. Pope Francis, Address to the Episcopal Conference of Switzerland on Their *Ad Limina* Visit, December 1, 2014, http://w2.vatican.va/content/francesco/en/speeches/2014/december/documents/papa-francesco_20141201_ad-limina-svizzera.html.

33. Malcolm Muggeridge, *Something Beautiful for God: Mother Teresa of Calcutta* (New York: Harper & Row, 1971), 83.

CHAPTER 3

1. Brian Kolodiejchuk, ed., *Come Be My Light* (New York: Image, 2007), 15.

2. Central Intelligence Agency, *The World Factbook*, https://www.cia.gov/library/publications/the-world-factbook/geos/in.html.

3. Ministry of Culture, *Anthropological Survey of India*, https://ansi.gov.in.

4. Rabindranath Tagore, *My Reminiscences* (New York: Macmillan, 1917), 91.

5. Brian Kolodiejchuk, ed., *Mother Teresa: A Call to Mercy; Hearts to Love, Hands to Serve* (New York: Image, 2016), 6

6. Kolodiejchuk, *Come Be My Light*, 14–15.

7. Skender Asani, Albert Ramaj, and Natasha Didenko, *Familjet Katolike Shqiptare në Shkup, Dokumente, Fotografi dhe Dëshmi* (Catholic Albanian Families in Skopje) (Skopje: Instituti I Trashëgimië Shpirtërore E Kulturore Të Shqiptarëve & Acta Non Verba, 2018), 341.

8. Asani, Ramaj, and Didenko, *Familjet Katolike*, 341.

9. *Kanuni i Lekë Dukagjinit/ The Code of Lekë Dukagjini*. Albanian Text Collected and Arranged by Shtjefën Gjeçovi. Translated, with an Introduction by Leonard Fox (New York: Gjonlekaj Publishing, 1989), 37.

10. Mike Barrett, "Searching for Radical Faith," *Christianity Today*, February 27, 2009, https://www.christianitytoday.com/ct/2009/february/30.36.html.

11. A Carmelite Nun, *John Paul I: The Smiling Pope* (Flemington, NJ: St. Teresa's Press, 1985), 31.

12. See the decree *Ad Gentes*, On the Mission Activity of the Church, chap. 1, no. 9, http://www.vatican.va/archive/hist_councils/ii_vatican_council/documents/vat-ii_decree_19651207_ad-gentes_en.html.

13. *Zani I Zojës Cernagore*, 1962, Vjeti I, No. 2, 15. All biographers of Mother Teresa identify Betika Kajnc, a Slovenian national, as a companion of Mother Teresa to the far-off India. See also *Blagovijest*, November–December 1932, which confirms Nasta Mëhilli as missionary and journey companion to India of Mother Teresa.

14. Asani, Ramaj, and Didenko, *Familjet Katolike*, 292.

15. Asani, Ramaj, and Didenko, *Familjet Katolike*, 292.

16. Lush Gjergji, *Madre Teresa. La Madre della Carita* (Bologna: Editrice Velar, 1990), 69.

17. Kolodiejchuk, *Come Be My Light*, 13.

18. Kathryn Spink, *The Miracle of Love: Mother Teresa of Calcutta, Her Missionaries of Charity, and her Co-workers* (San Francisco: Harper & Row, 1981), 17–18.

19. Asani, Ramaj, and Didenko, *Familjet Katolike Shqiptare në Shkup*, 286.

20. Asani, Ramaj, and Didenko, *Familjet Katolike Shqiptare në Shkup*, 314.

21. Benedict XV, Apostolic Letter *Maximum Illud*, November 30, 1919, https://w2.vatican.va/content/benedict-xv/it/apost_letters/documents/hf_ben-xv_apl_19191130_maximum-illud.html.

22. Benedict XV, *Maximum Illud*.

23. Saverio Gaeta, *Madre Teresa. Il Segreto della Santità* (Milan: Edizioni San Paolo, 2016), 23.

24. Kathleen Kudlinski, *Mother Teresa Friend of the Poor* (New York: Simon & Schuster, 2006), 67.

25. Julian S. Das, "Mother Teresa and the Jesuits," *Jivan—News and Views of Jesuits in India* (April 2016): 7.

26. William D Dinges, "'An Army of Youth': The Sodality Movement and the Practice of Apostolic Mission," *U.S. Catholic Historian* 19, no. 3, Popular Piety and Material Culture: Art, Film, and Liturgical Experience (Summer 2001): 36.

27. *Manual of the Sodality* (New York: Apostleship of Prayer, 1897), chap. 6, https://archive.org/stream/manualofthesodal00unknuoft/manualofthcsodal00unknuoft_djvu.txt.

28. Gjergji, *Madre Teresa*, 58–59.

29. Charles J. Borges, "India," in *The Blackwell Companion to Catholicism*, ed. James J. Buckley, Frederick Christian Bauerschmidt, and Trent Pomplun (Malden, MA: Wiley-Blackwell Publishing, 2007), 115.

30. Ines A. Murzaku, *Catholicism, Culture, Conversion: The History of the Jesuits in Albania (1841–1946)* (Rome: Orientalia Christiana Analecta, 277), 209.

31. Murzaku, *Catholicism, Culture, Conversion*, 217.

32. Asani, Ramaj, and Didenko, *Familjet Katolike*, 286.

33. Sister Teresa to *Blagovijest* (November 1932): 118.

34. John Padberg, ed., *The Constitutions of the Society of Jesus and Their Complementary Norms: A Complete English Translation of the Official Latin Texts* (St. Louis: Institute of Jesuit Sources, 1996), 3.

35. Laurence Lux-Sterritt, "Mary Ward and Her Female Society of Jesus in Counter-Reformation England," *Revue de l'histoire des Religions* 225 (2008): 7.

36. Gill K. Goulding, *A Church of Passion and Hope: The Formation of An Ecclesial Disposition from Ignatius Loyola to Pope Francis and the New Evangelization* (London: Bloomsbury, 2016), 151.

37. Pius XII to the World Congress of the Lay Apostolate, October 14, 1951, http://w2.vatican.va/content/pius-xii/fr/speeches/1951/documents/hf_p-xii_spe_19511014_apostolato-laici.html.

38. John Scally, "Mother Teresa, Who Becomes a Saint on Sunday, Began Her Life as a Nun in Dublin," *Irish Times*, September 2, 2016, https://www.irishtimes.com/opinion/mother-teresa-who-becomes-a-saint-on-sunday-began-her-life-as-a-nun-in-dublin-1.2777022.

39. Mother Teresa, interview by Nodlaig McCarthy, September 15, 1974, https://www.rte.ie/archives/2014/0915/643814-mother-teresa-remembers-time-in-rathfarnham/.

40. Raghu Rai and Navin Chawla, *Faith and Compassion: The Life and Work of Mother Teresa* (Shaftesbury, Dorset: Element Books, 1996), 26.

41. John Scally, *Mother Teresa: The Irish Connection* (Dublin: Poolbeg Books, 2010), 41.

42. Scally, *Mother Teresa*, 41.

43. Christine Burke, "Loreto Sisters Are Proud of Mother Teresa," https://www.loreto.org.au/loreto-sisters-proud-mother-teresa/.

44. Kolodiejchuk, *Come Be My Light*, 15

45. Pius XI, Homily at the Canonization Mass in Honor of St. Therese of the Child Jesus, May 17, 1925, https://w2.vatican.va/content/pius-xi/it/homilies/documents/hf_p-xi_hom_19250517_benedictus-deus.html. Available in English at https://www.ewtn.com/therese/readings/readng2.htm.

46. Second Vatican Council, Dogmatic Constitution on the Church *Lumen Gentium*, no. 17, http://www.vatican.va/archive/hist_councils/ii_vatican_council/documents/vat-ii_const_19641121_lumen-gentium_en.html.

47. Thérèse of Lisieux, *Story of a Soul: The Autobiography of St. Thérèse of Lisieux*, trans. John Clarke (Washington, DC: ICS Publications, 1996), 99.

48. Thérèse of Lisieux, *Story of a Soul*, 99.

49. Francis Broome, ed., *The Little Way for Every Day: Thoughts from Thérèse of Lisieux* (Mahwah, NJ: Paulist Press, 2014), 18.

50. Gjergji, *Madre Teresa*, 85.

51. Kolodiejchuk, *Come Be My Light*, 16.

52. St. Thérèse Lisieux, *Poems of St. Thérèse Lisieux*, trans. Alan Bancroft (London: HarperCollins, 1996), 98.

53. St. Bonaventure, *The Life of Christ*, trans. and ed. W. H. Hutchings (London: Rivingtons, 1888), 17.

54. Kolodiejchuk, *Come Be My Light*, 16–17.

55. Gjergji, *Madre Teresa*, 84–85.

56. Mark Twain, *Following the Equator: A Journey Around the World*, vol. 2 (New York: Harper), 231.

57. Twain, *Following the Equator*, 26.

58. Gjergji, *Madre Teresa*, 85.

59. Gjergji, *Madre Teresa*, 85.

60. Gaeta, *Madre Teresa*, 25.

61. Kolodiejchuk, *Come Be My Light*, 17.

62. Tagore, *My Reminiscences*, 91.

63. D. R. SarDesai, *India: The Definitive History* (Boulder, CO: Westview Press, 2008), 253.

64. SarDesai, *India*, 257.

65. Barbara D. Metcalf and Thomas R. Metcalf, *A Concise History of Modern India* (New York: Cambridge University Press, 2006), 169.

66. E. C. Dozey, *A Concise History of the Darjeeling District since 1835* (Calcutta: Art Press, 1922), 108.

67. Dozey, *Concise History of the Darjeeling District*, 37.

68. Jeff Kochler, *Darjeeling: The Colorful History and Precarious Fate of the World's Greatest Tea* (New York: Bloomsbury, 2015), 15.

69. Gaeta, *Madre Teresa*, 27.

70. Gjergji, *Madre Teresa*, 89.

71. N. Sundararajan, *Walking with Angels: Mother Teresa Florence Nightingale* (Chennai: Sura Books, 2004), 7.

72. Kolodiejchuk, *Come Be My Light*, 364n11.

73. *Saint Teresa of Calcutta: Memories of Her Years with Loreto (1928–1948)*, 4, accessed June 15, 2020, http://loreto.org.au/wp-content/uploads/2016/09/Mother-Teresa-Booklet.pdf.

74. Amy Ruth, *Mother Teresa* (Minneapolis: Learner Publications, 1999), 43.

75. *Saint Teresa of Calcutta: Memories of Her Years with Loreto (1928–1948)*, 4.

76. Ruth, *Mother Teresa*, 43.

77. Elaine McDonald, "From Mary Ward (1585–1645) to Michael (Frances) Corcoran (1846–1927): The Educational Legacy of the Loreto Order" (PhD diss., Dublin City University, 2008), 181.

78. Rai Chawla, *Faith and Compassion*, 27.

79. Kolodiejchuk, *Come Be My Light*, 19.

80. Kolodiejchuk, *Come Be My Light*, 19.

81. Cardinal Joseph Ratzinger, Homily on the Fourth Centenary of the Birth of Mary Ward, January 23, 1985, http://www.congregatiojesu.org/uploadspdf/en/Cardinal_Josef_Ratzinger_1985.pdf.

82. *Life of Mary Ward Foundress of the Institute of the B.V.M.* (London: Burns and Oates, 1909), 114.

83. *Life of Mary Ward Foundress of the Institute of the B.V.M.*, 57.

84. Kerry Walters, *St. Teresa of Calcutta: Missionary, Mother, Mystic* (Cincinnati: Franciscan Media, 2016), 16.

85. Ratzinger, Homily on the Fourth Centenary of the Birth of Mary Ward.

86. Kolodiejchuk, *Come Be My Light*, 20.

87. Mary Catharine Elizabeth Chambers, *The Life of Mary Ward (1585–1645)* (London: Burns and Oates, 1882), 403.

88. Kolodiejchuk, *Come Be My Light*, 20.

89. Kolodiejchuk, *Come Be My Light*, 25.

90. SarDesai, *India*, 304.

91. Gaeta, *Madre Teresa*, 33.

92. Metcalf and Metcalf, *Concise History of Modern India*, 209.

93. Kolodiejchuk, *Come Be My Light*, 28.

94. Egan, *Such a Vision of the Streets*, 24.

95. Egan, *Such a Vision of the Streets*, 24.

96. Rai and Chawla, *Faith and Compassion*, 29.

97. Kolodiejchuk, *Come Be My Light*, 39–40.

98. St. Augustine, *De diversis quaestionibus octoginta tribus*, 64, 4: PL 40, 56.

CHAPTER 4

1. Mother Teresa to Father Picachy, August 7, 1960. In Brian Kolodiejchuk, ed., *Come Be My Light* (New York: Image, 2007), 200.

2. "Mother Teresa Book Won't Halt Sainthood," *Chicago Tribune*, August 27, 2007, https://www.chicagotribune.com/news/ct-xpm-2007-08-27-0708260354-story.html?int=lat_digitaladshouse_bx-modal_acquisition-subscriber_ngux_display-ad-interstitial_bx-bonus-story____.

3. Geneviève Chénard, "Mother Teresa Doesn't Deserve Sainthood," *New York Times*, March 25, 2016, https://www.nytimes.com/roomfordebate/2016/03/25/should-mother-teresa-be-canonized/mother-teresa-doesnt-deserve-sainthood.

4. Serge Larivée, Carole Sénéchal, and Geneviève Chénard, "Les côtés ténébreux de Mère Teresa," *Studies in Religion/Sciences Religieuses* 42, no. 3 (2013): 337.

5. Larivée, Sénéchal, and Chénard, "Les côtés ténébreux de Mère Teresa," 335.

6. Christopher Hitchens, "Hitchens Takes on Mother Teresa," *Newsweek*, August 8, 2007, https://www.newsweek.com/hitchens-takes-mother-teresa-99721.

7. Hitchens, "Hitchens Takes on Mother Teresa."

8. Alfred Lord Tennyson, "From 'The Ancient Sage,'" *The Oxford Book of English Mystical Verse*, ed. D. H. S. Nicholson and A.H. E. Lee (Oxford: Clarendon Press, 1917), 168.

9. Eugene R. August, "Tennyson and Teilhard: The Faith of 'In Memoriam,'" *PMLA* 84, no. 2 (1969): 222.

10. Joseph Cardinal Ratzinger, *Introduction to Christianity* (San Francisco: Ignatius Press, 1990), 48.

11. Ratzinger, *Introduction to Christianity*, 48.

12. Paul Tillich, *Ultimate Concern: Tillich in Dialogue*, ed. D. Mackenzie Brown (New York: Harper and Row, 1965), 191.

13. John Paul II, "Master in the Faith," Apostolic Letter of His Holiness John Paul II to the Very Reverend Father Felipe Sainz De Baranda Superior General of the Order of the Discalced Brothers of the Blessed Virgin Mary of Mount Carmel on the Occasion of the IV Centenary of the Death of Saint John of the Cross, Doctor of the Church, https://www.ewtn.com/catholicism/library/master-in-the-faith-8924.

14. Homily of His Holiness John Paul II for the Inauguration of His Pontificate, October 22, 1978, http://w2.vatican.va/content/john-paul-ii/en/homilies/1978/documents/hf_jp-ii_hom_19781022_inizio-pontificato.html.

15. George Weigel, *Witness to Hope: The Biography of Pope John Paul II* (New York: Harper Collins, 1999), 86.

16. John Paul II, "Master in the Faith."

17. Weigel, *Witness to Hope*, 86.

18. John Paul II, "Master in the Faith."

19. Pope Francis, General Audience November 23, 2016, https://w2.vatican.va/content/francesco/en/audiences/2016/documents/papa-francesco_20161123_udienza-generale.html.

20. Brian Kolodiejchuk, ed., *Come Be My Light* (New York: Image, 2007), 39–40.

21. Lush Gjergji, *Madre Teresa. La Madre della Carita* (Bologna: Editrice Velar, 1990), 128–29.

22. Kolodiejchuk, *Come Be My Light*, 44.

23. Kolodiejchuk, *Come Be My Light*, 47.

24. Kolodiejchuk, *Come Be My Light*, 48.

25. Greg Watts, *Mother Teresa: Faith in the Darkness* (London: Oxford Hudson, 2009), 32.

26. Kolodiejchuk, *Come Be My Light*, 48.

27. Pope Pius XII, *Evangelii Praecones*, Encyclical on Promotion of Catholic Missions, June 2, 1951, http://w2.vatican.va/content/pius-xii/en/encyclicals/documents/hf_p-xii_enc_02061951_evangelii-praecones.html.

28. Kolodiejchuk, *Come Be My Light*, 122.

29. Kolodiejchuk, *Come Be My Light*, 54.

30. Kolodiejchuk, *Come Be My Light*, 72.

31. Kolodiejchuk, *Come Be My Light*, 210.

32. Robert M. Garrity, *Mother Teresa's Mysticism: A Christo-Ecclesio-Humano-centric Mysticism* (Hobe Sound, FL: Lectio Publishing, 2017), 31.

33. Barbara Brown Taylor, *Learning to Walk in the Dark* (New York: Harper Collins, 2014), 4.

34. Kolodiejchuk, *Come Be My Light*, 131.

35. Kolodiejchuk, *Come Be My Light*, 154.

36. Taylor Patrick O'Neill, "The Dark Night of Mother Teresa, The Three Ages of the Spiritual Life, and the Witness of the Mystics," in *Mother Teresa and the Mystics: Toward a Renewal of Spiritual Theology*, ed. Michael Dauphinais, Brian Kolodiejchuk, Roger W. Nutt (Ave Maria, FL: Sapientia Press, 2018), 188.

37. Kolodiejchuk, *Come Be My Light*, 158.

38. Kolodiejchuk, *Come Be My Light*, 164.

39. Weigel, *Witness to Hope*, 86.

40. St. Jerome, *Epist.* 108, 31 CSEL 55, 349.

41. St. Augustine, "Sermo de martyribus," *Revue Bénédictine* 51 (1939): 19.

42. Kolodiejchuk, *Come Be My Light*, 164.

43. Kolodiejchuk, *Come Be My Light*, 214.

44. Kolodiejchuk, *Come Be My Light*, 214.

45. Scolozzi, *Una Chiamata nella Chiamata*, 88.

46. Kolodiejchuk, *Come Be My Light*, 214.

47. Scolozzi, *Una Chiamata nella Chiamata*, 88.

48. O'Neill, "The Dark Night of Mother Teresa, 188–90.

49. O'Neill, "The Dark Night of Mother Teresa," 190.

50. Garrity, *Mother Teresa's Mysticism*, 71.

51. Michael Gorman, *Inhabiting the Cruciform God: Kenosis, Justification, and Theosis in Paul's Narrative Soteriology* (Grand Rapids: Eerdmans, 2009), 123.

52. Kolodiejchuk, *Come Be My Light*, 215–16.

53. Kolodiejchuk, *Come Be My Light*, 82.

54. Celia Kourie, "The Way of the Mystic: The Sanjuanist Stages of the Spiritual Path," *Theological Studies* 72, no. 4 (2016): 9.

55. O'Neill, "The Dark Night of Mother Teresa," 191.

56. Angelo Comastri, *Madre Teresa Una Goccia D'Acqua Pulita* (Milan: Paoline Editoriale, 2016), 64.

57. Cristina Siccardi, *Madre Teresa. Tutto Iniziò nella mia Terra* (Milan: Edizioni San Paolo, 2009), 260.

58. Kolodiejchuk, *Come Be My Light*, 177.

59. Garrity, *Mother Teresa's Mysticism*, 65.

60. Reginald Garrigou-Lagrange, *The Three Ages of Interior Life: Prelude of Eternal Life*, vol. 2 (St. Louis: Herder Book Co., 1948), 507.

61. Martin Bialas, *The Mysticism of the Passion in St. Paul of the Cross: An Investigation of Passioncentrism in the Spiritual Doctrine of the Founder of the Passionist Congregation* (San Francisco: Ignatius Press, 1990), 194n163.

62. Kolodiejchuk, *Come Be My Light*, 251.

63. Elizabeth of the Trinity, *I Have Found God: The Complete Works, Letters from Carmel*, vol. 2 (Washington, DC: ICS Publications, 2014), 105.

64. Kolodiejchuk, *Come Be My Light*, 98.

65. Scolozzi, *Una Chiamata nella Chiamata*, 89.

66. Scolozzi, *Una Chiamata nella Chiamata*, 89.

67. Benedict XVI, Homily, Apostolic Journey to France, September 15, 2008, https://w2.vatican.va/content/benedict-xvi/en/homilies/2008/documents/hf_ben-xvi_hom_20080915_lourdes-malati.html.

68. Benedict XVI, Homily, Apostolic Journey to France, September 15, 2008.

69. Kolodiejchuk, *Come Be My Light*, 222.

70. Benedict XVI, Homily, Apostolic Journey to France, September 15, 2008.

71. Pope Francis, Apostolic Exhortation *Gaudete et Exsultate*, March 19, 2019, http://w2.vatican.va/content/francesco/en/apost_exhortations/documents/papa-francesco_esortazione-ap_20180319_gaudete-et-exsultate.html#_ftnref101.

72. Kolodiejchuk, *Come Be My Light*, 236.

73. Paul Ekman and Wallace Friesen, "Felt, False, and Miserable Smiles," *Journal of Nonverbal Behavior* 6, no. 4 (Summer 1982): 245.

74. "Mother Teresa Gives Her First TV Interview in Ten Years," May 1993, minute 3:01, https://www.youtube.com/watch?v=xrppvaHZjXs.

75. Diane Mapes, "How to Spot a Fake Smile: It's All in the Eyes," *NBC News*, March 30, 2011, https://www.nbcnews.com/healthmain/how-spot-fake-smile-its-all-eyes-1C9386917.

76. Comastri, *Madre Teresa*, 49.

77. Comastri, *Madre Teresa*, 49.

78. Phyllis Zagano and C. Kevin Gillespie, "Embracing Darkness: A Theological and Psychological Case Study of Mother Teresa," *Spiritus: A Journal of Christian Spirituality* 10, no. 1 (Spring 2010): 71.

79. Elizabeth of the Trinity, *I Have Found God*, 105.

80. Scolozzi, *Una Chiamata nella Chiamata*, 28.

81. Kolodiejchuk, *Come Be My Light*, 139.

82. Mother Teresa, *In My Own Words* (Liguori, MO: Liguori Publications, 1996).

83. George W. Rutler, "Humility and the Host," *First Things*, March 1, 2018, https://www.firstthings.com/web-exclusives/2018/03/humility-and-the-host.

84. Vatican Council II, Pastoral Constitution on the Church in the Modern World *Gaudium et Spes*, December 7, 1965, http://www.vatican.va/archive/hist_councils/ii_vatican_council/documents/vat-ii_const_19651207_gaudium-et-spes_en.html.

CHAPTER 5

1. Mother Teresa, Nobel Peace Prize Acceptance Speech, December 10, 1979, https://www.nobelprize.org/prizes/peace/1979/teresa/26200-mother-teresa-acceptance-speech-1979/.

2. Mother Teresa, Nobel Peace Prize Acceptance Speech.

3. Valentino Salvoldi, *Madre Teresa, Emblema di Pace* (Gorle: Editrice Velar, 2014), Kindle loc. 194–195.

4. Mother Teresa, *A Call to Mercy: Hearts to Love, Hands to Serve*, ed. Brian Kolodiejchuk (New York: Crown, 2016).

5. Brian Kolodiejchuk, ed., *Come Be My Light* (New York: Image, 2007), 50.

6. *Rule of St. Benedict*, Chapter 33, http://archive.osb.org/rb/text/rbemjo1.html#33.

7. *Rule of St. Francis*, Chapter 1, https://ofm.org/wp-content/uploads/2017/05/The_Rule.pdf.

8. Francis of Assisi, *The Little Flowers of Saint Francis* (Mineola, NY: Dover, 2003), 148.

9. *Rule of St. Francis*, Chapter 6.

10. Francis of Assisi, *The Little Flowers of Saint Francis*, 85.

11. Charlotte Radler, "Detachment in Meister Eckhart and Its Significance for Buddhist-Christian Dialogue," *Buddhist-Christian Studies* 26 (2006): 113.

12. Mother Teresa, *Constitutions of the Missionaries of Charity* (Calcutta: Missionaries of Charity, 1988), 38.

13. Yves Congar, *Tradition and Traditions: An Historical and a Theological Essay* (London: Burns and Oates, 1966), 266.

14. Benedict XVI, Address to the Roman Curia, Thursday, December 22, 2005, http://www.vatican.va/holy_father/benedict_xvi/speeches/2005/december/documents/hf_ben_xvi_spe_20051222_roman-curia_en.html.

15. Vincent of Lérins, *The Commonitory* (Baltimore: Robinson, 1847), 71; also José Madoz, *El Concepto de la Tradicion en S. Vicente de Lerins* (Rome: Pontificia Università Gregoriana, 1933), 125–33.

16. Mother Teresa, *Constitutions of the Missionaries of Charity*, 32.

17. David Scott, *The Love That Made Mother Teresa: Special Canonization Edition* (Manchester, NH: Sophia Institute Press, 2016).

18. John Paul II, *Letter to Families*, February 2, 1994, https://w2.vatican.va/content/john-paul-ii/en/letters/1994/documents/hf_jp-ii_let_02021994_families.html.

19. Cristina Siccardi, *Madre Teresa. Tutto Iniziò nella Mia Terra* (Milan: San Paolo Edizioni, 2013), 41.

20. *Madre Teresa di Calcutta. Amiamo chi non e Amato* (Bologna: EMI, 2016), 12–13.

21. Second Vatican Council, Pastoral Constitution on the Church in the Modern World, *Gaudium et Spes*, "Fostering the Nobility of Marriage and the Family," chapter 1, no. 47, http://www.vatican.va/archive/hist_councils/ii_vatican_council/documents/vat-ii_cons_19651207_gaudium-et-spes_en.html.

22. Pietro Maranesi, "Pietro di Bernardone nella Vicenda Iniziale di Francesco: Analisi della 'Legenda trium sociorum,'" in *Collectanea Franciscana*, vol. 88, fasc. 1–2, 14.

23. Maranesi, "Pietro di Bernardone," 14.

24. Thomas of Celano, *The Lives of S. Francis of Assisi*, trans. A. G. Ferrers Howell (London: Methuen & Co., 1908), 3.

25. Salter E. Gurney, trans., *The Legend of Saint Francis by the Three Companions* (London: Aldine House, 1902), 8.

26. Thomas of Celano, *The Lives of S. Francis of Assisi*, 14.

27. Maranesi, "Pietro di Bernardone," 47.

28. Maranesi, "Pietro di Bernardone," 20.

29. Francis of Assisi, *The Little Flowers of Saint Francis*, 2.

30. *Rule of St. Francis*, Chapter 1.

31. Pope Francis, Papal Audience, June 17, 2019, https://www.vaticannews.va/en/pope/news/2019-06/pope-francis-conventual-franciscans-general-chapter.html.

32. Thomas of Celano, *The Lives of S. Francis of Assisi*, 147.

33. Gurney, *Legend of Saint Francis by the Three Companions*, 13.

34. Gurney, *Legend of Saint Francis by the Three Companions*, 15.

35. Thomas of Celano, *The Lives of S. Francis of Assisi*, 147.

36. Pope Francis, "Poverty, at the Heart of the Gospel, Is Not an Ideology," Morning Homily at Santa Marta, June 16, 2015, http://www.asianews.it/news-en/Pope:-Poverty,-at-the-heart-of-the-Gospel,-is-not-an-ideology-34524.html.

37. Mario Bertini, *Francesco e Teresa* (Milan: Edizioni Biblioteca Francescana, 2002), 20.

38. Scott, *The Love That Made Mother Teresa*.

39. Francis of Assisi, *The Testament of St. Francis*, https://ofm.org/wp-content/uploads/2016/11/Testament.pdf.

40. Pietro Maranesi, "La fragilità fonte di verità e di vita secondo Francesco di Assisi," *Italia Francescana* 82 (2007): 108.

41. Augustine Thompson, *Francis of Assisi* (Ithaca, NY: Cornell University Press, 2012), 19.

42. Pietro Maranesi, "Il servizio ai lebbrosi in san Francesco e nei francescani," *Italia Franciscana* 11 (2009): 13.

43. Saint Bonaventure, *The Life of Saint Francis of Assisi*, trans. E. Gurney Salter, chapter 2, 6, https://www.ecatholic2000.com/bonaventure/assisi/francis.shtml.

44. Bonaventure, *The Life of Saint Francis of Assisi*, chapter 1, 6.

45. Francis of Assisi, *The Little Flowers of Saint Francis*, 15.

46. Mother Teresa, *A Call to Mercy*, 111.

47. Angelo Comastri, *Madre Teresa, Una Goccia d'Acqua Pulita* (Milan: Paoline Editoriale, 2016), 41–42.

48. Comastri, *Madre Teresa*, 42.

49. Navin Chawla, *Mother Teresa: The Centenary Edition* (New Dehli: Penguin Books, 2002), 200.

50. Mother Teresa, *In My Own Words*.

51. Mother Teresa, *In My Own Words*.

52. Kolodiejchuk, *Come Be My Light*, 39–40.

53. Kolodiejchuk, *Come Be My Light*, 175.

54. Mother Teresa, *A Call to Mercy*, 36.

55. Scott, *The Love That Made Mother Teresa*.

56. Kolodiejchuk, *Come Be My Light*, 301.

57. Louise Chipley Slavicek, *Mother Teresa: Caring for the World's Poor* (New York: Chelsea House Publishers, 2007), 49.

58. Andrzej Grzybowski, Jarosław Sak, Krzysztof Korecki, "Misericordia and Leprosy in the 20th Century," *Clinics in Dermatology* 34 (2016): 13.

59. Elaine Murray Stone, *Mother Teresa: A Life of Love* (Mahwah, NJ: Paulist Press, 1999), 35.

60. Stone, *Mother Teresa: A Life of Love*, 35.

61. Grzybowski, Sak, and Korecki, "Misericordia and Leprosy," 13.

62. Renzo Allegri, *Conversations with Mother Teresa: A Personal Portrait of the Saint, Her Mission, and Her Great Love for God* (Frederick, MD: The Word Among Us Press, 2011), 98.

63. Stone, *Mother Teresa: A Life of Love*, 36.

64. Mother Teresa, *In My Own Words*.

65. M. G. Chitkara, *Mother Teresa* (New Dehli: APH Publishing, 1998), 123–24.

66. *Compendium of the Social Doctrine of the Catholic Church*, no. 287, http://www.vatican.va/roman_curia/pontifical_councils/justpeace/documents/rc_pc_justpeace_doc_20060526_compendio-dott-soc_en.html#The%20duty%20to%20work.

67. "Il Sari delle Suore di Madre Teresa Viene Confezionato dai Lebbrosi: Un Redattore di Fides ha Vissuto una Intera Giornata Con Le Suore di Madre Teresa. Domani il Suo Racconto in Esclusiva ai Nostri Abbonati con un Web-Book su Madre Teresa," Venerdì, 17 Ottobre 2003, http://www.fides.org/it/news/1310-IL_SARI_DELLE_SUORE_DI_MADRE_TERESA_VIENE_CONFEZIONATO_DAI_LEBBROSI_UN_REDATTORE_DI_FIDES_HA_VISSUTO_UNA_INTERA_GIORNATA_CON_LE_SUORE_DI_MADRE_TERESA_DOMANI_IL_SUO_RACCONTO_IN_ESCLUSIVA_AI_NOSTRI_ABBONATI_CON_UN_WEB_BOOK_SU_MADRE_TERESA.

68. Mother Teresa, *In My Own Words*.

69. Francis of Assisi, *The Little Flowers of Saint Francis*, 15.

70. Mother Teresa of Calcutta, Georges Gorrée, and Jean Barbier, *Tu mi Porti l'Amore, Scritti Spirituali* (Rome, Città Nuova Editrice, 2005), 65.

71. Mother Teresa, *In My Own Words*.

72. Gurney, *The Legend of Saint Francis*, 13.

73. Francis of Assisi, *The Little Flowers of Saint Francis*, 29–30.

74. Gurney, *The Legend of Saint Francis*, 49.

75. Gurney, *The Legend of Saint Francis*, 59–60.

76. Francis of Assisi, *The Little Flowers of Saint Francis*, 38.

77. Thomas of Celano, *The Lives of S. Francis of Assisi*, 56.

78. Thompson, *Francis of Assisi*, 87.

79. Thompson, *Francis of Assisi*, 71.

80. Thomas of Celano, *The Lives of S. Francis of Assisi*, 58.

81. Thomas of Celano, *The Lives of S. Francis of Assisi*, 23–24.

82. Mother Teresa, *In My Own Words*.

83. Kathryn Spink, *Mother Teresa: A Complete Authorized Biography* (San Francisco: HarperSanFrancisco, 1997), 3.

84. Lush Gjergji, *Mother Teresa: Her Life, Her Words* (Hyde Park, NY: New City Press, 1991), 12.

85. Mother Teresa, *In My Own Words*.

86. Kolodiejchuk, *Come Be My Light*, 314.

87. Daniel Jones, address to the United Nations, September 9, 2016, "The Fruit of Service Is Peace," http://webtv.un.org/search/leaving-no-one-behind-mother-teresa's-enduring-message-for-the-international-community-today/5122960370001.

88. *Madre Teresa di Calcutta. Amiamo chi non e Amato* (Bologna: EMI, 2016), 13.

89. Kolodiejchuk, *Come Be My Light*, 77.

90. Kolodiejchuk, *Come Be My Light*, 265.

91. Mother Teresa, *In My Own Words*.

92. Adrienne Wood, Magdalena Rychlowska, Sebastian Korb, and Paula Niedenthal, "Fashioning the Face: Sensorimotor Simulation Contributes to Facial Expression Recognition," *Trends in Cognitive Sciences* 20, no. 3 (March 2016): 227–40.

93. Scott, *The Love That Made Mother Teresa*.

94. Kolodiejchuk, *Come Be My Light*, 98.

95. Pope Pius XII, "Radiomessaggio di sua Santita Pio XII Rivolto ai Governanti ed ai Popoli nell'Imminente Pericolo della Guerra" (Radio Message of His Holiness Pope Pius XII Addressed to Governors and Peoples in the Imminent Danger of War), August 24, 1939, https://w2.vatican.va/content/pius-xii/it/speeches/1939/documents/hf_p-xii_spe_19390824_ora-grave.html.

96. Leonardo Sapienza, ed., *Paolo VI e Madre Teresa* (Rome: Edizioni Viverein, 2016), 121.

97. Sapienza, *Paolo VI e Madre Teresa*, 122.

98. Mother Teresa, *A Call to Mercy*, 14.

99. Fady Noun, "Mother Teresa, the War in Lebanon and the Rescue of 100 Orphans and Children with Disabilities," *Asia News.it*, September 2, 2016, http://www.asianews.it/news-en/Mother-Teresa%2C-the-war-in-Lebanon-and-the-rescue-of-100-orphans-and-children-with-disabilities-38470.html.

100. Noun, "Mother Teresa, the War in Lebanon and the Rescue of 100 Orphans and Children with Disabilities."

101. "Hospital Is Visited by Mother Teresa," *New York Times*, August 15, 1982, https://www.nytimes.com/1982/08/15/world/hospital-is-visited-by-mother-teresa.html.

102. Pat Williams and Jim Denney, *21 Great Leaders: Learn Their Lessons, Improve Your Influence* (Uhrichsville, OH: Shiloh Run Press, 2015), 213.

103. Kolodiejchuk, *Come Be My Light*, 317.

104. Kolodiejchuk, *Come Be My Light*, 311–12.

105. Scott, *The Love That Made Mother Teresa*.

106. Kolodiejchuk, *Come Be My Light*, 292.

107. Mother Teresa, The 42nd Annual National Prayer Breakfast, Congressional Record 140, no. 50, Monday, May 2, 1994, https://www.govinfo.gov/content/pkg/CREC-1994-05-02/html/CREC-1994-05-02-pt1-PgS16.htm.

108. Scott, *The Love That Made Mother Teresa*.

CHAPTER 6

1. Pope Paul VI, *Evangelii Nuntiandi*, Apostolic Exhortation, December 8, 1975, no. 41, http://w2.vatican.va/content/paul-vi/en/apost

_exhortations/documents/hf_p-vi_exh_19751208_evangelii-nuntiandi
.html.

2. Sacred Congregation for the Doctrine of Faith, *Norms Regarding the Manner of Proceeding in the Discernment of Presumed Apparitions or Revelations*, February 27, 1978, http://www.vatican.va/roman_curia/congregations/cfaith/documents/rc_con_cfaith_doc_19780225_norme-apparizioni_en.html.

3. Celia Kourie, "Mysticism: A Survey of Recent Issues," *Journal for the Study of Religion* 5, no. 2 (September 1992): 89.

4. Gelsomino Del Guercio, "Il mistero delle stimmate di Padre Pio. La parola ai tre medici che lo hanno visitato," *Aleteia*, March 7, 2018, https://it.aleteia.org/2018/03/07/giudizio-medici-su-stimmate-padre-pio/2/.

5. Renzo Allegri, *La Passione di Padre Pio* (Milan: Mondadori, 2015), https://padrepiopietr.wordpress.com/2016/09/07/scontro-storico.

6. Hotel San Michel San Giovanni Rotondo, "Le Indagini e la Condanna del Sant'Uficio: Le Stimmate, 1919–1931,"accessed June 24, 2020, http://www.albergosanmichele.com/le-indagini-e-la-condanna-del-sant-uffizio.html.

7. Angelo Maria Mischitelli, *Padre Pio. Un Uomo Un Santo* (Rome: Sovera Edizioni, 2015), 430.

8. Adolfo Affatato, *Padre Pio and I: Memoirs of a Spiritual Son* (2016).

9. John Paul II, Homily on the Beatification of Padre Pio of Pietrelcina, Rome, May 2, 1999, http://w2.vatican.va/content/john-paul-ii/en/homilies/1999/documents/hf_jp-ii_hom_02051999_padre-pio.html.

10. Angelo Devananda Scolozzi, *Una Chiamata nella Chiamata. Testimonianza dei Miei Ventun Anni di Vita Accanto a Madre Teresa di Calcutta* (Vatican City: Libreria Editrice Vaticana, 2014), 88.

11. Tyler Cabot, "The Rocky Road to Sainthood," *The Atlantic*, November 2005, https://www.theatlantic.com/magazine/archive/2005/11/the-rocky-road-to-sainthood/304302/.

12. Brian Kolodiejchuk, ed., *Come Be My Light* (New York: Image, 2007), 54–55.

13. Kolodiejchuk, *Come Be My Light*, 55.

14. Kolodiejchuk, *Come Be My Light*, 334.

15. Frank M. Rega, *Padre Pio and America* (Rockford, IL: Tan Books, 2005), 49.

16. Kolodiejchuk, *Come Be My Light*, 1–2.

17. *The Catechism of the Catholic Church*, http://www.vatican.va/archive/ccc_css/archive/catechism/p3s1c3a2.htm.

18. Hans Urs von Balthasar, *Our Task: A Report and a Plan* (San Francisco: Ignatius Press, 1994), 72.

19. von Balthasar, *Our Task*, 61.

20. Georges Chantraine, "Exegesis and Contemplation in the Work of Hans urs von Balthasar," in *Hans Urs von Balthasar: His Life and Work*, ed. David L. Schindler (San Francisco: Ignatius Press, 1991), 134.

21. Derek Sakowski, *The Ecclesiological Reality of Reception Considered as a Solution to the Debate over the Ontological Priority of the Universal Church* (Rome: Editrice Pontificia Università Gregoriana, 2014), 343.

22. Kolodiejchuk, *Come Be My Light*, 213.

23. Kolodiejchuk, *Come Be My Light*, 41.

24. Kolodiejchuk, *Come Be My Light*, 41.

25. Ignazio Ingrao, *Il segno di Padre Pio, Da Santo Perseguitato a Simbolo della Chiesa della Misericordia di Papa Francesco* (Milan: Edizioni Piemme, 2016), 14.

26. Ingrao, *Il segno di Padre Pio*, 18. Also, Domenico Agasso, "Quella Misteriosa Devozione di Bergoglio per Padre Pio," *La Stampa*, February 6, 2016, https://www.lastampa.it/vatican-insider/it/speciali/2016/02/06/news/quella-misteriosa-devozione-di-bergoglio-per-padre-pio-1.36560092.

27. Pope Francis, General Audience, Wednesday, December 13, 2017, http://w2.vatican.va/content/francesco/en/audiences/2017/documents/papa-francesco_20171213_udienza-generale.html.

28. Kolodiejchuk, *Come Be My Light*, 48.

29. Kolodiejchuk, *Come Be My Light*, 48.

30. Kolodiejchuk, *Come Be My Light*, 48–49.

31. Kolodiejchuk, *Come Be My Light*, 78.

32. Pope Benedict XVI, Dialogue with Priests, June 10, 2010, http://w2.vatican.va/content/benedict-xvi/en/speeches/2010/june/documents/hf_ben-xvi_spe_20100610_concl-anno-sac.html.

33. Kolodiejchuk, *Come Be My Light*, 84.

34. Congregation for Divine Worship, *Redemptionis Sacramentum*, no. 92, http://www.vatican.va/roman_curia/congregations/ccdds/documents/rc_con_ccdds_doc_20040423_redemptionis-sacramentum_en.html.

35. *Code of Canon Law*, "The Minister of the Most Holy Eucharist," art. 1, can. 900, http://www.vatican.va/archive/cod-iuris-canonici/

315

eng/documents/cic_lib4-cann879-958_en.html#THE_EUCHARISTIC
_CELEBRATION.

36. Kolodiejchuk, *Come Be My Light*, 162.

37. Mother Teresa, *A Call to Mercy* (New York: Random House, 2016), 135).

38. Mother Teresa, *Constitutions of the Missionaries of Charity* (Calcutta: Missionaries of Charity, 1988), 56.

39. Mother Teresa, *In My Own Words* (Liguori, MO: Liguori Publications, 1997).

40. Alessandro Gnocchi, *Padre Pio Santo Eremita: L'incontro con Dio sulle orme dei Padri del deserto* (Verona: Fede & Cultura, 2017).

41. Affatato, *Padre Pio and I.*

42. John Paul II, Homily on the Canonization of Padre Pio of Pietrelcina, Capuchin Priest, Rome, June 16, 2002, http://w2.vatican
.va/content/john-paul-ii/en/homilies/2002/documents/hf_jp-ii_hom
_20020616_padre-pio.html.

43. Affatato, *Padre Pio and I.*

44. Affatato, *Padre Pio and I.*

45. Affatato, *Padre Pio and I.*

46. St. Pius X, Exhortation "To All the Catholics of the World," August 2, 1914, *Acta Apostolicae Sedis* 6, no. 11, 373, https://www
.catholicworldreport.com/2014/07/28/st-pius-xs-plea-for-peace/.

47. Mother Teresa, *In My Own Words.*

48. Mother Teresa, "Priestly Celibacy: Sign of the Charity of Christ," http://www.vatican.va/roman_curia/congregations/cclergy/documents/rc
_con_cclergy_doc_01011993_sign_en.html#top.

49. Kolodiejchuk, *Come Be My Light*, 283.

50. Christopher Hitchens, "Mommie Dearest: The Pope Beatifies Mother Teresa, a Fanatic, a Fundamentalist, and a Fraud," *Slate*, October 20, 2003, https://slate.com/news-and-politics/2003/10/the-fanatic
-fraudulent-mother-teresa.html.

51. Pope Paul VI, Declaration *Inter Insigniores*, October 15, 1976, http://www.vatican.va/roman_curia/congregations/cfaith/documents/rc
_con_cfaith_doc_19761015_inter-insigniores_en.html.

52. Sebastian Vazhakala, Maria Giuseppina Scanziani, et al., *Vita con Madre Teresa, Testimonianze, Lettere, Immagini Inedite* (Chiasso: Elvetica Edizioni, 2003), 102.

53. "Mother Teresa Beyond Women Priests," accessed June 26, 2020, https://cmpaul.wordpress.com/2010/07/28/mother-teresa-beyond-women-priests/.

54. Bernardo Cervellera, ed., *Madre Teresa, la Misericordia per l'Asia e per il Mondo* (Siena: Edizioni Cantagalli, 2016), 54.

55. Cervellera, *Madre Teresa*, 54.

56. Kolodiejchuk, *Come Be My Light*, 334.

57. Antonio Maria Sicardi, OCD, "Saint Teresa of Child Jesus and the Priesthood," http://www.vatican.va/roman_curia/congregations/cclergy/documents/jub_preti_20000517_sicari_en.html.

58. Sicardi, "Saint Teresa of Child Jesus and the Priesthood."

59. Mother Teresa, *In My Own Words*.

60. Mother Teresa. *A Call to Mercy*, 319.

61. Philip Kosloski, "Mother Teresa: A Prayer for Priests," *Aleteia*, September 9, 2018, https://aleteia.org/2018/09/09/a-prayer-for-priests-written-by-mother-teresa/.

62. Gennaro Preziuso, *Padre Pio, l'Apostolo del Confessionale* (Rome: San Paolo, 1998), https://padrepiopietr.wordpress.com/2017/10/07/dalla-preghiera-allazione/#more-1640.

63. Preziuso, *Padre Pio, l'Apostolo del Confessionale*.

64. Kolodiejchuk, *Come Be My Light*, 286.

65. St. Basil of Caesarea, *To Eustathius the Physician*, Letter 189, accessed June 26, 2020, http://www.newadvent.org/fathers/3202189.htm.

66. Giovanni Chifari, "Padre Pio e la Misericordia: Coordinate Biblico-Teologiche," *La Stampa*, February 3, 2016.

67. Gnocchi, *Padre Pio Santo Eremita*.

68. Gnocchi, *Padre Pio Santo Eremita*.

69. Hans Urs von Balthasar, *New Elucidations* (San Francisco: Ignatius Press, 1986), 38.

70. Gnocchi, *Padre Pio Santo Eremita*.

71. Jeffrey P. Bishop, *The Anticipatory Corpse: Medicine, Power, and the Care of the Dying* (Notre Dame, IN: University of Notre Dame Press, 2011); Bharat Ranganathan, "Might Only Theology Save Medicine? Some Ideas from Ramsey," *Studies in Christian Ethics* 30, no. 1 (2017): 83–99; Farr Curlin, "Medicine's Dance with Death," *Public Discourse, The Journal of the Witherspoon Institute* (November 16, 2012).

72. Affatato, *Padre Pio and I*.

73. John Paul II, "Homily on the Beatification of Padre Pio of Pietrelcina," Rome, May 2, 1999, http://w2.vatican.va/content/john-paul

-ii/en/homilies/1999/documents/hf_jp-ii_hom_02051999_padre-pio
.html.

74. Francesco di Raimondo, *Padre Pio e Madre Teresa. L'Esperienza di un Collaboratore Medico* (Rome: Edizioni Borla, 2001), 56.

75. di Raimondo, *Padre Pio e Madre Teresa*, 57.

76. di Raimondo, *Padre Pio e Madre Teresa*, 45.

77. Jere d. Palazzolo, "St. (Padre) Pio Home for the Relief of Suffering in the USA: Responding to the Call," *The Linacre Quarterly* 83, no. 4 (2016): 458.

78. di Raimondo, *Padre Pio e Madre Teresa*, 81–82.

79. Mario Bertini and Folco Terzani, *La Santa. Accanto a Madre Teresa* (Brescia: Editrice La Scuola, 2016), 136.

80. Kolodiejchuk, *Come Be My Light*, 145.

81. Kolodiejchuk, *Come Be My Light*, 152.

82. Cristina Siccardi, *Madre Teresa. Tutto Iniziò nella mia Terra* (Milan: Edizioni San Paolo, 2009), 200.

83. Teresio Bosco, *Madre Teresa. La Carezza di Dio* (Turin: Editrice Elledici, 2016), 26.

84. Ellen Barry, "Kolkata Testifies to the Grace of Mother Teresa, Its New Saint," *New York Times*, September 4, 2016, https://www.nytimes .com/2016/09/05/world/asia/mother-teresa-kolkata-canonization-saint .html.

85. "Mother Teresa's Care for the Dying," *The Lancet* 344 (October 15, 1994): 1098.

86. William E. Phipps, "The Origin of Hospices/Hospitals," *Death Studies* 12, no. 2 (1988): 95.

87. Willliam A. Donohue, *Unmasking Mother Teresa's Critics* (Manchester, NH: Sophia Institute Press, 2016).

88. "Mother Teresa's Care for the Dying," 1098.

89. Mario Bertini and Folco Terzani, *La Santa. Accanto a Madre Teresa* (Brescia: Editrice La Scuola, 2016), 144.

90. Vijay Prashad, "Mother Teresa: Mirror of Bourgeois Guilt," *Economic and Political Weekly* 32, nos. 44/45 (November 8–14, 1997): 2856.

91. Bertini and Terzani, *La Santa*, 137.

92. Hiromi Josepha Kudo, *Mother Teresa a Saint from Skopje* (Gujarat, India: Gujarat Sahitya Prakash, 2006), 173.

93. Phipps, "The Origin of Hospices/Hospitals," 97.

94. John Paul II, "Address to Doctors and Patients," San Giovanni Rotondo, May 23, 1978, https://w2.vatican.va/content/john-paul-ii/it/

speeches/1987/may/documents/hf_jp-ii_spe_19870523_medici-malati
.html.

95. Kolodiejchuk, *Come Be My Light*, 146.

96. Palazzolo, "St. (Padre) Pio Home for the Relief of Suffering in the USA," 455.

97. Mother Teresa, *A Call to Mercy*, 40.

98. Mother Teresa, *A Call to Mercy*, 140.

99. Address of John Paul II on Occasion of the Meeting with Mother Theresa during the Visit to Nirmal Hriday Ashram, Calcutta (India), February 3, 1986, http://w2.vatican.va/content/john-paul-ii/en/speeches/1986/february/documents/hf_jp-ii_spe_19860203_nirmal-hriday.html.

100. di Raimondo, *Padre Pio e Madre Teresa*, 90.

101. di Raimondo, *Padre Pio e Madre Teresa*, 88.

102. Mother Teresa, *A Call to Mercy*, 84.

103. Beppe Amico, *Madre Teresa, La Santa dei Poveri* (Streetlib Srl., 2015), 120.

104. Ines A. Murzaku, "Padre Pio and Mother Teresa: Jubilee Patrons," *The Catholic Thing*, September 23, 2016, https://www.thecatholicthing.org/2016/09/23/padre-pio-and-mother-teresa-jubilee-patrons/.

CHAPTER 7

1. Juliusz Słowacki, "Our Slavic Pope" (1848), trans. Noel Clark, http://slowacki.chez.com/engslavp.htm.

2. George Weigel, *Witness to Hope: The Biography of Pope John Paul II 1920–2005* (New York: Harper Perennial, 2005), 513.

3. Orazio La Rocca, "Quel Giorno che Cambio la Storia, Parla il Segretario di Wojtyla," *Famiglia Cristiana*, October 16, 2018, http://www.famigliacristiana.it/articolo/la-testimonianza-del-cardinale-stanislao-dziwisz.aspx.

4. Felix Corley, "Soviet Reaction to the Election of Pope John Paul II," *Religion, State and Society* 22, no. 1 (1994): 40.

5. Paul Kengor, *The Divine Plan: John Paul II, Ronald Reagan, and the Dramatic End of the Cold War* (Intercollegiate Studies Institute).

6. John Paul II, First Greeting and Blessing to the Faithful, October 16, 1978, http://w2.vatican.va/content/john-paul-ii/it/speeches/1978/documents/hf_jp-ii_spe_19781016_primo-saluto.html.

7. John Paul II, Address in the Basilica of St. Francis of Assisi, Assisi, Italy, Sunday, November 5, 1978, http://w2.vatican.va/content/john-paul-ii/en/speeches/1978/documents/hf_jp-ii_spe_19781105_assisi.html.

8. John Paul II, *Ecclesia in Europa*, Post-Synodal Apostolic Exhortation, June 28, 2003, http://w2.vatican.va/content/john-paul-ii/en/apost_exhortations/documents/hf_jp-ii_exh_20030628_ecclesia-in-europa.html.

9. John Paul II, Homily, Apostolic Journey to Gniezno, Cathedral of Gniezno, June 3, 1979, https://w2.vatican.va/content/john-paul-ii/en/homilies/1979/documents/hf_jp-ii_hom_19790603_polonia-gniezno-cattedrale.html.

10. John Paul II, Homily, Apostolic Journey to Gniezno.

11. George Weigel, *The Final Revolution: The Resistance Church and the Collapse of Communism* (New York: Oxford University Press, 2003), 102.

12. John Paul II, Address, Chapel of the Apparitions of Fatima, Apostolic Visit to Portugal, May 12, 1982, https://w2.vatican.va/content/john-paul-ii/it/speeches/1982/may/documents/hf_jp-ii_spe_19820512_vescovo-leiria-fatima.html.

13. Aldino Cazzago, *Cristianesimo d'Oriente e d'Occidente in Giovanni Paolo II* (Milan: Jaca Book, 1996), 20.

14. Weigel, *The Final Revolution*, 95.

15. John Paul II, Homily, Victory Square, Warsaw, Poland, June 2, 1979, no. 4, https://w2.vatican.va/content/john-paul-ii/en/homilies/1979/documents/hf_jp-ii_hom_19790602_polonia-varsavia.html.

16. Weigel, *The Final Revolution*, 102.

17. John Paul II, Encyclical *Redemptor Hominis*, March 4, 1979, no. 17, http://w2.vatican.va/content/john-paul-ii/en/encyclicals/documents/hf_jp-ii_enc_04031979_redemptor-hominis.html.

18. Cardinal Stanislaw Dziwisz, *A Life with Karol: My Forty-Year Friendship with the Man Who became Pope* (New York: Doubleday, 2008), 174.

19. John Paul II, Encyclical *Centesimus Annus*, May 1, 1991, no. 44, http://www.vatican.va/holy_father/john_paul_ii/encyclicals/documents/hf_jp-ii_enc_01051991_centesimus-annus_en.html#-2J.

20. John Paul II, Address to the 34th General Assembly of the United Nations, October 2, 1979, no. 13, https://w2.vatican.va/content/john

-paul-ii/en/speeches/1979/october/documents/hf_jp-ii_spe_19791002
_general-assembly-onu.html.

21. Gerald J. Beyer, "John XXIII and John Paul II, the Human Rights Popes," *Ethos Quarterly of the John Paul II Institute at the Catholic University of Lublin* 27, no. 2/106 (2014): 82.

22. John Paul II, *Redemptor Hominis*, no. 17.

23. Pius XI, *Quadragesimo Anno*, May 15, 1931, https://w2.vatican.va/content/pius-xi/en/encyclicals/documents/hf_p-xi_enc_19310515_quadragesimo-anno.html.

24. "Three Men Look at Communism," *Christianity in the World Today*, November 25, 1957.

25. John Paul II, Homily for the Inauguration of His Pontificate, St. Peter's Square, October 22, 1978, http://w2.vatican.va/content/john-paul-ii/en/homilies/1978/documents/hf_jp-ii_hom_19781022_inizio-pontificato.html.

26. Andrea Tornielli, "Karol Wojtyla," *Il Foglio*, September 16, 2009, https://www.ilfoglio.it/ritratti/2009/09/16/news/karol-wojtyla-998/.

27. Weigel, *The Final Revolution*, 100.

28. Kengor, *The Divine Plan*.

29. Dziwisz, *A Life with Karol*, 179.

30. Central Intelligence Agency, *The World Factbook*, https://www.cia.gov/library/publications/the-world-factbook/geos/al.html.

31. Francesco Follo, *Meditiamo con Giovanni Paolo II* (Milan: Paoline Editoriale, 2007), 95.

32. Dziwisz, *A Life with Karol*, 175.

33. Tad Szulc, *Pope John Paul II: The Biography* (New York: Scribner, 1995), 261 and 433.

34. Dziwisz, *A Life with Karol*, 174.

35. Dziwisz, *A Life with Karol*, 175.

36. Dziwisz, *A Life with Karol*, 175.

37. Saverio Gaeta, *Madre Teresa: Il Segreto della Santita* (Milan: Edizioni San Paolo, 2016), 141.

38. Weigel, *Witness to Hope*, 513.

39. Gaeta, *Madre Teresa*, 141.

40. Don Lush Gjergji, "Papët dhe Nënë Tereza," *Illyria, The Albanian-American Newspaper*, March 14, 2016, http://illyriapress.com/papet-dhe-nena-tereze/.

41. Pier Giorgio Liverani, *Dateli a Me Madre Teresa e l'impegno per la Vita* (Rome: Città Nuova, 2003), 8.

42. Mario Bertini, *Sulle Strade di Madre Teresa* (Milan: Paoline Editoriale, 2003), 31–32.

43. Liverani, *Dateli a Me* (Rome: Città Nuova, 2003), 11.

44. Francesco Rapacioli, "Madre Teresa di Calcutta. 'Era più Teologa lei di Noi Teologi," August 25, 2010, http://xoomer.virgilio.it/dinajpur/b10c/banglanews435.htm#era.

45. Dziwisz, *A Life with Karol*, 137.

46. Andrew M. Essig and Jennifer L. Moore, "U.S.-Holy See Diplomacy: The Establishment of Formal Relations, 1984," *The Catholic Historical Review* 95, no. 4 (October 2009): 748.

47. Kengor, *The Divine Plan*.

48. Dziwisz, *A Life with Karol*, 173.

49. "Navarro-Valls: Eccezionale Sintonia tra Madre Teresa e Giovanni Paolo II," Alessandro Gisotti, Interview for Vatican Radio, August 30, 2016, http://www.archivioradiovaticana.va/storico/2016/08/30/navarro-valls_gande_sintonia_tra_madre_teresa_e_wojtyla/it-1254554.

50. Benedict XVI, Address, Visit to the Gift of Mary House, January 4, 2008, https://w2.vatican.va/content/benedict-xvi/en/speeches/2008/january/documents/hf_ben-xvi_spe_20080104_dono-maria.html.

51. "Navarro-Valls: Eccezionale Sintonia tra Madre Teresa e Giovanni Paolo II."

52. John Paul II, Apostolic Letter *Mulieris Dignitatem*, no. 31, http://w2.vatican.va/content/john-paul-ii/en/apost_letters/1988/documents/hf_jp-ii_apl_19880815_mulieris-dignitatem.html.

53. John Paul II, "Letter to Women," June 29, 1995, no. 4, https://w2.vatican.va/content/john-paul-ii/en/letters/1995/documents/hf_jp-ii_let_29061995_women.html.

54. John Paul II, "Letter to Women," no. 10.

55. John Freely, *The Grand Turk: Sultan Mehmet II—Conqueror of Constantinople and Master of an Empire* (New York: Overlook Press, 2009), 166.

56. Pope Francis, Holy Mass and Canonizations, Seventh Sunday of Easter, May 12, 2013, http://w2.vatican.va/content/francesco/en/homilies/2013/documents/papa-francesco_20130512_omelia-canonizzazioni.html.

57. John Paul II, Homily, Pastoral Visit to Otranto, October 5, 1980, https://w2.vatican.va/content/john-paul-ii/it/homilies/1980/documents/hf_jp-ii_hom_19801005_otranto.html.

58. George Weigel, "The Ostpolitik Failed. Get over It," *First Things*, July 20, 2016, https://www.firstthings.com/web-exclusives/2016/07/the -ostpolitik-failed-get-over-it.

59. Gjon Sinishta, "Grave Violation of Religious Rights in Albania," *Occasional Papers on Religion in Eastern Europe* 3, no. 5 (1983): 13.

60. John Paul II, Angelus, Pastoral Visit to Bari and Bitonto, February 26, 1984, https://w2.vatican.va/content/john-paul-ii/it/angelus/1984/ documents/hf_jp-ii_ang_19840226.html.

61. John Paul II, Address, Pastoral Visit to the Parish of Saint Gregory VII, April 27, 1986, https://w2.vatican.va/content/john-paul-ii/ it/speeches/1986/april/documents/hf_jp-ii_spe_19860427_parrocchia -s-gregorio-vii.html; also Alessandro Colombo, ed., *La Libertà Religiosa negli Insegnamenti di Giovanni Paolo II, 1978–1998* (Milan: Vita e Pensiero supplemento al quaderno n. 7, Settembre 2000): 131.

62. John Paul II, Address, Pastoral Visit to the Parish of Saint Gregory VII.

63. "Letër e Nënë Terezës e Shkruar në Gjuhën Shqipe," *Drita*, September 28, 2017, https://www.kultplus.com/trashegimia/leter-e-nene -terezes-e-shkruar-ne-gjuhen-shqipe-foto/.

64. "Mother Teresa of Calcutta (1910–1997)," accessed July 1, 2020, http://www.vatican.va/news_services/liturgy/saints/ns_lit_doc_20031019 _madre-teresa_en.html.

65. Fatjona Mejdini, "Nënë Tereza, Murgesha që Frikësoi Komunistët e Shqipërisë," *Reporter.al*, September 3, 2016, https://www.reporter .al/nene-tereza-murgesha-qe-frikesoi-komunistet-e-shqiperise/.

66. Mejdini, "Nënë Tereza."

67. Mejdini, "Nënë Tereza."

68. Tina Rosenberg, "The Habits of the Heart," *World Policy Journal* 11, no. 4 (Winter 1994/1995): 85.

69. Stephen Dowling, "The Cold War Bunkers That Cover a Country," BBC, November 2, 2018, http://www.bbc.com/future/story/ 20181102-the-cold-war-bunkers-that-cover-a-country.

70. Mejdini, "Nënë Tereza."

71. Gjovalin Shkurtaj, "Mother Teresa and Me: Visa for a Saint," Fox News, September 2, 2016, https://www.foxnews.com/opinion/ mother-teresa-and-me-visa-for-a-saint?.

72. Shkurtaj, "Mother Teresa and Me."

73. Kastriot Kotoni, "Zajmi: Vizita e parë e Nënë Terezës nën Survejimin e Sigurimit," *Shekulli*, September 4, 2016.

MOTHER TERESA

74. "Zbulohet letra e Nënë Terezës drejtuar Ramiz Alisë," *Dita*, August 27, 2016, http://www.gazetadita.al/zbulohet-letra-e-nene-terezes-drejtuar-ramiz-alise/.

75. Prof. Inis Kraja, daughter of a life-long friend of Bojaxhiu family, interview with author, April 24, 2017.

76. Alqi Koçiko, "Pjesa 'Tiranase' e Nënë Terezës," *Dita*, September 5, 2016.

77. Koçiko, "Pjesa 'Tiranase' e Nënë Terezës."

78. Inis Kraja, interview with author.

79. Inis Kraja, interview with author.

80. John Paul II, Address, Pastoral Visit to the Parish of Saint Gregory VII.

81. Walter Goodman, "Critic's Notebook; A Skeptical Look at Mother Teresa," *New York Times*, February 8, 1995.

82. "Rrëfimi I Nexhmije Hoxhës per Takimin me Nënë Terezën në Tiranë," *Tema*, September 4, 2016, http://www.gazetatema.net/2016/09/04/rrefimi-i-nexhmije-hoxhes-per-takimin-me-nene-terezen-ne-tirane/.

83. Dziwisz, *A Life with Karol*, 175.

84. John Paul II, Address, Pastoral Visit to the Parish of Saint Gregory VII.

85. Ines A. Murzaku, "*Ad maiorem Dei gloriam*: The Jesuits in Albania," *Occasional Papers on Religion in Eastern Europe* 37, no. 6 (2017): 116.

86. "1989, kur Nënë Tereza vinte për herë të parë në Tiranë," *Shqiptari I Italise*, September 1, 2016.

87. Denis R. Janz, *World Christianity and Marxism* (New York: Oxford University Press, 1998), 108; also "Dokument/ Kur Nënë Tereza shenjtërohej nga komunistët, asnjë fjalë për fetarizmin e saj," accessed July 2, 2020, http://www.time.al/18-09-06-Dokument-Kur-Nene-Tereza-shenjterohej-nga-komunistet-asnje-fjale-per-fetarizmin-e-saj/FAKSIMILE-Kur-Nene-Tereza-shenjterohej-nga-komunistet-asnje-fjale-per-fetarizmin-e-saj.aspx.

88. "Missionaries of Charity, Their Increasing Numbers throughout the World." In 1997, when Mother Teresa passed away, there were 3,914 sisters and 363 brothers serving the poor. In 2016, there are 5,161 sisters and 416 brothers in the midst of the marginalized. Rome Reports, September 2, 2016, https://www.romereports.com/en/2016/09/02/missionaries-of-charity-their-increasing-numbers-throughout-the-world/.

89. Willliam A. Donohue, *Unmasking Mother Teresa's Critics* (Manchester, NH: Sophia Institute Press, 2016).

324

90. Sarah Cahalan, "Envoy to Albania," *Notre Dame Magazine*, Autumn 2018, https://magazine.nd.edu/stories/envoy-to-albania/.

91. Ines A. Murzaku, "Mother Teresa Practiced Forgiveness in Personal Tragedy. Christopher Hitchens Attacked Her for It," *The Stream*, September 3, 2016, https://stream.org/mother-teresa-practiced-forgiveness-in-personal-tragedy-christopher-hitchens-attacked-her-for-it/.

92. "Nexhmija: Ju Tregoj Drekën me Nënë Terezën," *Shekulli*, September 6, 2010, http://www.ikubmagazine.com/ReadArticleNew.aspx?no=1009060075&l=en.

93. Mother Teresa, *A Call to Mercy* (New York: Random House, 2016), 250.

94. "Nexhmija: Ju Tregoj Drekën me Nënë Terezën."

95. Mother Teresa, *A Call to Mercy*, 252.

96. Mother Teresa to the President of Albania, Ramiz Alia, December 4, 1990. AQSH (The Central Archive of Albania), F. 498, V. 1990, D. 369, Fl. 3.

97. Dziwisz, *A Life with Karol*, 136.

98. Kengor, *The Divine Plan*.

99. John Paul II, Message to the Albanian Nation, April 25, 1993, https://w2.vatican.va/content/john-paul-ii/it/speeches/1993/april/documents/hf_jp-ii_spe_19930425_nazione-albanese.html.

100. John Paul II, Message to the Albanian Nation.

101. John Paul II, Message to the Albanian Nation.

102. John Paul II, *Regina Coeli*, Apostolic Visit to Albania, Scutari, April 25, 1993, https://w2.vatican.va/content/john-paul-ii/it/angelus/1993/documents/hf_jp-ii_reg_19930425.html?.

103. Francis, Apostolic Exhortation *Gaudete et Exsultate*, March 19, 2018, no. 6, http://w2.vatican.va/content/francesco/en/apost_exhortations/documents/papa-francesco_esortazione-ap_20180319_gaudete-et-exsultate.html#_ftnref94.

104. Dziwisz, *A Life with Karol*, 176.

105. Dziwisz, *A Life with Karol*, 176.

106. "Cronache," *Corriere della Sera*, October 18, 2003, https://www.corriere.it/Primo_Piano/Cronache/2003/10_Ottobre/18/madreteresa.shtml.

107. John Paul II, Homily on the Beatification of Mother Teresa of Calcutta, October 19, 2003, http://w2.vatican.va/content/john-paul-ii/en/homilies/2003/documents/hf_jp-ii_hom_20031019_mother-theresa.html.

CHAPTER 8

1. Francis, Prayer at Mother Teresa Memorial, Apostolic Journey to Bulgaria and North Macedonia, May 7, 2019, http://w2.vatican.va/content/francesco/en/prayers/documents/papa-francesco_preghiere_20190507_macedoniadelnord-preghiera.html.

2. Francis, Prayer at Mother Teresa Memorial.

3. According to *The World Fact Book* the religious percentages in North Macedonia are as follows: Macedonian Orthodox 64.8%, Muslim 33.3%, other Christian 0.4%, other and unspecified 1.5%. Central Intelligence Agency, accessed July 6, 2020, https://www.cia.gov/library/publications/the-world-factbook/geos/mk.html; Gerard O'Connell, "Pope Francis Makes History in North Macedonia," *America*, May 7, 2019, https://www.americamagazine.org/faith/2019/05/07/pope-francis-makes-history-north-macedonia.

4. "Papa: Madre Teresa ci aiuti ad essere attenti al grido dei poveri," *Vatican News*, May 7, 2019, https://www.vaticannews.va/it/papa/news/2019-05/papa-francesco-viaggio-macedonia-nord-memoriale-madre-teresa.html.

5. John Bingham, "Pope Francis: How Cardinals' Conclave Lobbying Campaign Paved Way for Argentine Pontiff," *The Telegraph*, November 22, 2014, https://www.telegraph.co.uk/news/religion/11248263/English-cardinal-Cormac-Murphy-OConnor-lobbied-for-Pope.html.

6. Francis, First Greeting, March 13, 2013, http://w2.vatican.va/content/francesco/en/speeches/2013/march/documents/papa-francesco_20130313_benedizione-urbi-et-orbi.html.

7. Geralamo Fazzini and Stefano Femminis, *Francesco Il Papa delle Prime Volte* (Milan: Edizioni San Paolo, 2018), 45.

8. Francis, Address, Pastoral Visit to Cagliari, September 22, 2013, http://w2.vatican.va/content/francesco/en/speeches/2013/september/documents/papa-francesco_20130922_lavoratori-cagliari.html.

9. Rosario Carello, *I Racconti di Papa Francesco. Una Biografia in 80 Parole* (Milan: Edizioni San Paolo, 2013), 69.

10. Francis, General Audience, Wednesday, March 11, 2015, https://w2.vatican.va/content/francesco/en/audiences/2015/documents/papa-francesco_20150311_udienza-generale.html.

11. Christopher Bellitto, *Ageless Wisdom: Lifetime Lessons from the Bible* (Mahwah, NJ: Paulist Press, 2016).

12. Luis Inostroza and Julia Helena Tábbita, "Informal Urban Development in the Greater Buenos Aires Area: A Quantitative-Spatial Assessment Based on Households' Physical Features Using GIS and Principal Component Analysis," *Procedia Engineering* 161 (2016): 2139.

13. Inostroza and Tábbita, "Informal Urban Development."

14. Silvina Premat, *Preti dalla fine del mondo: viaggio tra i "curas villeros" di Bergoglio* (Bologna: EMI, 2014).

15. Pedro Garcia junto al Padre Pepe Di Paola en Punto de Partida, 29 de Enero de 2014, www.puntodepartidatv.com and https://www.youtube.com/watch?v=NEI6JLVTLOI.

16. Premat, *Preti dalla fine del mondo*.

17. Premat, *Preti dalla fine del mondo*.

18. Premat, *Preti dalla fine del mondo*.

19. Jorge Mario Bergoglio, *Nei Tuoi Occhi è la Mia Parola: Omelie e Discorsi di Buenos Aires 1999–2013* (Milan: Rizzoli, 2016), loc. 10515–16 Kindle.

20. List of Popes, accessed July 6, 2020, http://w2.vatican.va/content/vatican/en/holy-father.html; Popes from Religious Orders, *Washington Post*, March 16, 2013.

21. John W. Padberg, ed., *The Constitutions of the Society of Jesus and Their Complementary Norms: A Complete English Translation of the Official Latin Texts*, No. 817 (Saint Louis: The Institute of Jesuit Sources, 1996), 413.

22. Padberg, *The Constitutions of the Society of Jesus*.

23. *Code of Canon Law*, Chapter VII, "Religious Raised to the Episcopate," Can. 705, http://www.vatican.va/archive/cod-iuris-canonici/eng/documents/cic_lib2-cann607-709_en.html#TITLE_II.

24. Ignatius of Loyola, *The Spiritual Exercises of Saint Ignatuis of Loyola*, trans. Elder Mullan SJ (New York: P. J. Kenedy and Sons, 1914), 12.

25. Ignatius of Loyola, *The Spiritual Exercises*, 38.

26. Austen Ivereigh, *The Great Reformer: Francis and the Making of a Radical Pope* (New York: Henry Holt and Company, 2014), 2.

27. "Perché i Papi Scelgono un Altro Nome?," *Focus*, March 13, 2013, https://www.focus.it/cultura/curiosita/perche-i-papi-scelgono-un-altro-nome.

28. Francis, Address to Representatives of the Communications Media, March 16, 2013, http://w2.vatican.va/content/francesco/en/speeches/2013/march/documents/papa-francesco_20130316_rappresentanti-media.html.

29. Francis, Homily at Mass for the Imposition of the Pallium and Bestowal of the Fisherman's Ring for the Beginning of the Petrine Ministry, March 19, 2013, http://w2.vatican.va/content/francesco/en/homilies/2013/documents/papa-francesco_20130319_omelia-inizio-pontificato.html.

30. James Corkery, "Francesco, Erede e Innovatore: Un Papa Argentino e Gesuita nella Tradizione Post-Conciliare," in *Dal Chiodo alla Chiave, La Teologia Fondamentale di Papa Francesco*, ed. Michelina Tenace (Vatican City: Libreria Editrice Vaticana, 2017), 135.

31. Corkery, "Francesco, Erede e Innovatore," 136.

32. Antonio Spadaro, "Wake Up the World: Conversation with Pope Francis about Religious Life," *La Civiltà Cattolica* 1 (2014): 3–17.

33. Philip Jenkins, "A Peripheral Vision," accessed July 7, 2020, http://www.patheos.com/blogs/anxiousbench/2014/02/a-peripheral-vision/.

34. Andrea Tornielli, "Tentazione sudamericana per il primo Papa extraeuropeo," interview with Cardinal Jorge Bergoglio, *La Stampa*, March 2, 2013, http://www.lastampa.it/2013/03/02/italia/cronache/tentazione-sudamericana-per-il-primo-papa-extraeuropeo-XvX5JzVJsZR6Sf99SmPAQJ/pagina.html.

35. Francis, *Evangelii Gaudium*, no. 236, http://w2.vatican.va/content/dam/francesco/pdf/apost_exhortations/documents/papa-francesco_esortazione-ap_20131124_evangelii-gaudium_en.pdf.

36. Bergoglio, *Nei tuoi occhi è la mia parola*.

37. John Paul II, Homily at Beatification of Six Servants of God, April 14, 2002, http://w2.vatican.va/content/john-paul-ii/en/homilies/2002/documents/hf_jp-ii_hom_20020414_beatification.html.

38. Bergoglio, *Nei tuoi occhi è la mia parola*.

39. Bergoglio, *Nei tuoi occhi è la mia parola*.

40. Bergoglio, *Nei tuoi occhi è la mia parola*.

41. Jorge Mario Bergoglio, *Il Senso della Vita. Dialoghi con Abraham Skorka e Marcelo Figueroa* (Milan: Mondadori, 2014), 43.

42. John Paul II, *Sollicitudo Rei Socialis*, December 30, 1987, no. 40, http://w2.vatican.va/content/john-paul-ii/en/encyclicals/documents/hf_jp-ii_enc_30121987_sollicitudo-rei-socialis.html.

43. Paul VI, *Populorum Progressio*, March 26, 1967, no. 48, http://w2.vatican.va/content/paul-vi/en/encyclicals/documents/hf_p-vi_enc_26031967_populorum.html.

44. Bergoglio, *Il Senso della Vita*, 44.

45. Mother Teresa, *In My Own Words* (Liguori, MO: Liguori Publications, 1997).

46. Mother Teresa, *A Call to Mercy* (New York: Random House, 2016), 112.

47. Francis, Homily at Opening of Holy Door for the Extraordinary Jubilee of Mercy, December 8, 2015, http://w2.vatican.va/content/francesco/en/homilies/2015/documents/papa-francesco_20151208_giubileo-omelia-apertura.html.

48. Elizabeth Dias, "A Francis Saint, a Teresa Pope," in *Mother Teresa: The Life and Works of a Modern Saint*, ed. David Van Biema (New York: Time, 2016), 7.

49. Francis, Homily at Canonization of Blessed Mother Teresa of Calcutta, September 4, 2016, http://w2.vatican.va/content/francesco/en/homilies/2016/documents/papa-francesco_20160904_omelia-canonizzazione-madre-teresa.html.

50. Francis, Angelus, Apostolic Journey to Tirana (Albania), September 21, 2014, http://w2.vatican.va/content/francesco/en/angelus/2014/documents/papa-francesco_angelus-albania_20140921.html.

51. Bergoglio, *Nei Tuoi Occhi è la Mia Parola*.

52. Bergoglio, *Nei Tuoi Occhi è la Mia Parola*.

53. Francis, Address, Visit to St. Francis of Assist Providence of God Hospital, Rio de Janeiro, July 24, 2013, http://w2.vatican.va/content/francesco/en/speeches/2013/july/documents/papa-francesco_20130724_gmg-ospedale-rio.html.

54. Francis, Address during the Meeting on the Family, October 4, 2014, http://w2.vatican.va/content/francesco/en/speeches/2014/october/documents/papa-francesco_20141004_incontro-per-la-famiglia.html.

55. "Patriarch Kirill Receives Piece of Francis of Assisi Relics as Birthday Gift from Pope," *Interfax Religion*, Moscow, November 23, 2016, http://www.interfax-religion.com/?act=news&div=13439.

56. "Patriarch Kirill Receives Piece of Francis of Assisi Relics."

57. "Patriarch Kirill Receives Piece of Francis of Assisi Relics."

58. Augustine Thompson, *Francis of Assisi: A New Biography* (Ithaca, NY: Cornell University Press), 157.

59. Francis, Encyclical Letter *Laudato Si'*, May 24, 2015, no. 1, http://w2.vatican.va/content/francesco/en/encyclicals/documents/papa-francesco_20150524_enciclica-laudato-si.html.

60. Francis, *Laudato Si'*, no. 11.

61. Francis, Address for World Day of Prayer for Peace, Assisi, September 20, 2016, http://w2.vatican.va/content/francesco/en/speeches/2016/september/documents/papa-francesco_20160920_assisi-preghiera-pace.html.

62. Francis, Message for Lent 2015, October 4, 2014, no. 2, http://w2.vatican.va/content/francesco/en/messages/lent/documents/papa-francesco_20141004_messaggio-quaresima2015.html.

63. Mother Teresa, *A Call to Mercy*, 106.

64. Mother Teresa, *A Call to Mercy*, 29.

65. Mother Teresa, *A Call to Mercy*, 37.

66. Hannah Brockhaus, "Pope Francis Discusses St. Therese's 'Little Way' in Talk with Religious Sisters," *National Catholic Register*, September 7, 2019, http://www.ncregister.com/daily-news/pope-discusses-st.-therese-little-way-in-talk-with-contemplative-nuns-in-ma.

67. Brockhaus, "Pope Francis Discusses St. Therese's 'Little Way.'"

68. Francis, Prayer at Mother Teresa Memorial, May 7, 2019, http://w2.vatican.va/content/francesco/en/prayers/documents/papa-francesco_preghiere_20190507_macedoniadelnord-preghiera.html.